INTERNATIONAL MIGRATION IN
THE NEW MILLENNIUM

DAMES

Dansk Center for Migration
og Etniske Studier

**EUROPEAN RESEARCH CENTRE
ON MIGRATION & ETHNIC RELATIONS**

International Migration in the New Millennium

Global Movement and Settlement

Edited by
DANIÈLE JOLY
Centre for Research in Ethnic Relations
University of Warwick

ASHGATE

© Danièle Joly 2004

Danièle Joly has asserted her right under the Copyright, Designs and Patents Act, 1988, to be identified as the editor of this work.

Published by
Ashgate Publishing Limited
Gower House
Croft Road
Aldershot
Hants GU11 3HR
England

Ashgate Publishing Company
Suite 420
101 Cherry Street
Burlington, VT 05401-4405
USA

Ashgate website: http://www.ashgate.com

British Library Cataloguing in Publication Data
International migration in the new millennium : global
    movement and settlement. - (Research in migration and
    ethnic relations series)
    1. Emigration and immigration 2. Immigrants - Cultural
    assimilation 3. Ethnic relations
    I. Joly, Danièle
    304.8'2

Library of Congress Cataloging-in-Publication Data
International migration in the new millennium : global movement and settlement / edited by
    Danièle Joly.
        p. cm. -- (Research in migration and ethnic relations series)
    Includes bibliographical references and index.
    ISBN 0-7546-0947-2
        1. Emigration and immigration. I. Joly, Danièle. II. Series.

JV6091.I574 2004
304.8'2--dc22   2003062016

ISBN   0 7546 0947 2

Printed and bound in Great Britain by Antony Rowe Ltd, Chippenham, Wilts.

Contents

List of Tables and Figures

Acknowledgements

This book developed from a conference which was sponsored by the UNESCO and the ISS. My warmest thanks go to Dr Serim Timur and Dr Leszek Kosinski.

For Nicolas

Introduction

Danièle Joly

The study of migration is undergoing a metamorphosis. This is motivated by an increasing awareness among scholars and practitioners that the old categories adopted do not match the field any more. Traditionally, the question of migration has been compartmentalised on the basis of discipline and stages or characteristics of the migration phenomenon. For instance, geographers and demographers have concentrated on migration patterns and flows while sociologists generally looked at processes of settlement and integration in receiving countries; asylum and refugees remained for a long time the preserve of lawyers. Migrants on arrival were considered a *tabula rasa* so that the causes of migration and their consequences were rarely linked despite the fact that the subjects involved were the same but at different poles of the trajectory. What is clearer today is that the interconnections weaving the fabric of international migration require a holistic and interdisciplinary approach (Joly, 2000; Brettell and Hollifield, 2000; Arango, chapter 1 in this book; Phizacklea, chapter 6 in this book;). This is strengthened by the diversified nature of migration at the end of the twentieth century which makes it more difficult to separate out international migration considered on the one hand as movement and, on the other hand, as the settlement of migrants and their interaction with majority society (often formulated as ethnic relations in much of the Anglo-Saxon literature). It has been argued that while migration was characterised historically by structured patterns of movement to traditional destinations, contemporary migration associated with globalisation, in contrast, is turbulent and fluid with multidirectional and reversible trajectory (Papastergiadis, 2000).

The backdrop to the migration phenomenon has been a panorama of far-reaching changes which have been taking place throughout the world towards the end of the twentieth century: the end of the Cold War, the consolidation of the European Union, the implementation of the neoliberal economic model. In Europe, the liberal model seriously undermined the welfare state at a high social cost which impacted most on the vulnerable members of society, many of whom are migrants and ethnic minorities. Neoliberalism proves to be even more unfettered in non-industrialised countries. Structural adjustment caused considerable economic and social dislocation worldwide, which has contributed to an enhancement of international migration. The turn of the century has witnessed an augmentation of military interventions headed by the USA, provoking waves of refugees in several parts of the world. Finally the 11 September events in the USA have not only led to greater conflicts and refugee movements in the Middle East and Asia but have also brought about an exacerbation of ethnic relations in industrialised countries where immigrants of Muslim origin have settled. With regard to Europe we are facing a reformulation of our societies which challenges traditional assumptions about a homogeneous national identity.

What is new is that the nation-state in crisis perceives itself as besieged from the outside by the globalisation of the economy and from inside by the challenge of ethnic and territorial minorities to its assumed homogeneity. The state is no longer capable of convincing its population or of imposing on it the national project and its uniformity, while the populations concerned are not ready to accept it. The institution of the state appears to have been weakened in many parts of the world. The nation-state proves unable to formulate a national project which meets or appears to meet the needs of the whole population, in the name of progress and living standard improvements (Donzelot, 1996). The social project in its communist, socialist or social-democratic forms is largely perceived to have failed. Institutions such as the school, the church, the trades unions and the political parties cannot fulfil their integration role as they used to (Wieviorka, 1996a, 1996b). The most serious consequences of this situation are the exclusionary processes resulting from it.

The ending of the post-war social democratic consensus bound up with the new hegemony of neoliberalism has involved the questioning of the viability of key institutions which promote social cohesion and cushion people in emergencies, such as the Welfare State. This has led to a re-examination of the notion of social rights (Marshall, 1950; Lister, 1990; O'Connor, 1993; Walby, 1994). Although neoliberalism does not remain unchallenged (King, 1996), the lack of 'social cohesion' resulting from it is a primary concern to some policy makers and to civil society. This is not only a European phenomenon but also extends throughout the developing world. The question of citizenship rights, in different forms, has become central to the debate about social integration or inclusion of ethnic minorities (Harvey, 1996; Martiniello, 1995; Morris, 1994; Turner, 1990).

Meanwhile, ethnicity has been acquiring a greater salience in Europe and worldwide: questions of identity, culture, religion and group difference keep rising to the top of the agenda. It is necessary to gain an understanding of why this is happening today, how these processes lead to social action, what forms of action they lead to and what the meaning of this action is. The formulation of those identities takes place through social interaction within a context of structural-cultural emergent properties (Archer, 1995; Carter and Sealey, 2001). Rather than being the property of a group or simply expressive of its aspirations, ethnicity may be regarded as a cultural emergent property whose provenance is to be found in specific social and historical circumstances (Joly et al., 2002). Ethnic mobilisation can constitute an important component of multicultural and antiracist strategies and provides an alternative focus for increasingly fragmented communities. At one level it is bound up with the way in which nationalisms are expressed either within or outside the nation state (Guibernau, 1995). Regional or sub-national particularism may provide a basis for collective action and identity. In some cases ethnic mobilisation has been an important tool for the furthering of group interests particularly vis-à-vis the local or national state (Rex and Drury, 1994). These forms of organisation can give rise to social networks which operate across borders and continents, attempting to maximise their resources within a structural and cultural framework of disadvantage. They may aim to further integration and participation in society while maintaining their group existence and identity. However, there are differentiations between ethnic groups in their strategies, aspirations and achievements. The majority society often creates additional problems through the reification of ethnicity, often depicting minority cultures as 'exotic' and static (Troyna, 1987). In addition, diasporic networks and consciousness demultiply the dimensions of ethnicity (Clifford, 1994; Brah, 1996). Finally the intersection of ethnicity, class, gender and other factors of differentiation adds to the complexity of the issue (Anthias, 1998).

In Europe society is built on a hierarchy of ethnicities and an inferior status attributed to minorities. It is founded on a relation of domination and discrimination and is to be found throughout the folds of society, in employment, in the schools, in the law, in the media: it is economic, political and ideological. Moreover, new legal categories have introduced differentiated statuses for foreign residents which involve unequal access to social rights and benefits. Asylum seekers and refugees have been particularly affected by these developments, so that it is possible to think in terms of a fundamental shift in the paradigm of asylum regimes (Joly, 1996). Most of the more recently arrived populations are refugees and are thus doubly disadvantaged: they are disempowered in their homeland and in the country of reception. They are both near and distant to their land of origin and their land of reception; they have to be considered in their relationship with different poles and are possibly the most modern agents in our society as a consequence of their 'strange-hood' (Joly, 1996).

The new modes of identity are not only those of minorities asserting themselves, they may also be those of the neofascist seeking the security of an 'ethnic purity' or the more ambiguous cultural racism of the 'new right' (Wieviorka, 1992). In the majority population ethnicity manifests itself as inward-looking rather than outward-looking, as traditional rather than modern, but new forms of this ethnicity are evolving within a modernity framework. The fragmentation of social life and the general crisis of society which leave political institutions impotent are posited as the fundamental reasons for the increase of racism (Alt, 1998). The economic recession, the crisis of the nation-state and the collapse of ideological projects create uncertainty and insecurity among the native majority population. One route followed is that of a closed ethnicity strengthening itself by the rejection of the outgroup (Miles 1993). The scapegoating, racialisation and criminalisation of the 'other' (Gilroy, 1982) is exacerbated, targeting ethnic minorities and refugees; racism expands its criterion based on phenotypical difference to the stigmatisation of cultural/religious difference (Modood, 1990). Demands are made for the prioritisation of natives' interests as a consequence of relative frustration processes (Willems, 1995). This phenomenon finds a mobilisation and a political expression in extreme right-wing parties such as the *Front National* in France and neo-fascist groups in Germany (Blaschke, 1998).

These questions are all the more critical because industrialised societies desperately need a large input of migrant labour to meet the needs of their economy resulting from their ageing demographic curve. A well publicised UN study (UNDP, 2000) predicts the need for a net migration of 13 Million a year into the European Union alone until 2050. Even if the magnitude of this figure can be questioned (Dobson et al., 2001), large numbers of migrants will have to be imported thus emphasising the importance of related issues pertaining to sending countries, receiving countries and the migrants themselves.

This book brings together contributions on international migration and on settlement/interaction of immigrants with majority society. It covers a selection of salient issues in the main regions of the world both from a theoretical and empirical perspective.

Joaquin Arango introduces a robust chapter on 'Theories of International Migration' (Chapter 1). Starting from the premise that international migration has emerged as a basic structural feature of almost all industrialised countries over the past three decades, he argues that although this stands as a testament to the strength and coherence of the forces causing migration, the theoretical basis for understanding these forces remains weak. In his view there is presently no single coherent theory of international migration. Instead there is a fragmented set of theories that have been developed largely in isolation from each other, and sometimes these theories are further segmented by disciplinary boundaries. According to Arango, however, the current trends and patterns in migration are such as to suggest that a full understanding of all the processes involved will not be possible if a single level of analysis is focused on, or if too much reliance is placed on the tools of one discipline alone. Instead, the complex and multifaceted nature of migration should be reflected in a sophisticated theory incorporating a variety of perspectives, levels and assumptions.

Through examining the major existing models which describe the initiation of international migratory movement, and then considering theories which attempt to account for the persistence of transnational population flows over time and space, the leading contemporary theories of international migration are explicated and integrated. The various theories are examined separately, their conceptual frameworks are compared and contrasted in order that areas of logical inconsistency and substantive disagreement can be revealed. This chapter attempts to throw critical light onto the theories involved, emphasising their activity and their reactive explanatory value. Although the propositions, assumptions and hypotheses arising from each of these perspectives are not inherently contradictory, each carries with it different implications for policy formulation. Arango concludes that only through evaluating and integrating the various theories and models will it be possible to construct an accurate and comprehensive theory of international migration for the new millennium.

Marek Okólski examines 'New Migration Movements in Central and Eastern Europe' (Chapter 2) and notes that in the 1990s Central and Eastern Europe in particular, have significantly contributed to the magnitude and variation of global movements of the population as a result of a multitude of political, socioeconomic and cultural factors. This is due to the transforming and already rapidly growing economies of Central and Eastern Europe which have become a magnet for many migrants from outside the region. In Okolski's opinion, their inflow, combined with as remarkably high intraregional mobility of the population of Central and Eastern European countries seems to justify recent references to the region as a new migration pole on the global scale. He also identifies the diversification of political and economic developments in particular countries of the region which has led to the emergence of clear sub-regional migration poles within Central and Eastern Europe. Despite lower than expected outflows to the West after 1990, Okolski notes that migration pressures exerted by the region are still considerable, and he maps out the types of flows: asylum seekers, ethnicity-driven migrants, persons taking part in incomplete migration and migrant workers.

Ronald Skeldon (Chapter 3) writing on 'Migration, the Asian Financial Crisis and its Aftermath' considers the impact that the economic crisis in Asia since mid 1997 may have had upon population movements in the region. The rapid development of parts of East and South-east Asia over the last decade gave rise to the importation of foreign labour demand to meet demand in sectors of those economies. Although one consequence of the crisis, and the associated increasing unemployment, might have been to slow or even reverse the importation of foreign labour, Skeldon argues that little direct evidence of such a trend is observed even if there are indeed changes in the nature of migration systems in Asia. In his view some of these changes are due to long term structural shifts in the nature of the economies themselves and it is difficult to identify specific 'crisis effects' on migration apart from a few knee-jerk, and essentially slow, deportations of foreign labour. The rising unemployment has not been the greatest in those sectors where immigrant labour is mainly found and, for a variety of reasons, it is virtually impossible to substitute newly employed domestic labour for imported foreign labour. He notes that consequences of the crisis may be increased exploitation of migrant labour and rises in the proportion of undocumented migrants. The number of highly skilled migrants is likely to have declined. However, a return to the village of unemployed domestic rural-to-urban migrants does not appear to have occurred to any great extent as the urban informal economies have burgeoned. While the immediate economic effects of the crisis are now diminishing, certain flashpoints for migration in the region remain.

In 'Economic Integration, Labour Market and International Migration: the Mercosur Case' (Chapter 4), **Neide Patarra** examines the relationship between the economy and migration in Latin America. She places the understanding of international migration within the new international context where production restructuring, financial readjustment, market globalisation, labour market precariousness, reduction of state actions with external debt crisis, public sector disability, among other features are presenting serious challenges for developing countries to regain sustained growth. One main aspect she emphasizes is that efforts to create common markets to face the situation implies new modalities of population movements in a context of increasing circulation of goods but not free circulation of labour. The chapter explores these ideas with reference to the Mercosur case, involving mainly Argentina, Paraguay, Uruguay and Brazil, four countries in South Cone Latin America. It is divided into three parts: the first summarises historical trends, confluences and disparities among the countries; socioeconomic indicators show the current situation and its implications in the context of economic migration. The second part deals particularly with international migration in the region, considering separately past and recent trends in each one of the countries. Migration towards the first world and intraregional migration consist of a wide variety of movements, including circularity, seasonality, temporality and so on. The third part considers the particularities of the Treaty that created the Mercosur common market and its organisation. In spite of the agreements signed, Mercosur governments do not have adequate channels for dealing with social problems. Compatibility between labour and migration laws, the welfare issue, social security, access to public services (mainly school and health), compatibility of retirement benefits, among other dimensions, are quite urgent in the context of increasing and diversifying population movements.

Oladele O. Arowolo deals with 'Return Migration in Africa' in Chapter 5. This chapter presents a regional perspective on the issue of return migration and the complex problem of reintegration into civil society. The Africa region is the focus, with emphasis on Sub-Saharan Africa (SSA). The author argues that future patterns of migration in SSA will most probably be dominated by refugees and clandestine workers, and the political and economic situations giving rise to such migrants are likely to remain unstable. He indicates that the changing political, economic, and environmental situations which propel such migratory movements are also potent factors in return migration. Following the wars of independence and cessation of civil conflicts, many countries in the region have been facing the problem of reintegrating the returnees into civil society. Arowolo notes that most of the organised schemes for the rehabilitation of returnees tend to be a spontaneous response to emergency situations and are largely donor driven. The focus of most such schemes is the repatriation process itself, rather than the reintegration process. The chapter reviews the main issues concerning reintegration, and presents a programme approach to national strategies for social, economic and political reintegration of returnees.

Annie Phizacklea develops a gendered perspective in migration in Chapter 6. She looks critically at the way in which the household is reified in many accounts of migration and why a gendered 'unpacking' of the institution allows to retain it as a central unit without its reification. She argues that while social networks may be critical for an understanding of some migrations they play a less central role for women in certain parts of the world, for instance Southeast Asia, where migration has become institutionalised from the state down. Considerable evidence shows that for women at least, intermediaries such as employment agencies and brokers may be of more critical significance in facilitating, even institutionalising transnational migration.

Phizacklea gives pointers to the main weaknesses in extant theorising from a gendered perspective. Through a case study of domestic workers she indicates that despite the harrowing conditions experienced by many women in the maid's industry worldwide their migration represents an attempt to bring a better life to themselves and their families in the face of prodigious external constraint.

Danièle Joly in 'Between Exile and Ethnicity' (Chapter 7), seeks to establish refugees in their country of exile/settlement as social types distinct from labour migrants. She looks at the notion of ethnic groups and their strategies as a theoretical tool for an understanding of refugees. The refugees' positioning within the structure of conflict in their country of origin is posited as a determining factor of their modes of settlement. She identifies two large categories: *Odyssean* refugees who nurtured a collective project in the land of origin and took it with them in the land of exile; and *Rubicon* refugees who did not partake of a collective project oriented towards the homeland or who have forsaken it. The chapter focuses on refugees in Western Europe.

Chan Kwok Bun in his chapter on 'Interrogating Identity, Ethnicity and Diaspora: Three Case Studies of the Ethnic Chinese' (Chapter 8) draws on fieldwork in Hong Kong, Thailand and Singapore, combining research on ethnic identity of the Chinese with research on Chinese business networks, to reflect on the ethnic Chinese experiences in the three countries. He interrogates words such as Chinese diaspora, identity, ethnicity, and Chineseness. A critique is made of existing conceptualisations of these terms, and offers an alternative interpretation of what it means to be Chinese in the postmodern world: ethnic Chinese constitute a majority of the population in Singapore; in Thailand, ethnic Chinese are a significant minority group in economic terms. The Chinese population of Hong Kong have experienced the transfer of the colony from Britain to China in 1997, and attention is drawn to the changing and multiple identities of Hong Kongers since then. Not entirely satisfied with the Chinese diaspora term but not able to find a substitute, the author considers the meaning of being hyphenated, to carry one's home on one's back, to exist in a transit, third zone 'where words do not stick', because it is better to remain nameless when language fails. The author concludes that ethnic Chinese do not constitute a diaspora in the way that Jewish or Greek people are deemed to. It may be possible to talk in terms of diasporas, with a pluralistic form or structures, but not a single unified diaspora of Chinese the world over.

Michel Wieviorka in his chapter on 'Ethnicity, Racism and Discrimination' (Chapter 9) first differentiates these two concepts analytically and then proceeds to examine their manifestation and relationship in the context of European societies. He notes the rise of both ethnicity and racism in our societies and concludes that the conditions which promote racism in a hypermodern society in which cultural identities (i.e., ethnicities) are many and varied and graded are related to the way in which the latter are dealt with politically. He argues that when universalism results in their visible existence being forbidden, or when communitarianism challenges universal values, there is more likelihood of racism flourishing than when an attempt is made to find ways of articulating the two demands: respect for difference and the maintenance of universal values.

Thomas Faist, considering 'Dual Citizenship as Overlapping Membership' (Chapter 10), notes that dual citizenship has increased dramatically over the past decades. More and more states are tolerating or even accepting dual membership for various reasons. This trend is disconcerting because citizenship and political loyalty to sovereign states were thought to be indivisible until very recently. The author argues that the new developments cast doubt on the assumption that overlapping citizenship violates the principle of popular sovereignty and that multiple ties and loyalties of citizens in border-crossing spaces or even world society contradict state sovereignty. The argument put forward is that dual citizenship is neither an evil nor an intrinsic value in political communities. In Faist's opinion dual citizenship is tied to genuine links of citizens into various sovereign political communities. He posits that three perspectives shed light on dual citizenship: national, postnational and transstate approaches: analytically, a transstate perspective can best describe relatively dense and continuous border-crossing ties as overlapping membership of citizens across several political communities; in contrast to national concepts, a transstate view grasps the integrative potentials of reciprocity and solidarity in border-crossing spaces for bounded political communities. Faist concludes that one useful attribute of a transstate perspective is that it does not make unwarranted assumptions about a quantum leap in collective identity from the 'nation' to 'Europe' or even 'humanity', as assumed by views such as postnational membership, suprastate citizenship and global democracy.

References

Alt, J. (1998) 'Racism within the General Crisis of Western Civilisation', in D. Joly (ed.), *Scapegoats and Social Actors*, Basingstoke: Macmillan.

Anthias, F. (1998), 'Connecting Ethnicity, "Race", Gender and Class in Ethnic Relations Research', in D. Joly (ed.), *Scapegoats and Social Actors*, Basingstoke: Macmillan.

Archer, M.S. (1995), *Realist Social Theory: A Morphogenetic Approach*, Cambridge: Cambridge University Press.

Blaschke, J. (1998), 'New Racism in Germany', in D. Joly (ed.), *Scapegoats and Social Actors*, Basingstoke: Macmillan.

Brah, A. (1996), *Cartographies of Diaspora*, London: Routledge.

Brettell, C. and Hollifield, J. (eds) (2000), *Migration Theory: Falling across Disciplines*, New York: Routledge.

Carter, B. and Sealey, A. (2001) 'Social Categories and Sociolinguistics: Applying a Realist Approach', *International Journal of the Sociology of Language*, 152, pp. 1–19.

Clifford, J. (1994), 'Diasporas', *Cultural Anthropology*, 9 (3), pp. 302–38.

Dobson, J. et al. (2001), *International Migration and the UK. Recent Patterns and Trends*, Home Office RDS Occasional Paper No. 75, December.

Donzelot, J. (1996), 'L'avenir du social', *Esprit*, 219 (March), pp. 58–81.

Gilroy, P. (1982), 'Steppin' out of Babylon – Race, Class and Autonomy', in *The Empire Strikes Back: Race and Racism in 70s Britain*, Centre for Contemporary Cultural Studies, Hutchinson.

Guibernau, M. (1995), *Nationalisms: The Nation-state and Nationalism in the Twentieth Century*, Cambridge: Polity.

Harvey, D, (1996) *Justice, Nature and the Geography of Difference*, Oxford: Blackwells.

Joly, D. (1996), *Haven or Hell? Asylum Policies and Refugees in Europe*, Basingstoke: Macmillan.

Joly, D. (2000), 'Some Structural Effects of Migration in Receiving and Sending Countries', *International Migration*, 38 (5) (December), pp. 25–40.

Joly, D., Carter, R., Owen, D. and Arulampalam, W. (2002), *The Social Dynamics of Migration*, University of Warwick: unpublished.

King, P. (ed.) (1996), *Socialism and the Common Good*, London: New Fabian Essays, Frank Cass.

Lister, R. (1990), *The Exclusive Society: Citizenship and the Poor*, London: Child Poverty Action Group.

Marshall, T.H. (1950), *Citizenship and Social Class*, Cambridge: Cambridge University Press.

Martiniello, M. (1995), *Migration, Citizenship and Ethno-national Identities in the European Union*, Aldershot: Avebury.

Miles, R. (1993), *Racism after 'Race Relations'*, London: Routledge.

Modood, T. (1990) 'British Asian Muslims and the Rushdie Affair', *The Political Quarterly*, 62 (2) (April), pp. 143–60.

Morris, L. (1994) *Dangerous Classes: the Underclass and Social Citizenship*, London: Routledge.

O'Connor, J. (1993) 'Gender, Class and Citizenship in the Comparative Analysis of Welfare State Regimes: Theoretical and Methodological Issues', *British Journal of Sociology*, 44, pp. 501–18.

Papastergiadis, N. (2000), *The Turbulence of Migration: Globalization, Deterritorialization and Hybridity*, Oxford: Polity Press.

Rex, J. and Drury, B. (eds) (1994), *Ethnic Mobilisation in a Multi-cultural Europe*, Aldershot: Ashgate.

Troyna, B. (1987), '"Swann's Song": the Origins, Ideology and Implications of "Education for All"', in T.S. Chivers (ed.), *Race and Culture in Education*, Berkshire: NFER-Nelson.

Turner, B. (1990), 'Outline of a Theory of Citizenship', *Sociology*, 24 (2), pp. 189–218.

UNDP (2000), *Replacement Migration: Is it a Solution to Declining and Ageing Populations?*, http://www.un.org/esa/population/migration.

Walby, S. (1994) 'Is Citizenship Gendered?', *Sociology*, 28 (3), pp. 379–95.

Wieviorka, M. (1992), *La France raciste*, Paris: Seuil.

Wieviorka, M (1996a), 'Violence, Culture and Democracy – A European Perspective', *Public Culture*, 8 (2), pp. 329–54.

Wieviorka, M. (1996b), *Une Société fragmentée? Le Multiculturalisme en debat*, Paris: La Découverte.

Willems, H. (1995), 'Right-wing Extremism, Racism or Youth Violence? Explaining Violence against Foreigners in Germany', *New Community*, 21 (4), October.

PART I
INTERNATIONAL MIGRATION

Chapter 1

Theories of International Migration

Joaquin Arango

Introduction

Ever since the dawn of the age of mass migration, well over a century ago, scholars have endeavoured to provide general explanations for the phenomenon of human migration, more or less abstracted from its specific occurrence. Economics, sociology and geography have been the most propitious disciplinary grounds, but by no means the only ones. The end results of such efforts have been models, analytical frameworks, conceptual approaches, empirical generalisations, simple notions, and only seldom real theories. A number of these explanations were not originally conceived to explain migration, but rather born to explain other facets of human behaviour and then imported and adapted for the explanation of migration. Efforts at theory building have not been cumulative: the relatively short history of theorising about migration takes the form of a string of separate, generally unconnected theories, models or frameworks, rather than a cumulative sequence of contributions that build upon previous blocks.

If the success of such efforts had to be measured by their ability to erect a general theory of migration, if could be easily concluded that none has been successful. Indeed, there is no such thing as a general theory of migration. But it is highly doubtful that this could be a good yardstick, as the level of aggregation at which such an overarching and all-encompassing theory should operate would be so high as to render it useless for all practical purposes. Migration is too diverse and multifaceted to be explained by a single theory. Efforts at theory building should be rather evaluated by their potential to guide research and provide cogent hypotheses to be tested against empirical evidence, and by their contribution to a better understanding of specific facets, dimensions and processes of migration. From this vantage point, there can be no doubt that students of migration can count nowadays on a much richer reservoir of conceptual and theoretical approaches than ever before from which to draw upon. Yet, the overall palette of theoretical contributions still mixes light and shade.

The pages that follow aim to provide a succinct description and a critical evaluation of the major contemporary explanations of migration. A preliminary caveat is in order: the terms *theory* and *explanation* will be liberally construed all along, and extended to all sorts of conceptual and analytical approaches, although not to typologies. Without detracting from the epoch-making significance of a few outstanding forerunners – above all *The Laws of Migration* by Ernest-George Ravenstein (1885–89), the undisputed founding father of modern thinking about migration, and the seminal *The Polish Peasant in Europe and America*, by William Thomas and Florian Znaniecki (1918–20), probably the most impressive book ever written on the subject of migration – theory building in this realm is practically a matter of the second half of the twentieth century, and especially of its last third. Most contributions prior to the 1960s have nowadays only a historical, if not purely archeological, interest with the exception of a number of contributions to the vocabulary of migration.

This survey starts with the neoclassical explanation of migration, the first theory worthy of its name. Seen in retrospect, its appearance represented a true watershed in the short history of thinking about migration, which it presided over in the 1960s and 1970s. Special attention is bestowed upon its increasing difficulties to come to terms with the rapidly changing reality of international migration since the mid-1970s. An array of new or renovated theories and conceptual frameworks has flourished in the last quarter of the century with that aim, mirroring the increasing relevance socially and politically accorded to the phenomenon. After a critical evaluation of both contributions and shortcomings, some reasons will be put forward that may help to understand the relative weaknesses of theoretical thinking about migration, and some areas which deserve greater attention will be suggested.

The Neoclassical Explanation

In the course of the third quarter of the twentieth century, rapid and sustained economic growth, the increasing internationalisation of economic activity, decolonisation, and emergent processes of economic development in the Third World, all brought about an intensification of migration, both internal and international. Thinking about migration at that time tended to mirror both the overall climate of the period and the characteristics of migration flows. It is hardly surprising that the major contributions to migration theorising in this period should come from the realm of economics. The general primacy of economic motivations in migration had already been recognised by Ravenstein several decades before, when he wrote that:

> bad or oppressive laws, heavy taxation, an unattractive climate, uncongenial social surroundings, and even compulsion (slave trade, transportation), all have produced and are still producing currents of migration, but none of these currents can compare in volume with that which arises from the desire inherent in most men to 'better' themselves in material respects (Ravenstein 1889, p. 286).

Such a primacy was paramount in the third quarter of the century, after the hectic period of massive resettlement of displaced populations and accommodation to new borders that followed World War II.

The direct predecessor of the neoclassical theory, and probably the first instance of a truly theoretical explanation of migration, was W. Arthur Lewis' model of 'economic development with unlimited supply of labour', an influential model of development in dual economies in which migration plays a pivotal role (Lewis, 1954). 'Dual' economies are economies in development, usually in post-colonial contexts, in which a modern sector, connected with the outside world, coexists with a traditional one which relies on subsistence agriculture for survival. When the modern sector expands, it draws labour from the traditional sector, where it is unlimited, in the sense that its marginal productivity equals zero. Lewis estimated that a 'cliff' of about 30 per cent was bound to exist between the wages of the two sectors, and that that differential would suffice for workers to move. For the advanced sector, having at its disposal an unlimited supply of migrant labour makes it possible to expand while keeping wages low, thus securing a high rate of profit. For the traditional sector, outmigration is the only way to get rid of surplus labour and to proceed in the production function towards higher capital-output ratios, and thus constitutes the precondition to embark in a process of development, out of economic backwardness. Therefore, in Lewis's model, migration is a crucial mechanism of development for the economy as a whole, exploiting the potential of growth inherent in economic disparities, and both sectors, traditional and modern, sending and receiving, greatly benefit from it.

Even though Lewis placed himself in what was known at the time as 'development economics', his model contained in a nutshell the basic elements of the equilibrium models which would dominate the social sciences, and migration theorising within it, at least in the ensuing two decades. Yet, it was not primarily a theory of migration, but a model of development.

The first theory about migration, and probably the most influential so far, was the theory of migration that emanates from neoclassical economics, based on such familiar tenets as rational choice, utility maximisation, expected net returns, factor mobility and wage differentials. A paradigm so versatile, which has been applied to so many dimensions of human behaviour, and whose influence still spills over from economics to other social sciences, could hardly disregard migration, to which it seems to fit naturally.

Simple, elegant and akin to common sense, it has the advantage of combining a micro perspective of individual decision-making and a macro counterpart of structural determinants. At a macro level, it is a theory about the spatial redistribution of the factors of production responding to different relative prices (Ranis and Fei, 1961; Harris and Todaro, 1970; Todaro, 1976). Migration results from the uneven geographical distribution of labour and capital. In some countries, or regions, labour is scarce relative to capital, and its price – the wage level – is correspondingly high, while in other countries or regions the opposite obtains. As a result, workers tend to go from countries or regions where labour is abundant and wages low to labour-scarce countries where wages are high. In so doing, they contribute to the redistribution of the factors of production and to the equalisation of wages between countries in the long run, redressing original inequalities. It can be concluded, therefore, that in the neoclassical view, the origin of migration is to be sought in disparities in wage rates between countries, which in turn mirror income and welfare disparities. Migration will bring about the elimination of wage differentials, and this disappearance will in turn entail the cessation of migration.

The reasons why individuals respond to structural differences between countries or regions and engage in migration is explained by the micro version of neoclassical theory (Todaro, 1969, 1976). Migration is the result of individual decisions made by rational actors who seek to improve their well-being by moving to places where the reward of their labour will be higher than the one they get at home, in a measure sufficient to offset the tangible and intangible costs involved in the move. It is therefore an individual, spontaneous, and voluntary act, which rests on the comparison between the present situation of the actor and the expected net gain of moving, and results from a cost-benefit calculus. It follows that migrants will tend to go to the destination where a higher net return is expected, after pondering all the available alternatives. Insofar as it implies incurring certain costs in order to reap higher returns from one's labour, migration constitutes a form of investment in human capital (Sjaastad, 1962).

In the third quarter of the twentieth century, the predominance of the neoclassical persuasion – and of its correlates, the functionalist paradigm in sociology and, more generally, modernisation theory – was contested, with limited success, by a school of thought located at the opposite side of the ideological spectrum that saw social processes in terms of conflict rather than equilibrium. In the 1960s and 1970s, this historical-structural inspiration, with its strong Marxist overtones, was embodied in dependency theory, which posited that the evolution of capitalism had given way to an international order composed of core industrialised countries and peripheral agrarian ones linked by uneven and asymmetrical relations. The advancement of the former rested on their exploitation of the latter, whose development was primarily hampered by their subordinate status. Underdevelopment was thus seen as a by-product of development. Dependency theory had little to say about migration, and that little was more about the rural-urban variety (Singer, 1973) than about its international counterpart. The latter constituted one of the mechanisms through which inequalities between countries were perpetuated and reinforced, especially through the brain drain.

Yet, the relative demise of the neoclassical explanation of migration in the course of the last quarter of the twentieth century would not be caused by the rather ineffectual challenge of dependency theory, but by its own intrinsic shortcomings, magnified by the profound changes undergone by the nature and characteristics of international migration since the mid-1970s. These changes have increased the heterogeneity and complexity of the phenomenon and have given rise to a migratory reality not very congenial with the neoclassical world.

The Challenge of a Changing Reality

The contemporary problems of the neoclassical theory of migration do not stem primarily from its insufficiencies as a theory, but rather from its difficulties to come to terms with reality.

The first fact that runs counter to the neoclassical explanation is why so few people move, given the huge differences in income, wages and levels of welfare that exist among countries. This is clearly the Achilles heel of neoclassical theory. If migration flows between countries were to conform to the prescriptions of neoclassical theory, the number of international migrants should be many times higher than the one that obtains in reality. In fact, economic disparities are important, no doubt, but by no means sufficient for migration flows to take place. In fact, they do not explain much nowadays.

The second, connected problem of the theory is its inability to explain differential migration. In itself, it fails to explain why some countries have relatively high outmigration rates and others, structurally similar, do not. The same can be said, *mutatis mutandis*, of different immigration rates among receiving countries. The reasonable corollary that can be inferred from the theory – that the volume of migration between sets of sending and receiving areas should be in keeping with the magnitude of economic imbalances separating them – does not hold either.

No doubt, these shortcomings of the neoclassical explanation of migration can be partly traced to its one-dimensionality, and more precisely to the exclusion of the political dimension when it has risen to pre-eminence. Being in essence a theory of the mobility of factors of production in accordance with relative prices, the neoclassical theory is increasingly at odds, when not incapable to come to terms, with a world bristling with barriers which severely curtail the movement of labour. Certainly, the contemporary international system – in which the free circulation of workers is the exception and restriction the rule – hardly conforms to the image of an ideal environment in which individuals move freely and spontaneously to pursue their own interests and maximise utility. Generalised restrictive admission policies reduce mobility and deter would-be migrants, in a measure impossible to ascertain but likely to be very large. Although in theory this factor – in cases where there is a possibility of overcoming entry restrictions – could be included in the calculus of the would-be migrant, taken both as an additional cost and as an aggravation of the uncertainty of the investment implied by migration, in practice its influence is so overriding that it deprives the theory of any use. It is true that almost everything can be translated into costs and benefits, and even that a value in monetary terms can be attached to it, but the price of such effort may often be the practical irrelevance, close to tautology, of finding that people move to enhance their well-being. In practice, the cost of overcoming entry obstacles is often so staggering that it dissuades the majority of those who might be candidates for migration if economic considerations alone were at play. In cases when such barriers cannot be overcome, it would make little sense to explain the decision to stay on the basis of the neoclassical calculus. Therefore, political factors are nowadays much more influential than differential wages in determining mobility or immobility, and the selectivity of migration can be explained more in terms of legal entitlements, or of personal characteristics in the case of undocumented moves, than in terms of wage differentials. As a result, when applied to international movements in the contemporary world, the neoclassical explanation floats between the obvious and the unrealistic.

Obviously, the explanation of internal migration, where mobility is normally unrestricted and the costs of cultural adaptation lower, is a different matter. The paradigm can also be successfully applied to the past, when entry barriers were less prominent than in the present.

Yet, the insufficiencies of the paradigm do not stem only from restrictive entry policies. It can also be unable to explain reality even in spaces where mobility is unfettered. To mention only one example, the case of the European Union – where the principle of free movement for nationals of the 15 member states coincides nowadays with a very limited volume of labour migration, despite the fact that important differences in levels of wages and welfare still remain – casts doubts about the general propensity to move whenever wage differentials clearly offset the cost of moving, as posited by the theory. The scant labour mobility between European Union countries in the present day suggests that such a propensity is not independent of absolute levels of income or welfare at home, and that beyond a certain threshold in welfare it declines to the point of vanishing. Therefore, the idea that migration only ceases when wage differentials have been reduced to the mere cost of moving does not seem to hold. Neither does the correlative prescription of the theory that posits that migration will bring about an equalisation of levels of welfare between countries. Whatever the data that are used, the idea that international migration has brought about a significant reduction in economic disparities among sending and receiving countries in recent decades seems hard to sustain.

Indeed, the neoclassical theory of migration has often been criticised on the grounds that it downplays non-economic factors – particularly cultural determinants, which are bound to be influential in such an existential decision as migration – that it mechanically reduces the determinants of migration, that it treats migrants and societies as if they were homogeneous, and that its perspective is static. In addition, it equates migrants with workers, and disregards all migration that is not labour migration.

Indeed, the theory has been criticised even by some of its initial proponents. A number of relevant amendments or improvements were introduced from an early date. The most relevant one was Michael Todaro's addition of a coefficient that accounts for the probability of finding employment – or of being unemployed – at destination in the calculation of the expected wage advantage (Todaro, 1969). Yet, this and other refinements to meet objections have not been sufficient to solve its difficult relations with a changing reality, especially in the international sphere.

The Contemporary Mosaic

In the last quarter of the twentieth century, *grosso modo*, international migration has undergone deep changes: *inter alia*, flows have become more global and heterogeneous in composition; Asia, Africa and Latin America have replaced Europe as the major region of origin; both the relative volume and the nature of labour demand in receiving societies have changed; restrictive admission policies have proliferated; new forms of migration based upon entitlements have become paramount; undocumented flows and clandestine traffics have acquired an increasing saliency; social integration in the receiving society has become less linear; and transnational spaces and communities have emerged. There are signs that suggest that international migration may be entering a new era. And since theories usually follow facts, these changes may have ushered into a new era in the ways of thinking about migration as well. The effects of such changes is compounded by the fact that thinking about migration seems to be presided over nowadays by the reality of international migration, while in the past it often mirrored internal migration.

As a result both of increasing interest in migration and in order to come to terms with this increasingly complex and different reality, an array of conceptual and theoretical approaches have either developed anew, or been invigorated with new air, or else brought to bear and adapted from other areas of human behaviour. Indeed, rather than new migration theories *qua se*, they are either modified versions of previous strands or adaptations of theoretical frameworks built for different purposes. They do not amount to a new paradigm, but rather form a colourful, variegated mosaic (Massey et al., 1998).

The New Economics of Labour Migration

One of the new theories, probably the most migration-specific of all – the new economics of labour migration – has developed out of the neoclassical tradition. Associated primarily with the name of Oded Stark (Stark, 1991), it can be seen either as an inside criticism of the micro version of neoclassical theory, cast in its same mould and altering only a few tenets, or as a variant of it that refines and enriches it with a number of amendments and additions. It shares with the latter its basic cornerstone, rational choice, but differs from it in that the actor who seeks to enhance its utility is more the family or the household than the individual migrant. Migration is a family strategy geared not so much to maximise income as to diversify sources of income, in order to minimise risks – such as unemployment, loss of income, or crop failures – and loosen constraints, given the imperfections that usually plague credit and insurance markets in sending countries. Insofar as migrants aim to maximise income, they do not necessarily do so in absolute terms, but rather relative to other households in its reference group, thus retaking the old notion of relative deprivation (Stark and Taylor, 1989). From this it can inferred that the more unequal the distribution of income in a given community, the more intensely relative deprivation will be felt, and the more incentives will there be for further migration to occur. In this connection, the new economics of migration lends attention to income distribution, contrary to the neoclassical explanation.

The new economics of migration presents a number of improvements over neoclassical theory. To start with, the central importance accorded to wage differentials is considerably downplayed: they do not necessarily entail migration and they are not indispensable for migration to occur. In addition, it highlights the role of families and households, underlines the importance of remittances, and pays more attention to information and to the complex interdependence between migrants and the context in which they operate. The pivotal role that the family often plays in migration had already been pointed out by Jacob Mincer, but in a different perspective and with different purposes, underlining the fact that often it is not so much workers as complete families who migrate (Mincer, 1978).

Yet, it is doubtful whether the disparate ingredients that make up the new economics of migration are sufficiently woven and logically integrated as to constitute a coherent theory, or whether it is no more than a critical, sophisticated variant of neoclassical theory. In any case, if anything detracts seriously from the value of the new economics of migration it is not so much its possible lack of theoretical autonomy as its limited applicability. The contexts of migration it describes seem to be rather peculiar ones, characterised by decades-long migration relationships. Indeed, although some of the evidence presented relates at times to other world regions, the new economics of migration seems to draw its inspiration, as well as the bulk of the evidence on which it rests, from a small number of rural villages in Mexico. Its versatility vis-à-vis other, less established migration contexts – especially those that involve considerable degrees of societal disorganisation, not to speak of life-threatening circumstances – looks uncertain at best. It is not applicable either to the movement of complete households, as Mincer's model was. Finally, the new economics of migration concerns itself only with the causes of migration on the sending side.

Dual Labour Market Theory

The opposite happens with another theory which contributes to a better understanding of contemporary realities, Michael Piore's dual labour market theory, insofar as it pays attention only to the receiving end of migration and places its explanation at the macro level of structural determinants. According to the theory, international migration is caused by a permanent demand for foreign labour that stems from certain intrinsic characteristics of advanced industrial societies, which in turn result in the segmentation of their labour markets. For a number of reasons, highly developed economies require foreign workers to take up jobs which native workers refuse and that are no longer filled – if they ever were – by women and teenagers. Piore mentions four factors responsible for such demand, which is satisfied by means of recruitment.

It can be said that both the starting point of dual labour market theory – the fact that in advanced economies there is a permanent demand for foreign labour – and the basic explanation for such demand – that native workers in advanced societies shun low-paid, unstable, unskilled, dangerous, demeaning, low-prestige jobs – are well-known empirical observations. In fact, the merit of the theory lies in explaining in a complex and technical way why all this happens. More precisely, although structured in a different way, the theory explains i) why in advanced economies there are unstable and low-productivity jobs; ii) why local workers shun such jobs; iii) why the local workers' reluctance to occupy unattractive jobs cannot be solved through standard markets mechanisms, that is, by raising the wages attached to such jobs; iv) why foreign workers from low-income countries are willing to accept such jobs; and, finally, v) why such structural labour demand can no longer be filled as before by women and teenagers.

In advanced economies there are unstable jobs due to the dualisation of the economy in a capital-intensive primary sector and a labour-intensive, low-productivity secondary sector, which gives way to a segmented labour market. Local workers shun such jobs because they confer low status and prestige and promise scant upward mobility, and because they entail motivation problems. The local workers' reluctance to occupy unattractive jobs cannot be solved through standard markets mechanisms, that is, raising the wages attached to such jobs because raising salaries at the bottom of the occupational scale would require proportionately raising wages at the following echelons, in order to respect the occupational hierarchy, and that would result in structural inflation. Foreign workers from low-income countries, especially temporary ones or those who entertain prospects of returning home some day, are willing to accept such jobs because low wages are usually high if compared with standards back home, and because the status and prestige that counts for them are the ones they have at home. Finally, such structural labour demand for entry-level jobs can no longer be filled as before by women and teenagers because female work has lost its secondary, dependent status in favour of an autonomous, career-oriented one, and lower fertility and longer education have diminished the availability of youngsters (Massey et al., 1998, p. 33).

The value of dual labour markets theory lies not so much in providing a general explanation of the causes of international migration, but rather in highlighting an important factor for the occurrence of international migration, namely the structural demand for foreign labour which is inherent in the economic structure of contemporary advanced societies. It also provides cogent explanations for such demand – although certainly not the only plausible ones – which help to understand, among other things, the apparently anomalous coexistence of a chronic demand for foreign labour with significant rates of structural unemployment in a number of receiving countries. Another merit is its contribution to dispel the idea that immigrant workers necessarily compete with native ones and affect the latter's level of wages and employment prospects.

Indeed, as a general explanation of the causes of international migration, dual labour markets theory is far from flawless. In the first place, a theory that posits that all international migration is demand-driven and excludes altogether 'push' factors cannot aspire to explain but a part of reality. Stating that most migrants end up finding employment at destination is one thing, and positing that migration flows are triggered by such demand a different one. Secondly, in our days immigration flows do not seem to result primarily, let alone uniquely, from recruitment practices, especially in the advanced economies that the theory envisages, such as those of North America or Western Europe. No doubt, recruitment was an important mechanism of immigration in those societies in the third quarter of the century, in the decades that preceded the formulation of the theory, and it is still practised today, particularly in the Persian Gulf and Asia-Pacific regions. But in advanced industrial economies most migrants come on their own initiative, and not necessarily to fill pre-existing jobs. In many cases, immigrants constitute a supply of labour that creates its own demand, that is, jobs that would not exist without their previous presence. Finally, the theory does not explain differential immigration rates, that is, why different advanced industrial economies, which have similar economic structures, exhibit rates of immigration that may vary by a factor of ten, say between Denmark or Norway on the one hand and Switzerland or Canada on the other.

World System Theory

Both the focus on macro social processes and the idea that highly developed economies need foreign labour to work for low wages in certain sectors are shared by world system theory, although its explanation of international migration does not so much rest on this demand, but rather in the dislocations brought about by capitalist penetration in less developed countries. A number of scholars, among them Alejandro Portes and Saskia Sassen, have put forth historical-structural explanations of international migration (Portes and Walton, 1981; Sassen, 1988). The conceptual cornerstone of world system theory is the notion of a 'modern world system' coined in the mid-1970s by historian-sociologist Immanuel Wallerstein, a world system of European hegemony that took shape since the sixteenth century and which consists of three concentric spheres – core states, semiperiphery and peripheral areas (Wallerstein, 1974). World system theory belongs in the historical-structural tradition that inspired in the 1960s dependency theory, although it differs in many respects from the latter. Yet, it shares with it the view of migration as one more product of the domination exerted by core countries over peripheral areas, in the context of international relationships fraught with conflict and tension. Migration also stems from inequality – in this case an unbalanced international order – but, contrary to equilibrium models, it reinforces it instead of leading to its redressing.

The kernel of the explanation of international migration has to be found primarily in the extension of the capitalist mode of production from core countries to peripheral ones, and the ensuing incorporation of new regions into an increasingly unified world economy. In the past this penetration was assisted by colonial regimes; in the present it is assured by neo-colonial regimes and multinational corporations, and direct foreign investment plays a crucial role in it. In order to counteract a declining rate of profit as domestic wages rise, and to accrue additional benefits, core countries intervene in peripheral ones in search of raw materials and to profit from cheap labour (Massey et al., 1998). This penetration, in combination with processes of modernisation and commercialisation of agriculture, entails the substitution of capitalist practices and processes for traditional ones, especially in agriculture and manufacturing.

A number of dislocations and disruptions ensue, including the displacement of workers who lose their traditional ways of life. Typically a large labour surplus develops that the still small non-agricultural sector is incapable of absorbing. This leads to migration to the cities, and to the swelling there of a traditional tertiary sector characterised by an extremely low productivity. An uprooted proletariat, prone to move abroad, is thus first created and in turn siphoned to the core countries through the same channels that were opened by the economic penetration, and through the cultural, transportation and communication links that followed. In the core countries migrants find employment in certain sectors which rely on cheap labour to maintain a high rate of profit. Migration thus operates as a global labour supply system (Sassen, 1988).

World system theory may shed light on the importance of past and present linkages between countries at different stages of development, and about some mechanisms of development which cause uprootedness. It also lends some flesh to the commonsense empirical observation that migration often connects countries that were linked in the past by colonial bonds, on account of the many vestiges left by such bonds.

Rather than being a theory of migration, world systems theory is a grand historical generalisation, a by-product of an univocal, reductionist and sense-loaded interpretation of history in which all countries pass through similar processes, as if following a grand script or some rigid laws of historical development. It is only applicable at the global level (Papademetriou and Martin, 1991, p. 10), and migrants are little more that passive pawns in the play of great powers and world processes presided over by the logic of capital accumulation. It may provide a background for the study of specific migration relationships between countries, but not so much for its investigation, as it is an explanation given *ex ante*, and formulated in a way that cannot be subject to empirical test. In addition, it seems difficult to reconcile with the increasing tendency towards the diversification of migration flows and paths, which runs parallel to the process of globalisation and questions the validity of one of the basic tenets of world system theory, as migration flows between hitherto unconnected or weakly connected countries are increasingly frequent, thus not following the very channels of penetration that allegedly created uprootedness.

Migration Networks

Few things, if any, are as characteristic of the contemporary way of looking into migration as the central attention accorded to migration networks, a notion that has a long tradition, going back to Thomas and Znaniecki (1918–20). What is new is the central role that they play in the investigation and the explanation of migration. The notion is so well known that it does not require much elaboration. Migration networks can be defined as sets of interpersonal relations that link migrants or returned migrants with relatives, friends or fellow countrymen at home. They convey information, provide financial assistance, facilitate employment and accommodation, and give support in various forms. In so doing, they reduce the costs and uncertainty of migration and therefore facilitate it (Massey et al., 1998, pp. 42–3). Networks can also induce migration through demonstration effects.

Migration networks can be seen as a form of social capital, insofar as they are social relations that permit access to other goods of economic significance, such as employment or higher wages. This viewpoint was first suggested by Douglas Massey (Massey et al., 1987), drawing on social capital theory, associated to such prominent names as James Coleman and Pierre Bourdieu. Likewise, as it has been suggested, this larger framework might also accommodate other intermediary institutions – such as smuggling rings or benevolent, humanitarian groups – which, with different purposes and aims, assist migrants to overcome entry barriers. Yet, the inclusion of such institution in the notion of social capital, which is made up of interpersonal ties, does not seem as straightforward as in the case of networks.

The importance of social networks for migration can hardly be overstated. It can be safely said that networks rank among the most important explanatory factors of migration. Many migrants move because others with whom they are connected migrated before. Migration networks have a multiplier effect, which is implicit in the formerly fashionable expression 'chain migration'. Moreover, the capital role that networks have usually played in migration flows is greatly enhanced nowadays in a world in which circulation is widely restricted. On the one hand, family reunion accounts for a substantial part of immigration flows in many countries. On the other, the importance of social networks is bound to increase as entry into receiving countries becomes more difficult, on account of their capacity to reduce the costs and risks of moving, including uncertainty.

In addition, networks are the main mechanism that makes migration a self-perpetuating phenomenon. Indeed, networks are cumulative in nature. They tend to grow ever larger and denser, as every move constitutes a resource for those who stay back, and facilitate further moves, which in turn widen the networks and the probability of their further expansion. The development of social networks may explain the continuation of migration independently from the causes that led to the initial movement. In fact, social networks may often be the foremost predictor of future flows. Because of this, migration networks may contribute to the explanation of differential migration. Yet, experience shows that an ever expanding dynamics cannot go forever. At some moment a saturation point must be reached, after which deceleration sets in. The dynamics of migration networks growth and stagnation constitute an area that calls for further investigation.

Last but not least, networks constitute an intermediate, relational level that stands between the micro level of individual decision-making and the macro level of structural determinants (Faist, 1997), thus contributing to bridge a gap that is one of the major limitations in migration thinking. Yet, all this notwithstanding, theorising about migration networks has not gone beyond the stage of a conceptual framework.

Systems Approach

Ever since the seminal contribution of Akin Mabogunje, in his study of rural-urban migration in Africa (1972), a systems approach has repeatedly been proposed as a fruitful, comprehensive framework for the study of migration. Migration systems are spaces characterised by the relatively stable association of a group of receiving countries with a number of areas of origin. Such association does not only result from migration flows, but is buttressed by connections and links of a varied nature. These linkages, and their multiple interactions, constitute the most appropriate context for the analysis of migration. Such a framework should ultimately be able to integrate the contributions of the remaining theoretical explanations, together with all the relevant actors in the process of migration, including networks and intermediary institutions, and some usually neglected dimensions, particularly the state (Kritz, Lim and Zlotnik, 1992).

Nevertheless, the migration systems' approach to migration, which aspired to draw on the analytic power of general system analysis, is as yet no more than a desideratum which has never been fulfilled, at least as far as international migration is concerned. It has hardly gone beyond the identification of international migration systems, at a purely descriptive level (United Nations, 1998, p. 147). Moreover, such identification has confined itself so far to the most stable part of the system, the countries that stand at the receiving end. The same can be said about the enumeration of the elements that define the existence of a migration system, such as relative structural homogeneity, geographic contiguity or proximity, similarity of policies, and common belonging to supranational organisations (Zlotnik, 1992). While no one would deny the advisability of studying migration flows as part of other flows and exchanges of various natures, the fact is that the full potential of the approach still remains at the stage of promise.

Migration as Self-sustaining and Self-perpetuating

A third theoretical strand that has received fresh consideration in recent times is the idea that migration is a self-sustaining and self-perpetuating phenomenon. This idea was first put forth by Gunnar Myrdal several decades ago, under the label 'cumulative causation', in the context of the 'backwash effects' put in motion by uneven development on underdeveloped areas. Douglas Massey has recently revived and enlarged the notion, identifying several factors and mechanisms that are responsible for the self-perpetuation of migration. The basic idea is that migration changes reality in a way that induces subsequent moves through a number of socioeconomic processes. The most important of them all, the expansion of networks, has already been referred to. Other relevant mechanisms which stem from migration and which in turn induce further migration include relative deprivation, the development of a culture of migration, a perverse distribution of human capital, and the stigmatisation of jobs usually performed by immigrants (Massey et al., 1998).

A Critical Evaluation

Recent theoretical contributions are leading to a better understanding of the causes of migration, and of the mechanisms that contribute to its self-perpetuation. Yet, the overall picture is still far from satisfactory. A number of clouds obscure the sky of migration theorising.

To start with, it can be surmised that the focus of existing theories may be somewhat misplaced. The first and foremost, often the only, dimension of migration that theories have aimed at explaining is why people move, or variants of the same question, such as what determines the volume of migration; that is, root causes, not even proximate determinants. This is clearly the case with neoclassical theory, the new economics of migration, world system theory, dual labour markets, and even the venerable 'push-pull' framework, even if only in abstract terms. Yet, it is not clear that investigating the causes constitutes the most useful and interesting line of enquiry nowadays.

As stated before, the usefulness of theories that try to explain why people move is in our days dimmed by their inability to explain why so few people move. Clearly, theories of migration should not only look to mobility but also to immobility, not only to centrifugal forces but also to centripetal ones. The classic pair 'push' and 'pull' should at least be complemented with 'retain' and 'repel'. The existence of centripetal forces that lead to staying has been generally ignored by theories, although there are signs of increasing interest in them in very recent years (Hammar et al., 1997). This implies that more attention than hitherto should be bestowed upon family types, kinship systems, social systems, and social structures in general. Much the same can be said about the cultural dimensions and contexts of migration, including, but not stopping there, the costs of cultural adaptation.

In addition to social and cultural factors, it is obvious that the explanation of limited mobility has to be sought in the realm of politics, more precisely in the crucial role played by states. The relevance of the political dimension nowadays can hardly be overstated. Nothing shapes migratory flows and types more than admission policies. As Kingsley Davis aptly put it, migration is a creature of policy (Davis, 1988, p. 259). Any theory built primarily with economic materials is bound to be in trouble in an international migration scene in which political considerations and the states intervene so prominently. In some of the most important contemporary migratory regions labour migration is severely curtailed – although a number of exceptions are generally recognised – and the largest migration flows result from legal entitlements, such us family reunion and asylum. Clearly, politics and the state are usually missing in theories of migration, and it is urgent to bring them back (Zolberg, 1989). In particular, the powerful impact of admission restrictions on processes, determinants and selectivity should be incorporated as an essential ingredient in models.

Some doubts can be raised as well about the usefulness of the over-arching emphasis put so far on the causes of migration. International migration is both very complex and straightforward. On the one hand, providing general answers apt to account for an endless variety of situations is exceedingly difficult. As both surveys and life histories show, the causes of migration are legion. General answers are bound to be reductionist. On the other hand, migration is rather straightforward. If something is in abundance, it is reason to move, and quite a few reasons can be taken for granted.

The time seems to have come to switch the bulk of theoretical attention away from causes and onto other dimensions of migration which are of paramount interest, both in intellectual and in policy terms, such as processes and consequences, including modes of migrant incorporation and societal transformations associated with international migration; the 'unsettled relationship' between migration and development, as Papademetriou and Martin rightly labelled it; social structures, including family and kinship ties; emerging processes of transnationalisation and their implications; and the state and the political context in which migration takes place, to mention but a few. In addition, refugees, traditionally overlooked on account of the exclusionary emphasis on voluntary migration, have to be included as essential actors in the theoretical explanation of migration. More thought should be devoted to migration networks and linkages of various types which stand between the macro and the micro dimensions.

All the above notwithstanding, dissatisfaction with existing migration theories, insofar as it is felt, may also have to do with matters of style. Existing theories generally promise more than they deliver. They tend to be partial and limited, in the sense that they are useful to explain a facet, or a dimension, or shed light on a particular feature, or are applicable to certain types of migration in certain contexts and not to others. To begin with, most theories only explain labour migration, and this is a considerable limitation in a contemporary scene in which other forms of migration are prominent. This partiality would not need to imply any problem in itself, were it not for the fact that – as it often happens in the social sciences – theories tend to make 'grand claims', out of proportion with their applicability and explanatory potential. The ambition to provide *the* explanation for migration, or for international migration for that matter, often betrays them. The aspiration at general applicability that can be presumed of a theory is generally neither met nor disclaimed.

Finally, migration theories generally suffer from epistemological fragility. If by theory is meant a set of logically interconnected propositions from which empirically testable statements can be formally derived, then almost no theory about migration meets these standards, with a couple of exceptions at best. But even if the standards are considerably lowered, most would still not qualify as a theory, whatever their empirical relevance and heuristic value. All of them provide useful points of view, but there should be more than that to qualify as a theory. Were it a purely formal matter, a question of logical status, it would not matter much. Yet, such weaknesses are far from inconsequential, as they have to do with the very nature and usefulness of theories, affect their ability to guide empirical research, and diminish their testability. It has to be added that this fragility tends to plague the social sciences as a whole.

Rather than fulfilling the function of guiding empirical research and providing testable hypotheses that can be contrasted with facts, existing migration theories are mainly useful for providing explanations *ex-post*. The starting point is usually one or more commonsense, empirical observations, which are then dressed in more or less formal and abstract terms with fitting explanations, drawn at times from the general reservoir of the social sciences. In so doing, theories or conceptual frameworks play the function of upgrading the formal status of empirical observations. In some cases, they are not abstract enough to go beyond empirical generalisation. Paraphrasing a famous metaphor that related theories with street lamps, in the case of migration existing theories are more useful to lean on them than to provide illumination. This may explain the fact that efforts at theorising have not led to cumulative advances in knowledge.

Concluding Remarks

In the course of the second half of the twentieth century, and especially in its last quarter, our understanding of the complexities of migration has made considerable progress. However, this deepened understanding has resulted more from empirical research, often divorced from theory, than from the enlightening effect of theories. It is true that the reservoir of theories, and especially of conceptual frameworks, available nowadays represents a clear improvement over the state of things which prevailed a few decades ago. Yet, as a whole, the contribution of theories to the knowledge of migration is still limited, more than what could be reasonably expected from theories. The wealth of forms and processes constantly revealed by empirical research, the dynamism manifested by an ever-changing reality, contrast with the limitations of theory building.

Such limitations are part and parcel of the general difficulties that the social sciences experience when trying to explain human behaviour, affected by a large number of interrelated variables.

But, in addition to that, in the case of migration they have to do with difficulties that are inherent in the phenomenon under scrutiny. Indeed, migration is hard to define, difficult to measure, multifaceted and multiform, and resistant to theory building (Arango, 1985), 'opaque to theoretical reasoning in general, and to formal models in particular' (Davis, 1988, p. 245). The first two obstacles make for ambiguity and oppose operationalisation. The third calls for interdisciplinary approaches which seldom happen.

Perhaps the greatest difficulty of studying migration lies in its extreme diversity, in terms of forms, types, processes, actors, motivations, socioeconomic and cultural contexts, and so on. It is no wonder that theories are at odds when trying to account for such complexity. As Anthony Fielding put it, 'perhaps migration is another "chaotic concept", one that needs to be "unpacked" so that each part can be seen in its proper historical and social context so that its significance in each context can be separately understood' (Fielding, 1983, p. 3).

This 'unpacking' calls for a better integration of theory and empirical research. While there are no simple and easy prescriptions for such a reconciliation, it could greatly benefit, *inter alia*, from case studies with a theoretical flair which focus on the specific – relying on a deep understanding of the societies involved – while making explicit the underlying assumptions on which they rest and contrasting them with reality, very much as Thomas and Znanicki did 80 years ago.

References

Arango, J. (1985), 'Las "Leyes de las Migraciones" de E.G. Ravenstein, cien años después', *Revista Española de Investigaciones Sociológicas*, 32, pp. 7–26.

Davis, K. (1988), 'Social Science Approaches to International Migration', in M.S. Teitelbaum and J.M. Winter (eds), *Population and Resources in Western Intellectual Traditions*, New York: The Population Council, pp. 245–61.

Faist, T. (1997), 'The Crucial Meso-level', in T. Hammar, G. Brochmann, K. Tamas and T. Faist (eds), *International Migration, Immobility and Development*, Oxford: Berg.

Fawcett, J.T. (1989), 'Networks, Linkages, and Migration Systems', *International Migration Review*, 23, pp. 671–80.

Fielding, A. (1983), 'The "Impasse in Migration Theory" Revisited', IBG/Royal Dutch G.S., *Conference on International Migration*, Soesterberg.

Gurak, D.T. and Caces, F. (1992), 'Migration Networks and the Shaping of Migration Systems', in M. Kritz, L.L. Lim and H. Zlotnik (eds), *International Migration Systems: A Global Approach*, Oxford: Clarendon Press, pp. 150–76.

Hammar, T., Brochmann, G., Tamas, K. and Faist, T. (eds) (1997), *International Migration, Immobility and Development*, Oxford: Berg.

Harris, J.R. and Todaro, M.P. (1970), 'Migration, Unemployment and Development: a Two Sector Analysis, *American Economic Review*, 60, pp. 126–42.

Kritz, M., Lim, L.L. and Zlotnik, H. (1992), *International Migration Systems. A Global Approach*, Oxford: Clarendon Press.

Lee, E.S. (1966), 'A Theory of Migration', *Demography*, 3 (1), pp. 47–57.

Lewis, W.A. (1954), 'Economic Development with Unlimited Supplies of Labour', *Manchester School of Economic and Social Studies*, 22, pp. 139–91.

Mabogunje, A.L. (1972), *Man, Space and the Environment*, New York: Oxford University Press.

Massey, D.S., Alarcón, R., Durand, J. and González, H. (1987), *Return to Aztlan: The Social Process of International Migration from Western Mexico*, Berkeley and Los Angeles: University of California Press.

Massey, D.S., Arango, J., Hugo, G., Kouaouci, A., Pellegrino, A. and Taylor, J.E. (1993), 'Theories of International Migration: A Review and Appraisal', *Population and Development Review*, 19 (3), pp. 431–66.

Massey, D.S., Arango, J., Hugo, G., Kouaouci, A., Pellegrino, A. and Taylor, J.E. (1998), *Worlds in Motion. Understanding International Migration at the End of the Millenium*, Oxford: Clarendon Press.

Mincer, J. (1978), 'Family Migration Decisions', *Journal of Political Economy*, 86 (5), pp. 749–73.

Papademetriou, D.G. and Martin, P.L. (1991), *The Unsettled Relationship: Labor Migration and Economic Development*, New York: Greenwood Press.

Piore, M.J. (1979), *Birds of Passage: Migrant Labor in Industrial Societies*, Cambridge: Cambridge University Press.

Portes, A. and Walton, J. (1981), *Labor, Class, and the International System*, New York: Academic Press.

Ranis, G. and Fei, J.C.H. (1961), 'A Theory of Economic Development', *American Economic Review*, 51, pp. 533–65.

Ravenstein, E.G. (1885), 'The Laws of Migration', *Journal of the Royal Statistical Society*, 48, pp. 167–227.

Ravenstein, E.G. (1889), 'The Laws of Migration', *Journal of the Royal Statistical Society*, 52, pp. 241–301.

Sassen, S. (1988). *The Mobility of Labor and Capital: A Study in International Investment and Labor Flow*, Cambridge: Cambridge University Press.

Singer, P. (1973), *Economia política da urbanizaçao*, Sao Paulo: Editora Brasiliense – Ediçoes Cebrap.

Sjaastad, L.A. (1962), 'The Costs and Returns of Human Migration', *Journal of Political Economy*, 705, pp. 80–93.

Stark, O. (1991), *The Migration of Labor*, Cambridge: Basil Blackwell.

Stark, O. and Taylor, J.E. (1989), 'Relative Deprivation and International Migration', *Demography*, 26 (1), pp. 1–14.

Thomas, W.I. and Znaniecki, F. (1918–20), *The Polish Peasant in Europe and America*, Boston: William Badger.

Todaro, M.P. (1969), 'A Model of Labor Migration and Urban Unemployment in Less Developed Countries', *American Economic Review*, March.

Todaro, M.P. (1976). *Internal Migration in Developing Countries*, Geneva: International Labor Office.

United Nations (1998), 'Recommendations on Statistics of International Migration', Rev. 1, Series M, No. 58.

Wallerstein, I. (1974), *The Modern World-System. Capitalist Agriculture and the Origins of the European World-Economy in the Sixteenth Century*, New York: Academic Press.

Zlotnik, H. (1992), 'Empirical Identification of International Migration Systems', in M. Kritz, L.L. Lim and H. Zlotnik (eds), *International Migration Systems. A Global Approach*, Oxford: Clarendon Press, pp. 19–40.

Zolberg, A. (1989), 'The Next Waves: Migration Theory for a Changing World', *International Migration Review*, 23 (3), pp. 403–30.

Chapter 2

New Migration Movements in Central and Eastern Europe[1]

Marek Okólski

Introduction

The last quarter of the twentieth century was often referred to as the 'era of migration'. Although statistical evidence does not unequivocally validate this popular view, it seems obvious that the flows and countries of migrants' origin and destination have become more diversified in that period (Zlotnik, 1998).

By all accounts, the contribution of Central and Eastern Europe (CEE) to those trends, especially over the last dozen years, was very substantial. Moreover, the population of Central and East European countries (CEECs) was among those very few that recently, since 1988 or so, experienced significant rise in the volume of migrant flows (Okólski, 1998).

This conclusion, however, would hardly be plausible, if legitimate at all, when referred to official statistics of CEECs. Those statistics are based on outdated concepts, which do not reflect newly shaped reality and recognise as migration only the movements of persons for permanent residence in another country. According to the official statistics of CEECs, the flows of migrants in the 1990s were rather low and stable, if not declining (Slovakia). The annual inflow ranged from approximately 1,000 (Bulgaria, Romania) to 10,000–15,000 (the Czech Republic and Hungary). The trends and levels with respect to the outflow were only a little more differentiated; whereas the Czech Republic, Hungary and Slovakia hardly recorded any meaningful emigration (the actual numbers below 1,000 on a yearly basis), emigration from Bulgaria, Poland and Romania reached a considerable size (between 25,000 and 60,000), with Bulgaria maintaining a relatively stable (the highest in the region) level and the remaining two showing a gradual decline since 1995 (Okólski, 1999a).

In the real world, meanwhile, the settlement migration has become a tiny part of all movements observed in CEE in recent period, giving way to many other, previously insignificant or unknown, forms of international mobility.

The changes in population movements in CEE came as a surprise because over most of the post-World War II period not only migration but any kind of international travelling took only a vestigial size in that region. The conspicuous shift from non-mobility to high-intensity migration regime in CEE followed the collapse of communist rule, and the opening up of external borders of all CEECs to foreign travelling.

Basic Trends and Issues

East to West Migration

Once the Central and East Europeans started to move abroad freely, the migration analysts scoffed at various gloomy predictions. The leitmotif of those predictions was that the revolution in CEE would have activated a huge migration potential in that region, and the main direction of inevitable large flows of people will be from East to West. Some sources spoke of millions persons, mainly from the ex-USSR to be involved in those movements.

Indeed, it appeared in the early 1990s that the East–West flows started to be a prevalent component of European migration. Seen from the West European perspective, that new trend was nearly obvious and expected, in view of the gradual lifting, since 1989, of major barriers that in the past prevented great numbers of Central and East Europeans from moving to the West. That expectation found strong support in the experience of a number of East–West emigration episodes, which have taken place since the post-Stalinist thaw of the mid-1950s. According to that experience, whenever the 'opportunities allowed', a massive mobilisation of people ready to emigrate took place, and almost instantly the number of emigrants from the East multiplied.

More importantly, European migration statistics for the late 1980s and early 1990s seemed to confirm the above prediction. Between 1985 and 1990 not only did the flows of people from East to West increase but in addition that increase was generally (with the distinct exception of Italy and Spain) faster than the growth of the immigration from the South. The early 1990s saw a continuation (if not – in the case of certain countries of the East – acceleration) of that trend. In addition, an increased presence of the citizens of CEECs in the West was reflected in many other (not strictly migration) records. The number of tourists has virtually multiplied everywhere in Western Europe, and some Western countries recorded intensified inflow of asylum seekers or seasonal workers from the East.

It quickly turned out, however, that the 1990s would not be a decade of East–West population movements. As early as around 1992 or 1993 westbound migration from the East started to slow down. In Germany, which probably receives from two-thirds to three-quarters of all Central and Eastern European migrants coming to the European Union, net migration in the case of Poles (a predominant nationality among the region's outmigrants) has been declining gradually since 1990, in the case of Hungary since 1992, and in the case of Bulgaria and Romania since 1993, whereas in the case of the Russian Federation it has remained relatively stable.

Concomitant was a shift from permanent to temporary migration and a decline in the number of asylum seekers' flow. All in all, despite liberalised regulations and step-by-step implemented freedom of movements in the home countries, and actually increased mobility of the Central and Eastern European population, its outflow to the West has begun to decrease, even before climbing to any spectacularly high level. The main reason behind this remarkable trend seems to be the West's abandonment of a policy of (politically-motivated) preferential treatment for Central and Eastern European migrants, and submitting those migrants to the newly-developed restrictive rules of 'fortress Europe' after 1990.

True, the mainstream of migration statistics, be it of countries of origin or destination, hardly reflects East to West ethnically driven flows, which erupted in the late 1980s, after a long spell of the levelling off that followed the post-World War II intensified movements. Leaving aside involuntary movements caused by ethnic cleansing within the former FSR Yugoslavia, two major directions of the migration of ethnic background seem to have dominated the trend:

- ethnic Germans from CEE (chiefly Poland, Romania and ex-USSR) to Germany; and
- ethnic Jews from the ex-USSR to Israel, Germany and the United States.

Other, less important, directions comprised ethnic Finns and Greeks from the former Soviet Union and ethnic Turks from Bulgaria.

It might be estimated that between 1989 and 1998 the two directions that crucially contributed to the ethnically motivated outflow from CEE, embraced as many as approximately 3.8 million persons, including 2.6 million ethnic Germans and 1.2 million ethnic Jews (along with their family members). Taken as a whole, it was probably one of the most sizeable waves of migrants observed in Europe over the last ten years or so. The fact that a large part of those movements is hardly accounted for in statistics and analyses of international migration, implies a severe bias in our understanding of contemporary East–West population flows.

With a distinct exception of the outflow from Bosnia and Kosovo, much of the recent East–West ethnic movements have been occurring under circumstances of no aggravating tension or no nagging need to leave the country of origin. Moreover a large part of migrants comprised persons whose ancestors had settled in the countries of origin generations ago, and who had been weakly tied to their symbolic 'homelands'. It seems therefore legitimate to tentatively conclude that, perceived within a broad perspective of contemporary migration trends, those ethnicity-driven flows of people may somehow seem an anachronism. On the other hand, it might be noted that active promotion, if not recruitment of migrants, pursued by government agencies or non-government organisations (NGOs) representing the countries of destination has been instrumental for this phenomenon to realise.

The description of recent East–West migration trend would be even more biased if no mention was made of the outflow of refugees and persons in need of temporary protection from the former Yugoslavia. At the peak time of asylum seekers arrivals in Western Europe (1993) that single country contributed to nearly one-third of the total (recorded in 19 countries of European Economic Area). Altogether, between 1991 and 1999 more than one million people from the former Yugoslavia sought some form of protection in the West (Baucic, 1999). On the other hand, the flow of those persons needs to be perceived from different perspective than just lifting of the 'iron curtain' in the former communist countries.

Even though all forms of population movements from East to West (including flow of regular migrants and asylum seekers, and 'repatriation' of ethnic groups) would be accounted for, the estimated overall number of citizens of CEECs who have moved to the West since 1988 seems much below the expectations expressed around 1990.

Other Movements

Taking a different perspective than the East to West migration, however, population movements in the post-communist CEE in the 1990s were indeed so conspicuous to deserve to be placed among the key developments in European migration. Besides the somewhat traditional outflow to Western countries, I have here in mind three new migration phenomena of similarly great importance in the region: firstly, an enormous intensification of international flows within the region; secondly, an influx of people from outside the region; and, thirdly, westbound transit migration. It is precisely the high intensity and great diversity of those flows that recently have led international migration analysts to describe Central and Eastern Europe ever more frequently as a 'new migration pole' or a 'new migration space' in the global arena.

Intraregional movements Convergent diagnoses prepared by many research centres attest to a considerably increased and indeed already very high international mobility of the region's population. They show, for instance, that from 1987 to 1994 about one third of Western and central Ukrainian households were involved in relocations of that kind, while before 1987 foreign travel had been a rarity, and cases of migration noted by researchers had for the most part been connected with redeployments of Red Army units (Pirozhkov et al., 1997). A similar proportion found for Polish households suggests that in the 1990s nearly half of the population occasionally benefited from proceeds gained as a result of migration (Frejka et al., 1998).

I will now restrict myself to a succinct indication of basic elements of those movements (Okólski 1998).

The first of them, and most important in terms of numbers, are voluntary resettlement flows between the countries that have emerged from the former USSR. Between 1991 and 1997 they involved about 10 million people, and at their peak in 1994 over one million people flowed into Russia itself from the other former Soviet republics, while nearly a quarter of a million left Russia for the other former republics.

The second element is a stream of refugees or persons in need of temporary protection. Although displaced persons from the former FSR Yugoslavia (over three millions by late 1999, including over 1.3 million outside the former Yugoslav borders) have taken refuge mainly in the West, yet the list of the top 25 receiving states includes six CEECs. Hungary itself has offered refuge to nearly 80,000 former Yugoslav citizens. A stream of displaced persons from the areas of the former USSR affected by civil wars or exacerbated ethnic or national conflicts has assumed even greater proportions. Russia has received most of them, nearly one million by early 1996. A mass outflow of Romanian citizens, principally Roma and persons of Hungarian nationality, has also been of some importance in this context. Hungary, for example, has become the receiving country for some 60,000 Romanian asylum seekers.

Migrations in search of employment are the third important component of internal Central and Eastern European migrations. There are two forms of such flows: an official one, documented with adequate permits; and an unofficial one, falling into the category of incomplete migration. Legal migrations for work occur between all the countries of the region, with inflows decidedly prevailing in some of them and outflows in others.

Finally, the fourth element of the international intraregional mobility is relatively new form, which might be termed incomplete migration. It involves persons described sometimes as 'false tourists', characterised by a flexible employment situation and, generally, a relatively low social status, persons ready to go abroad almost at any time and taking up various simple and extremely low-paid jobs, usually for short periods of time and without the permit required. The basic forms of employment are petty trade, household help, renovation and construction services, fruit picking, assistance at harvest, and sewing. Such persons are continually in touch with the members of their households remaining at home and actually spend most of their time with them. It is a transitory form of spatial mobility, with its source in structural imbalances on the domestic labour markets of many of the countries in the region, and in particular in a relative surplus of rural population. It substitutes, in part at least, the formerly widespread commuting from the country to nearby towns, or short-distance seasonal (internal) labour migrations. According to one estimate, in 1995 some 800,000 people came to Poland from Ukraine alone in such capacity.

It might therefore be concluded, in view of the foregoing discussion, that the flows that have their origins in the fall of communist system in Europe have recently began to shape the all-European migration trends. Owing to a close geographical proximity and the common history, a predominant proportion of migrants, exiles, asylum seekers and (more or less genuine) tourists from CEE preferred moving within that region to leaving for anywhere else.

The phenomenon of the flow of irregular workers is completely new to CEE and results from the increasing internal economic diversification of the region. Though very recent, it has already assumed large proportions and numerous forms. For instance, in the Czech Republic and Hungary such workers (among whom Ukrainians prevail) are for the most part employed under several months' contracts, while in Poland and Russia under contracts for performance of a specific task, sometimes executed in the course of several days or weeks. One estimate quotes the number of 100,000 to 200,000 irregular foreign workers in the Czech Republic in 1997, as compared to 125,000 aliens holding work permits (Drbohlav, 1998). In Poland, a mere 18,000 foreigners were employed legally at the same time, while a few hundred thousand (probably over half a million) worked without permission.

The inflow to CEE The second important stream turning CEE into a region of migration influx is the immigration of aliens, sometimes whole families, coming to stay for longer periods, often with the intention to settle down. Though the settlement process is usually extended over many years, some countries of the region already have communities of foreigners, numbering from several thousand to between 10,000 and 50,000 people, of nationalities rarely found in these countries before 1990. The spectacular examples are: the Chinese community in Hungary, the Chinese and Vietnamese communities in the Czech Republic, and the Vietnamese and Armenian communities in Poland. A certain influx of nationals of Western countries, particularly high-class specialists posted by their companies and young graduates who find it difficult to begin a career in their home countries, seems to be a qualitatively important novelty. In order to help imagine the volume of this influx, one may quote an estimated number of Western migrants in the Czech Republic in 1997. While slightly over 15,000 of them were holders of long-term residence permits, and about 9,000 of business or work permits, as many as 30,000 to 40,000 were employed without the permit required (Drbohlav, 1998).

As a result of these trends, some of the countries: Croatia, the Czech Republic, Slovakia and Hungary have become net immigration countries, and in some of their areas, multinational communities have flourished, with Prague, where foreigners already account for over 10 per cent of the population, being the most significant example. Other countries, such as Lithuania, Poland and Romania follow suit, with their emigration systematically diminishing and immigration growing.

It seems evident from the above considerations that the influx of people into CEECs is characterised by a high degree of illegality. Illegality in a variety of shades, incidentally: sometimes illegal border crossing occurs, in other cases the permitted period of stay is exceeded, in yet others there is unregistered stay or activity. It is often the case that whole migrant families reside in a host country without legalisation for as long as several years, which slowly forces them out to the margin of society, preventing them from getting a proper education and regular employment, from participation in the social security and health care systems, not to mention other forms of participation in public life.

Transit migration Proceeding to the third important group of flows of migrants observed in the countries of the region, that is westbound transit, one should note in the first place its strictly illicit nature. Furthermore, the transit in question is increasingly supported by a vast network of trafficking organisations operating on an international scale.

Thanks to their newly-liberalised migration policies facilitating border crossing, convenient geographic situation and lack of experience in combating illegal migration, CEECs have made an excellent waiting room before the final stage of a migrant's journey from his home country to the target country (which mostly turns out to be Germany). This role falls principally to the Czech Republic and Poland as countries bordering Germany, the most important target country in European migrations. The other countries of the region play the role of mobilisation centres or intermediate links in migrant trafficking. Of particular significance in this context are the countries of the Commonwealth of Independent States (CIS), with considerable stretches of their borders poorly marked or unguarded. Thus, the present-day westbound transit migration is a common problem for the countries of the region.

According to estimates by CEECs, some 150,000 to 250,000 migrants from Asia and Africa stay in their territories at any given time, awaiting trafficking into the West. According to a recent estimate by Tajikistan, 'the first transit country' for many of the trafficked migrants, about 20,000 Afghan nationals stay in its territory at any given time, prepared for a further organised journey (Olimova, 1998). The numbers of migrants in traffic staying in the territories of countries such as Russia, Ukraine and Belarus are even considerably greater. Another example presents Poland where in 1997 alone, some 1,600 convoys with illegal migrants in transit were detained, including 215 in excess of 10 people. An estimated 30,000 to 50,000 migrants are trafficked annually from Poland to Germany (Okólski, 1999b). Reports from the Czech Republic allow a similar estimate. While the ethnic composition of the group of trafficked migrants varies considerably, the inhabitants of the Indian subcontinent (Afghanistan, Bangladesh, India, Pakistan and Sri Lanka) have recently prevailed. Persons with Algerian, Chinese, Iraqi, Iranian, Somali and Vietnamese passports are often found among them as well.

The trafficking in aliens into some of the CEECs, including occasional smuggling from the West, is a relatively new derivative phenomenon. The latter occurrence may be illustrated by the smuggling of Vietnamese (awaiting deportation to their country from Germany) into Poland. The trafficking in Ukrainian and Romanian minors and bringing them into Hungary for the purpose of prostitution, and the trafficking in Vietnamese nationals and inserting them in Poland in connection with illegal employment at firms owned by other Vietnamese are, for example, relatively large-scale phenomena.

Migrant trafficking is becoming a highly profitable and, at the same time, well-organised illegal activity, in which use is made of modern technologies (including heavy military equipment) and of international connections between criminal groups, as well as of links between offenders and the border guards or the police. Given its profitability and the high, definitely not diminishing, demand for the services of trafficking networks on the part of potential migrants, it may be expected to become a lasting phenomenon.

Summary of Recent Trends

Summing up this description of the new migration phenomena in CEE, the following conclusions may be drawn:

- while the international mobility of the residents of the region has grown considerably, the main flows are directed into the countries of the region;
- forms or types of migration flows and the links of the region with the other parts of the globe have become greatly diversified;
- it follows from the two characteristics mentioned above that the region has become a new important unit in the global migration space;
- besides common features accounting for similarity between the countries of the region, there are characteristics clearly distinguishing countries from one another;
- there are strong migration magnets in the region (the Czech Republic, Poland, Russia and Hungary), as well as outmigration areas, sending out migrants attracted by the aforementioned magnets, or by other ones outside the region (Belarus, Bulgaria, Moldova, Romania and Ukraine), and countries experiencing migration on a very moderate scale (Lithuania and Slovakia);
- in terms of the intensity of migration flows, the following types of countries may be distinguished: the first, with strong inflow but weak outflow (the Czech Republic and Hungary); the second, with strong inflow and outflow (Croatia, Poland, Russia and Romania); the third, with weak inflow but strong outflow (Albania, Belarus, Bulgaria, Moldova and Ukraine); and the fourth, with weak inflow and outflow (Lithuania and Slovakia);
- finally, there is a small number of countries in the region (mainly Russia) where large masses of displaced persons have emerged, awaiting return home or a further journey, that is, a phenomenon being a starting point for further intensified migration, while some other countries (mainly Bosnia and Kosovo) remain largely abandoned by persons in need of temporary refuge, and thus are bound to experience an intensive wave of returns in the future; on the other hand, in some countries (such as Poland, Russia and

Hungary), unlike most of the others, embryos of new, permanent migrant communities have emerged, which in turn means that these countries will need to solve the problems of integration of aliens.

Major Consequences and Challenges

Separateness or Marginalisation of Migrants

New trends in international migration in CEE have found the region largely inexperienced and unprepared to cope with its size, diversity and dynamics. Side effects of the transition to democratic state and market economy have rather universally comprised various gaps in legal regulations, weakening of the state administration and law enforcement, booming of the shadow economy, etc. One of the distinct outcomes of this situation is the difficulty of migrants to integrate in the host society or at least benefit from its basic social and economic institutions. Moreover, over the 1990s the situation has tended to worsen.

Irregularity One important symptom of such tendency appears to be a very high volume and persistence of irregular migration. This pertains to border crossing, migrant's stay in the host country, legitimacy of migrant's employment and certain other, probably less important, aspects. An overwhelming proportion of persons who travel within, from, to or through CEE move for a different purpose than presumed or officially declared, and many of them overstay without due authorisation. A large part of travelling foreigners resort to forged documents, mostly tourist vouchers, business letters or personal invitations, but sometimes also passports, visas or work permits.

As a consequence, while abroad, foreigners are often in a precarious situation. They are unprotected by their own state and exposed to abuse and exploitation in the host country. On the other hand, irregularity of migration fuels activities of local criminal groups, corruption of police and administration, functioning of shadow economy, and so on, either in countries of origin or destination. Mainly for those reasons relatively great number of foreigners, despite their recurrent visits to the same countries of destination, remain literally alien or marginalised in those countries.

Transnationality At least three symptoms involving the 'alienation' of migrants might be related to the transnationalism of migrants' situation: the growing enclaves of highly skilled migrants, the setting up of the embryo of ethnic enclaves and the persistence of split living arrangements of people involved in incomplete migration.

As much as in all Western countries, a growing importance might be ascribed to the flows of people for whom social integration in the host country is not an issue. Those flows embrace persons who are either (actually and willingly) short-term migrants and by definition do not seek social integration, or those who come for a relatively long stay (for example, exceeding one year) but the basic function (and the main purpose) of their movement precludes that kind of integration or makes it a matter of relatively low priority. Below I reflect on the latter.

Typically, long-term migrants whose social integration in the host country is not a prerequisite for performing/achieving major objectives of their migration, while its absence does not in any significant way harm the migrant or the host country, include the diplomatic personnel and foreign students. In the last decade or so, however, this is also (increasingly) the case of the highly skilled employees of transnational corporations (TNCs), the representatives of various international NGOs and other international service providers. This trend has also been visible in CEE (OECD, 1998).

From the analysis pertaining to the post-1990 experts' flows from West to East it is evident that the highly skilled migrants identify themselves with a multiplicity of functions, in particular with the restructuring of company, branch and national economy, therefore linking the transformation of CEE to the globalisation process, but they are hardly involved in the public life of destination countries (Rudolph and Hillmann, 1997).

Also, symptoms of the setting up of transnational migrant communities whose founding principle is not necessarily tight social integration with the host country but which have been built upon the ethnic origin of migrants rather than their skills were recently observed in CEE. Nyiri (1997), for instance, has described the process of organisation of the new overseas Chinese communities in Hungary whose major trait is the high level of internal integration and their strong political and economic affiliation with China. For those communities relations with the host society do not seem of primary importance. They have been created thanks to the worldwide Chinese commercial web, interwoven through traditional family links, which invests large capital in various destination countries and is capable of flexibly moving the stock and distribution centre from one country to another. This pattern leading to, as Habermas puts it, 'deterritorialised nationalism' presents the host societies with a risk of rejection of their political culture by migrant communities.

Still, the phenomenon of incomplete migration poses more complex problems for migrants and sending/receiving societies. By incomplete migration I understand the specific outcome of an unfinished 'mobility transition' (Zelinski, 1971) in countries of CEE, which left a large part of the rural population halfway through between its employment in agriculture and residence in town, and prevented a considerable proportion of the inhabitants of small towns from moving to large urban centres. Its origins might be sought in the radical slowing down of outflow from the rural areas and peripheral towns and the strong increase in commuting, because the failure of initial 'socialist' industrialisation in the 1950s and 1960s denied urban housing opportunities to workers recruited in the countryside and small towns for urban labour force as manual or low-skilled workers. After the expiration of demand for low-skilled commuters or seasonal industrial workers in the late 1960s and throughout the 1970s, many persons (predominantly Poles) who found themselves in such situation begun income-seeking activities (mainly, petty trade) in neighbouring former socialist countries. This evolved towards the present form of the phenomenon, popular in many countries of CEE (for example, Poland, Romania, Slovakia and Ukraine), which is characterised by the following traits:

- migrants enter the host country under the guise of tourists to trade or work informally;
- migration is considered by the household as an alternative and supplementary source of income, often within the household strategy of income diversification and the minimising of risks;
- although each flow involves only weeks or days spent in the host country, the migrants do that repeatedly and in effect many of them work for a considerable part of the year outside the home country.

Due to the very low cost of living of the migrants households, incomplete migration – despite low migrants' pay – has proved to be a relatively efficient way of earning money under transitory circumstances. On the other hand, the result of that phenomenon is *inter alia* the prolonged precariousness of migrants' economic situation, family life and, generally, social role. It deprives the migrants from any form of integration in the host country, and at the same time, in the case of people from the rural areas, sustains their socially marginal position in the home country, or, in the case of the inhabitants of urban areas, contributes to their marginalisation (Frejka et al., 1998).

Though it might be argued that people who resort to that mobility create another form (strikingly different from that represented by the privileged highly skilled professionals) of transnational migrants, the function of their movements is only peripheral. The solution to the problem of transnational marginalisation of those migrants might not come instantly nor easily. On the contrary, many factors such as their low level of education, an accrued strong habit of flexible behaviours, the demanding socioeconomic milieu of the transforming home country, and the existence – in frequent cases – of a 'safety niche' composed of a family house and a subsistence-oriented plot of land supported by extended and strong family ties, suggest – for the life perspective – that a great proportion of the persons taking part in incomplete migration will neither be able to cope with the challenges of the coming modern society nor will they be sufficiently covered by the protective umbrella of the state. Therefore, coming to terms with the transnational marginalisation of current migrants from CEECs might require the passing of the generation involved.

Prolonged temporariness of foreigners in precarious situation   Due to 'undefined circumstances' of the early transition period, including excessively flexible rules of foreigners' admission, poor border control (in many cases, especially on the territory of the former Soviet Union, the lack of check points), inefficient monitoring of foreigners' sojourn and employment, and so on, the region has become an attractive destination for many migrants from Africa and Asia seeking refuge, for whatever reason. In the course of time, with more and more consolidated efforts by the Central or Eastern European states to cope with new migration reality, however, a substantial part of those migrants, originally heading for the West, have had to remain within CEE. Various estimates speak of hundreds of thousand of such people staying, usually unwillingly, on the territory of CEECs, typically in Russia, Ukraine and Belarus.

A peculiarity of this phenomenon is that, on the one hand, the migrants belong to the poor and a majority of them cannot afford returning home (for some of them that would be dangerous, anyway), and, on the other hand the host countries of CEE lack financial resources, expertise and, in some cases, institutions to resolve the problem. In effect, the migrants (usually young individuals but also couples with minor children), whose situation often is irregular, have for years a *de facto* temporary legal status and live in makeshift arrangements. They are detached from *inter alia* labour market, social security, educational system and cultural life.

Many of those persons have been for years submitted to admission procedures, including those related to the refugee status, with a slight chance of succeeding or even being transferred to a country outside of CEE. One of the main factors that perpetuates the precarious situation of migrants who arrived from the South is their conglomerate-type composition. Namely, these comprise a mix of the former (of the pre-transition period) students or migrant workers, the people who in the early 1990s 'accidentally' found themselves in CEE, genuine refugees or other kinds of asylum seekers, and migrants assisted by trafficking organisations. Recently, members of all these groups, including trafficked migrants, in increasing quantities, attempt to use the resources and facilities of refugee protection and humanitarian agencies. Due to this, in some countries of the region the asylum system is said to be at stake, as it has become increasingly difficult to distinguish *bona fide* refugee from any other category of migrants originating in Africa and Asia, and provide a proper assistance to those entitled.

Adverse Effects of the Outflow of Privileged Ethnic Groups

By privileged ethnic groups I mean those whose members are actively, in an organised way (usually, legally) recruited in the countries of origin and supported in the countries of destination. Only a handful of ethnic groups living in CEE (primarily Germans and Jews) benefit from being in such situation.

What seems striking as far as those voluntary East–West movements are concerned is the fact that the ethnic entitlement for resettlement was usually not strictly observed. For instance, the share of ethnic Jews among those who emigrated from Russia to Israel is said to have fallen below 50 per cent in the late 1990s (Tolts, 1999), which resembles the proportion of ethnic Germans among *Aussiedler* population from Poland admitted by Germany in the 1980s, especially 1989 and 1990 (Frejka et al., 1998). On the other hand, and more importantly, that migration is demographically and socially highly selective, and, among other things, involves a heavy brain drain. For example, between 1994 and 1996 migrants with a university degree constituted more than a half of all ethnic migrants from that country who arrived in Canada, more than 45 per cent in the United States, one third in Israel, one fifth in Greece and one sixth in Germany (de Tinguy, 1997). Conspicuously, in the 1990s, Germany, making an unusual exception to its internal regulations, admitted around 60,000 Jews originating from the ex-USSR of whom a large majority were highly skilled. Among those who settled in Berlin almost three quarters (of the adult immigrants) were university graduates or university students, and engineering and medicine were the most common professions among them (Doomernik, 1997).

Illegal Business of Migration

In a recent paper Salt (1998, p. 4) has developed the concept of the migration business as 'a system of institutionalised networks consisting of organisations, agents and individuals each of which stands to gain some form of remuneration. In other words, there are vested interests in the promotion of migration'.

Below I leave aside the public business of migration and a large part of the private component of that business whose relevance to CEE is still limited, and focus entirely on the illegitimate (thus undesirable) side of the latter.

A major part of that illegal business consists of trafficking in persons or, in its reduced form smuggling of migrants. The importance of that phenomenon lies in the fact that for a large majority of the residents of many countries in the South (or – to a lesser extent – the East) no alternative option currently exists if they strive to migrate to the West. On the other hand, the activities of trafficking networks increasingly affect the numbers of actual migrants, as well as the selection of destination countries and the routes attended. It might therefore be argued that trafficking in persons is or might soon become a significant factor contributing to the emergence of a new geographic pattern of migration.

In contrast to many other illegitimate acts observed in the process of migration, an individual act of trafficking affects more than just one society, and its consequences are probably more comprehensive and far reaching. Its prevention and combating seem even more arduous than other forms of illicit migrants' behaviours. This is because trafficking in migrants involves international groups of organised crime and is closely linked with other illegal activities of those groups, and – last but not least – yields high profits.

As indicated in this chapter, the countries of CEE have recently become a major transit ground and vestibule (and, in growing instances, a destination) for tens of thousands (annually) of foreigners smuggled or trafficked into Western Europe. A survey conducted in 1998 in Poland revealed the existence of two basic premises facilitating further growth of that phenomenon: the world-wide availability of contact points reaching out most remote and most hardly accessible localities in Africa and Asia, and the well co-ordinated and effective functioning of the trafficking organisations (Okólski, 1999b).

Despite the enormously high price of the trafficking, relative to the affluence of all countries of migrants' origin, a mechanism is observed according to which increasingly money is paid to a trafficker by a future migrant's employer beforehand or, after successful arrival to the target country by those, usually, relatives or other coethnics, who commit themselves to the migrant's insertion at the ultimate destination. Another important finding reveals the significant role of the 'Russian' criminal networks in running trafficking organisations. At least one-third of all studied cases displayed a very similar pattern: an unattended trip (often, Aeroflot flight) to Moscow or another city in the ex-USSR is followed after a varying waiting period for the building of the migrant's group, by an escorted trip to Kiev, Minsk or Vilnius, and, usually after the rearrangement of the group, an illegal entering of Poland. Those migrants explicitly pointed to travel arrangements, document issuance, transportation network, hiding on the route and border crossing as facilitated by Russian authorities such as official tourist agents, diplomatic representatives, airline staff, policemen, military and border guard officers, who apparently collaborated closely with the traffickers. In turn, while in Poland a large part of the trafficked migrants is introduced to the government refugee services and – for the time when the final trafficking operation is prepared – placed in one of the refugee reception centres. Gradually, migrants – in newly composed groups – are further trafficked to Germany and other Western countries (Okólski, 1999b).

Such *modus operandi* of migrant trafficking organisations brings a number of immediate, detrimental and socially unwanted, consequences for a country of transit or destination, which *inter alia* include the penetration of foreign (international) criminal networks and, as has already been suggested, the undermining of the national asylum system. It spreads the corruption of officials, increases the incidence of crime and involves violations of human (migrants') rights, particularly the right to asylum. The costs of combating that phenomenon are immense.

The problem of migrant trafficking owes very much to a coincidence of two major political trends ongoing in Europe: the opening up of the former socialist countries to population movements (in the aftermath of the collapse of the communist system in Europe) and the closing of western European borders for the migrants from the South (and certain countries of the East). An effective solution of this problem does not seem feasible without a concerted counteraction on the part of both segments of the continent, and, ultimately, arriving at a common European migration policy, including the idea of uniform external borders.

Propensity to Migrate for Work to the West and Some Other Issues related to Expected EU Enlargement

As regards the transformation period, the complete freedom of movement the residents of CEE have generally acquired seems to be of particular consequence in terms of the general laws of migration and the dynamics of the migration process itself. Foreign travel is no longer conditional, as was formerly the case, upon a discretionary decision by the public administration. Thus, its direction and the time of absence from the home country have no impact on the future freedom of migration by a given individual or members of his family. While abroad, a Central or Eastern European is no longer, as it was the case in the past, under the pressure of the exceptionality of the situation, and generally does not seek to settle down there or to extend his stay until the limits of tolerance of the host country. Therefore, a general opinion may be voiced that in many countries of the region the tendency to settle down abroad or to long-term migration, including mass outflow of members of distinct groups, such as ethnic minorities, political opposition or elites, has dwindled. Moreover, for a large proportion of the population, particularly for high-class specialists or dynamic and ambitious representatives of the young generation, foreign travel, including travel to the West, is no longer primarily an opportunity to earn an additional income, and often involves considerable spending abroad.

It seems to be a more general tendency, as the attraction of Western labour markets has diminished for the Central and Eastern European labour force. It is common knowledge that what used to be and still remains relatively widely available in the West is seasonal or irregular employment, or employment offered in what is known as the secondary/inferior segment of the labour market, suffering from a shortage of domestic labour because of low pay and difficult working conditions. Meanwhile, interest in offers of employment coming from that segment has recently started to diminish slowly even within CEE. However, the principal factor weakening the desire to take up second-rate jobs abroad is a radical change in the 'labour migration economics'. The reason is an increase in direct costs of migration, for example, the actualisation of fares (that is, a significant rise in the prices of tickets) of national airlines, and a truly dramatic rise in its indirect costs, that is, the costs of the opportunities lost in the home country (earnings, a job security, social insurance and so on). At the same time, the benefits from migration have decreased, primarily due to a decline in the purchasing power of proceeds earned abroad and transferred home. Before 1990, $1,000, a sum by no means exorbitant and transferable even on a monthly basis by a hard-working and hard-saving worker could be equivalent to about 30 monthly salaries, that is, to a two years and six months' remuneration in CEE, while today in a number of the countries of the region it would merely correspond to three to five months' earnings. For many this is already too little, considering the costs of migration.

Although the future enlargement of the European Union is still ahead of us, most likely by more than five years, the fact of the possible accession of six new countries, including five countries of CEE seems to have already affected thinking of the changes in the migration trends, if not actual migration phenomena in Europe. A possibility of the future eastbound extension of the external borders of the EU has stimulated the adaptation of candidate countries' migration regulations to the 'European standards' and the tightening of the borders of the Czech Republic, Hungary and Poland. This resulted in the deceleration of the pace of the foreigners' inflow, more efficient control over the movements of the citizens of countries allowed visa-free entry and probably also reduction in illegal immigration to these countries. On the other hand, a tendency is observed among certain groups of migrants arrived in those countries to settle and eventually acquire citizenship of the host country (for example, in the case of Vietnamese in Poland). Such tendency might to some degree be linked with the expectations among migrants from the countries with limited access to the European Union that once the Czech Republic, Hungary and Poland (along with other three candidates) are granted the full membership in the EU, those immigrants will be able to automatically benefit from the free movement right within the Union. Nevertheless this phenomenon seems so far to be of a negligible magnitude.

Whereas the control over the inflow of foreigners to whom the EU restrictions apply is largely considered manageable in the candidate countries of CEE, more clouds seem to surround the issue of the future propensity of the citizens of those countries to seek employment in other EU countries provided the institutional barriers are abolished. Poland might serve as an illustration of the probable acute migration pressure. It might be so for at least two reasons. A primary consideration is demographic. Between 2001 and 2010 the working age population is expected to grow by nearly 700,000 in Poland while the corresponding total of 15 countries of the EU may decline by over 1,100,000. The second argument pertains to a necessity of restructuring of the Polish (highly fragmented and inefficient) agriculture, which presently gives employment to around 20 per cent of the labour force. Coming down with that percentage to the current level of Portugal (just above 10 per cent) by the year 2010 would have required freeing of some 2 million agricultural workers. Spectacular as they may seem, however, these arguments are largely dubious: the above quoted increase in the size of working age population in Poland will be a combination of a tremendous rise in the 'immobile' age group (45 or over) and a decline (by a little more than 600,000) in the 'mobile' group (up to the age 45) whereas a majority of the redundant agricultural labour will most likely (again predominantly due to the ageing) become the pensioners.

Recent analyses strongly posit that no significant increase in migration for work in the EU labour market is likely from the candidate countries after their accession (for example, Hars, 1998; Okólski and Stola, 1998). This seems in keeping with an earlier conclusion arrived at by Tapinos (1994, p. 220): 'Legal barriers cannot be regarded as the main obstacles preventing migration' and therefore 'the fear of mass immigration resulting solely from the removal of legal barriers in Central and Eastern Europe is probably unfounded'.

However, the current political debate suggests a very careful approach of the EU countries to that issue. In view of this, following a very comprehensive analysis of the economic and political realities in the EU and Central and Eastern Europe, Morawska (1999) offers the probable scenario of the admission process which assumes that the accession will take place in 2005, the transitional ten-year period after the formal admission will be introduced, and repeated delays in allowing the free international movements of persons will take place afterwards. This in turn, irrespective of the underlying rationale and harmful effects for the future development of Central and Eastern European countries and the future integration of Europe, would make the issue of the migration consequences of the accession irrelevant, at least in one generation perspective.

Final Comment: a Need for Comprehensive and Stable Policy

It seems evident from the foregoing analysis that, emerged after an abrupt political and socioeconomic change around 1990, the migration phenomena and trends in CEE are still in the making. By all means, the countries of the region urgently require refined migration policies and more coordinated international collaboration, both with the partners from within CEE, countries from outside of the region and international organisations. The policies should reflect the new migration realities but also domestic and international priorities.

One of the premises of successful implementation of that goal would be the completing of legislative work, that is, enacting laws that are still missing, and the amending or harmonising of the existing laws to make them conform to international principles, conventions and other documents, to bilateral and multilateral inter-government agreements, and particularly to the provisions stipulated by major documents of the European Union, such as the Treaty of Amsterdam.

Two major issues seem to pertain to the flow of migrants: effective control of the border in CEECs and channelling a bulk of irregular into regular flow. In other words, by better control on entry many unwanted foreigners might be prevented from coming whereas by skilful modifications of eligibility rules (e.g. concerning seasonal migrant workers) many so far irregularly arriving foreigners might be transferred to the regularity.

As far as the matter of migrants' stay in CEECs is concerned, two other problems call for particular attention. One of those problems, which stem from the legacy of recent past, might be formulated as follows: the status of undocumented migrants or those who over a long time now continue to be in a provisory legal situation should be determined as soon as possible, and those migrants should either be given full civil rights in the country of actual residence or effectively expelled (sent back to their home country). Another problem, which is much more future oriented, assumes the developing of a stable and sound set of the principles of migrants' integration. Until this moment no country in CEE has ever undertaken to do so. An enormous complexity and urgency of the issue of migrants integration, including such elements as the resettlement of ethnic groups, especially persons repatriated from abroad, the insertion (in terms of geographic, social and economic space) of refugees or asylum seekers, finding appropriate socio-occupational niches for other categories of migrants (experts, students, workers), etc., seems to present one of the greatest challenges and at the same time the most demanding tests of maturity for new democracies of CEE.

Note

1   This chapter draws on parts of the author's plenary lecture entitled 'Migration Pressures on Europe' and presented to the *European Population Conference* (The Hague, 30 August–3 September 1999), and on his keynote introduction entitled 'Emergence of the Countries of Central and Eastern Europe as Countries of Immigration and Transit' presented to the *Council of Europe Colloquy on Migration in Central and Eastern Europe: New Challenges* (Warsaw, 17–19 December, 1998).

References

Baucic, I. (1999), 'The Balkan Crisis and Refugees', UNESCO/ISSC/University of Warwick Conference on International Migration: *Towards the New Millennium. Global and Regional Perspectives*, Coventry, 16–18 September.

de Tinguy, A. (1997), 'Dix Ans de Migrations Est-Ouest: Quelles Tendances?', *International Conference on Central and Eastern Europe – New Migration Space*, Pultusk (Poland), 11–13 December.

Doomernik, J. (1997), *Going West. Soviet Jewish Immigrants in Berlin since 1990*, Aldershot: Avebury.

Drbohlav, D. (1998), 'Labour Migration in the Czech Republic', UNESCO Seminar on *International Migration in Central and Eastern Europe at the Threshold of Millennium: New Trends and Emerging Issues*, Moscow, 8–10 September.

Frejka, T., Okólski, M. and Sword, K. (eds) (1998), *In-Depth Studies on Migration in Central and Eastern Europe: the Case of Poland*, New York: United Nations.

Hars, A. (1998), 'Hungary and the Enlargement of the European Union. Comments on Causes and Consequences of Labour Migration', unpublished paper.

Morawska, E. (1999), 'Transnational Migrations in the Enlarged European Union: a Perspective from East Central Europe', Reflection Group on Long-term Implications of EU Enlargement: the Nature of the New Border, Florence, 25 February.

Nyiri, P. (1997), 'Organisation and Integration in a New Overseas Chinese Community – Hungary, 1989–1997', *International Conference on Central and Eastern Europe – New Migration Space*, Pultusk (Poland), 11–13 December.

OECD (1998), *Trends in International Migration. SOPEMI Annual Report*, Paris: OECD.

Okólski, M. (1998), 'Regional Dimension of International Migration in Central and Eastern Europe', *Genus*, LIV (1–2), pp. 11–36.

Okólski, M. (1999a), 'Migration Pressures on Europe', in D. Van de Kaa, H. Leridon, G. Gesano and M. Okólski (eds), *European Populations: Unity in Diversity*, Dordrecht: Kluwer.

Okólski, M. (1999b), 'Migrant Trafficking in Poland: Actors, Mechanisms and Combating', Preliminary results of the IOM/ISS study, Institute for Social Studies, Warsaw, 15 February.

Okólski, M. and Stola, D. (1998), 'Migration between Poland and EU: the Perspective of Poland's Future Membership of EU', in P. Korcelli (ed.), *Changes in Migration in Poland as a Consequence of the Accession to the European Union*, Warsaw: PWN [in Polish].

Olimova, S. (1998), 'Irregular Migration and Migrant Trafficking in Tajikistan: Evidence from a First Transit Country', IOM Regional Seminar on *Migrant Trafficking Through the Baltic States and Neighbouring Countries*, Vilnius, 17–18 September.

Pirozhkov, S., Malinovska, O. and Marchenko, N. (1997), *External Migration in Ukraine: Causes, Effects and Strategies*, Kiev: IOM [in Ukrainian].

Rudolph, H. and Hillmann, F. (1997), 'The Invisible Hand Needs Visible Hand', in K. Koser (ed.), *The New Realities*, Houndmills: Macmillan.

Salt, J. (1997), 'Reconceptualising Migration and Migration Space', *International Conference on Central and Eastern Europe – New Migration Space*, Pultusk (Poland), 11–13 December.

Tapinos, G. (1994), 'Regional Economic Integration and Its Effects on Employment and Migration', in *Migration and Development: New Partnership for Co-operation*, Paris: OECD.

Tolts, M. (1999), 'Russian Jewish Migration in the Post-Soviet Era', *European Population Conference*, The Hague, 30 August–3 September.

Zelinski, W. (1971), 'The Hypothesis of the Mobility Transition' *Geographical Review*, 61, pp. 219–49.

Zlotnik, H. (1998), 'International Migration 1965–1996: an Overview', *Population and Development Review*, 20 (2), pp. 429–68.

Chapter 3

Migration, the Asian Financial Crisis and its Aftermath[*]

Ronald Skeldon

Introduction

The economic crisis of the Asian region that began in the middle of 1997 heralded the apparent end of a period of rapid economic growth and was expected to alter, even reverse, migration patterns that had emerged during the first half of the 1990s: migration patterns that were increasingly focused on destinations within Asia itself. While it is common to speak of an 'Asian crisis' it is important to keep in mind that the crisis was centred in East and Southeast Asia, with relatively few repercussions in the countries of South or Central Asia. In the epicentre of the crisis, the World Bank's East Asian 'miracle economies' of Japan, three of the four 'tigers', Hong Kong, South Korea and Singapore, together with the economies of Indonesia, Malaysia and Thailand, which had grown at perhaps the highest and most sustained rates of economic growth in history, appeared to go into economic freefall. Between 1960 and 1985, these economies demonstrated a growth in GNP per capita of 5.5 per cent per annum, with double-digit growth not uncommon for particular countries for particular years. In 1998, all of the East and Southeast Asian economies, with the notable exceptions of China and Taiwan, entered into recession or negligible growth (Table 3.1). The recession was deepest in Indonesia and Thailand. Regional currencies depreciated significantly, in the case of the Indonesian ringgit by over 60 per cent in 1998 alone. Regional stock markets plunged, and banks and financial institutions failed on an unprecedented scale in South Korea and Thailand.

Yet, despite the depth of the recession, most economies recovered far more quickly than was thought possible at the time. By 1999, only Thailand technically remained in recession and the majority of the other economies had resumed their path of rapid growth. By 2001, Thailand had resumed positive, if slow, growth and projections of 1.5 to 2.5 per cent were being made for 2002 (Chalamwong, 2002). Only Japan remained mired in low or negative growth,

Table 3.1   Growth in per capita GDP, 1997–2000, Asian economies

	1997	1998	1999	2000
China	8.8	7.8	7.8	8.0
Hong Kong	5.0	−5.3	3.0	10.5
Taiwan	6.7	4.6	5.4	5.9
Indonesia	4.7	−16.7	2.6	4.4
Malaysia	7.5	−7.5	5.8	8.3
Philippines	5.2	−0.5	3.3	4.0
Singapore	8.5	0.1	5.9	9.9
Thailand	−1.5	−10.0	−0.8	−8.8
Japan	1.8	−1.1	0.8	1.5
South Korea	5.0	−6.7	10.9	8.8

Source: Country papers presented at the *Workshop on International Migration and Labour Market in Asia*, Tokyo, OECD and Japan Institute of Labour, 4–5 February 2002, supplemented by data in *Key Indicators of Developing Asian and Pacific Countries, 2001*, New York, Oxford University Press, 2001.

although its problems long predated the Asian crisis having their origins in the bubble economy of the 1980s that ended in the early 1990s. The Japanese economy was technically in recession during the third and fourth quarters of 2001 (Iguchi, 2002).

The Social Impact of the Crisis

The figures on economic growth throw light on but one dimension of the crisis and its aftermath. Unemployment provides insight of a different nature. Levels unquestionably rose in the countries worst affected by the crisis. Data of the time suggested that these doubled in early 1998 in Indonesia, South Korea and Thailand (*The Economist*, 25 April 1998). Labour force data from Thailand showed that, although the number of unemployed actually decreased from around 354,000 in 1996 to 292,000 in 1997, their number increased markedly in 1998 to 1,138,000, which still represented but 3.4 per cent of the labour force (Gray 1999). Using different estimates, the ILO expected unemployment in Thailand to exceed 1.9 million in 1999, up from 1.4 million in early 1998. The total number of unemployed in Indonesia has already probably reached almost 15 million and must surely have been a factor in the unrest in that country in 1998. Even in Hong Kong, an economy which had one of the tightest labour markets in Asia, unemployment in the second quarter of 1998 was estimated at 4.8 per cent, the highest level in two decades.

Of greater interest is what has occurred to unemployment since the immediate aftermath of the crisis. With the exceptions of South Korea and China, unemployment has persisted at high levels, even increasing markedly in some economies from 2000. The figures for China are almost certainly underestimates: some 26 million workers have been laid off from state enterprises since 1998 and the real rate in 2002 may be in excess of 20 per cent in some sectors.[1] That is, despite improvement in economic growth, unemployment has emerged as a structural feature of many Asian economies. Rising labour costs are forcing companies to relocate to cheaper areas. Although the largest of those cheaper areas is China, restructuring from centralised planning has still meant that unemployment has risen rather than fallen.

Table 3.2   Levels of unemployment, Asian economies, 1996–2001

	1996	1997	1998	1999	2000	2001
Taiwan	2.6	2.7	2.7	2.9	3.0	4.4
Hong Kong	2.8	2.2	2.7	2.9	3.4	6.7
Japan	3.4	3.4	4.1	4.7	4.7	5.5
Korea	2.0	2.6	6.8	6.3	4.2	
Singapore	3.0	2.4	3.2	4.6	4.4	5.0
Indonesia	4.9	4.7	5.5	6.4	6.1	
Malaysia	2.5	2.4	3.2	3.0	3.1	
Philippines	8.6	8.7	10.1	9.7	12.0	
Thailand	1.1	0.9	3.4	3.0	2.4	
China	3.0	3.1	3.1	3.1	3.1	

Source: Country papers presented at the *Workshop on International Migration and Labour Market in Asia*, Tokyo, OECD and Japan Institute of Labour, 4–5 February 2002, supplemented by information from Asian Development Bank, *Key Indicators of Developing Asian and Pacific Countries, 2001*, New York, Oxford University Press, 2001.

Poverty, too, increased following the crisis. The incidence of poverty in Thailand, having declined steadily from 32.6 per cent in 1988, representing 17.9 million people, to 11.4 per cent in 1996, representing 6.8 million, increased to 12.9 per cent in 1998 (NESDB, 1999, p. 4). The crisis was estimated in the same source to have been directly responsible for an increase of 1.5 million in the number of poor, who reached 7.9 million in 1998. The increase in poverty in Indonesia was much greater. Having declined from about 54.2 million in 1976 through 30 million in 1987 and 22.5 million in 1996, the number of poor rose to some 80 million in 1998. ILO estimates place the number of poor much higher, at almost 99 million, although that estimate is not comparable to the numbers for earlier periods (Feridhanusetyawan, 1999, p. 76). Taking a longer-term perspective, poverty still appears to have declined over the decade of the 1990s in Thailand and the Philippines, although it rose in Indonesia. The percentage of the population below national poverty lines declined in Thailand and the Philippines from 27.2 and 45.3 per cent in 1990 to 15.9 and 39.4 per cent respectively, while it rose from 15.1 to 18.2 per cent over the same period in Indonesia.[2]

Changing Patterns of Migration in East and Southeast Asia

Before attempting to assess what impact the crisis and its aftermath may have had on population migration in East and Southeast Asia, some background to the major shifts that occurred in the patterns of movement in the region before the crisis is necessary. It is important to realise that the movements of peoples are not new in Asia but have brought about a mixing of cultures throughout that region's long history. There have been, however, significant fluctuations in volume and direction of those population movements in the past and we can surely expect further fluctuations in the future. It has been argued that our time is 'the age of migration' (Castles and Miller, 1993) and while international movements in Asia and elsewhere have unquestionably become a major concern as the twentieth century comes to a close, the actual proportions of the population which are moving neither appears to have increased markedly over the recent past nor seems unduly large when compared with previous 'ages of migration' (see Zlotnik, 1998). Some even argue the real migration question of our present global era is why it is that more people do not move (Hammar et al., 1997). Nevertheless, many of the types of population movement today are not captured by systems of data collection and our figures are underestimates. Many people move short term and it is probably true to conclude that more people are moving in a greater variety of ways than ever before. However, on a per capita basis, the volumes of movement from Asia today are still low when compared with the proportions leaving European populations a century ago. When we consider the implications of the recent crisis affecting Asia, it is important not to forget that such crises are not new.

Although the movement of labour was a ubiquitous feature of Asian societies, there was considerable variation from one part of that vast area to another. Any discussion of anything 'Asian', irrespective of the topic, immediately runs into the issue of regional differences, and migration is certainly no exception. Just as there have been critical differences in migration over time, so too are there differences over space. The movement of indentured labour, for example, affected only relatively few areas around the periphery of the continent where colonial or foreign penetration and influence were most intense. The emigration of the Chinese was essentially from three provinces in southern China, Guangdong, Fujian, and Zhejiang, and concentrated from specific districts within those provinces (see Pan, 1998). Similarly, the emigration from India came from a number of clearly defined source areas rather than being evenly drawn from the Indian population as a whole (see Clarke et al., 1990, p. 12).

Little international migration occurred either among or from Asian countries from the early 1950s to the early 1970s. One of the earlier major flows was of contract labour migrants primarily to the oil-rich countries of the Middle East. The evolution of this system from a dependence upon regional sources of Arab labour, through to the countries of South Asia, and then to the countries of Southeast and East Asia has been well told elsewhere (Arnold and Shah, 1986; Gunatilleke, 1986; Findlay, 1994, ch. 5). From the late 1980s, and accelerating after the Gulf War of 1990–91, there was a shift in direction in labour migration towards destinations within Asia itself and particularly towards those economies that had exhibited rapid and sustained economic growth – Japan and the 'tiger' economies of South Korea, Taiwan, Hong Kong, Singapore, Malaysia, Brunei and even Thailand.

Associated with the economic growth in these economies had been a transition to lower fertility (Table 3.3). The rapid employment creation and the slowing in growth of the labour forces in several of these countries saw a transition from labour-surplus to labour-deficit economies and a shift from labour export to the importation of labour in what has been called a 'migration transition' (see the essays in Abella, 1994, especially that by Fields). While the search for specific 'turning points' might prove elusive, the general shift from participation in systems of labour emigration to labour immigration is particularly clear for South Korea and Taiwan. Thailand has emerged as a country of major immigration as well as emigration.

It is worth pointing out that the socialist economies of China and Viet Nam followed a different path. There, workers went to the then Soviet Union and the countries of Eastern Europe where some still remain although, with

Table 3.3   Fertility levels in Asian economies, 1980–1999

	1980	1990	1999
Taiwan	2.5	1.8	1.6
Hong Kong	2.0	1.3	1.0
Japan	1.8	1.5	1.5
Korea	2.6	1.8	1.6
Singapore	1.9	1.7	1.5
Indonesia	4.3	3.0	2.6
Malaysia	4.2	3.8	3.0
Philippines	4.8	4.1	3.3
Thailand	3.5	2.2	1.9
China	2.5	2.1	1.9
Vietnam	5.0	3.6	2.3

Source: Asian Development Bank, *Key Indicators of Developing Asian and Pacific Countries, 2001*, New York, Oxford University Press, 2001.

the demise of the Soviet Union and the opening up of the Chinese and Vietnamese economies, migrant labourers have increasingly being going to capitalist countries and competing with the more well-established source areas of Asian migrants.

The magnitude of the change in destination is clearly seen for the three major exporters of contract labour in the Southeast Asian region: Indonesia, the Philippines and Thailand. In 1980, 84 per cent of overseas contract workers from the Philippines went to the Middle East, with only 11 per cent going to other Asian countries. The corresponding figures for Indonesia were 74 and 8 per cent, and for Thailand 97 and 3 per cent respectively. By 1994, Asian countries were the destination of 36 per cent of overseas contract workers from the Philippines, 36 per cent of those from Indonesia and 89 per cent of those from Thailand (data cited in Hugo, 1998b). The switch for Thailand is most dramatic and occurred in the late 1980s. Part of the reason for the more rapid shift for Thailand was political, with Saudi Arabia barring the recruitment of Thai workers because of a theft of jewels belonging the Saudi Royal family by a Thai worker, which illustrates the fragility of the overseas contract labour market and the extent to which political considerations can affect flows. In both the remaining labour movements to the Middle East and in the regional flows to Asian destinations, there has been an increasing feminisation of the flows consequent upon the rising demand for labour in service occupations in a broad range of activities, including domestic workers, nurses and entertainers of all sorts.

The numbers involved in the contract labour migrant system are large. In 1994, the annual number of contract workers going overseas from Indonesia was 141,287, from the Philippines 555,226 (plus another 154,376 based at sea), and from Thailand 169,764 (Huguet 1995). By 2000, these numbers had increased to 435,219, 643,304 and 183,023 respectively.[3] Perhaps more impressive, however, has been the growth in the number of migrants in the Asian countries themselves. Accurate numbers are impossible to ascertain at this stage owing to the importance of undocumented migrants, who may indeed account for the greater proportion of total workers. The International Labour Organisation (ILO, 1998, p. 28) estimated that there were, before the crisis, probably some 2.5 million foreign workers in Malaysia, including 1 million who were undocumented, perhaps over 1 million in Thailand, although the estimates fluctuated widely, about 1.4 million in Japan and 450,000 in Singapore. The greater part of the build-up in these numbers took place in the 1990s, with the number of workers in Malaysia doubling in the five years from 1992.

The Impact of the Crisis on Migration

The key question relates to the fate of the labour migrants in Asia in the face of rising levels of domestic unemployment. The ready solution was to expel the foreign workers and replace them with the domestic workers made redundant by the crisis and by structural changes in the economies. This solution not only appeared to be economically rational but might relieve domestic political pressures that had built up from the newly unemployed themselves. However, given that the financial crisis affected both areas of origin and areas of destination of migration, there was an equal temptation to 'export' domestic unemployment overseas. Several governments in the region sought to place newly redundant labour in more dynamic economies. Yet, despite attempts to reduce, restrict or accelerate migration, relatively few dramatic changes appear to have occurred in the numbers of migrants in Asian economies with the exception of the country hardest hit, Indonesia, from which migration has indeed accelerated.

The stock of foreign workers increased steadily throughout the 1990s in Japan, Hong Kong, Singapore, Taiwan and South Korea (Table 3.4). Only in South Korea can an 'Asian financial crisis' effect be seen, with a sharp reduction in the number of foreign workers during 1998. The situation among those economies lower down the development hierarchy is different. There,

Table 3.4   Official estimates of the total number of foreign workers in Asian economies, 1996–2000

	1996	1997	1998	1999	2000
Taiwan		245,697	255,606	278,000	326,515
Hong Kong[1]	164,300	171,000	180,600	193,700	216,790
Japan[2]	610,000	630,000	660,000	670,000	710,000
South Korea[2]	210,494	245,399	157,689	217,384	285,506
Singapore				530,000	612,233
Indonesia[3]	24,868	24,359	21,307	14,863	16,836
Malaysia[2]	745,239	1,471,645	1,127,652	818,677	799,685
Philippines[3]	4,333	6,055	5,335	5,956	
Thailand[2]	1,033,863	1,125,780	1,103,546	1,089,656	1,102,612
China[3]	80,000	82,000	83,000	85,000	

Notes

1   Includes an estimate of foreign domestic workers only; there are no stock figures for the highly skilled.
2   Includes estimates of undocumented workers.
3   Estimate of foreign experts only, primarily professionals, the highly skilled and teachers.

Source: Country papers presented at the *Workshop on International Migration and Labour Market in Asia*, Tokyo, OECD and Japan Institute of Labour, 4–5 February 2002.

the crisis effect was more marked in population migration, with the numbers of foreign workers declining in Malaysia and Thailand as well as in Indonesia. Here, however, considerable caution needs to be used in the interpretation of the available figures. In contrast to Japan and the tiger economies, data-gathering systems are not as well developed in these Southeast Asian nations. More important is the fact that the long land and sea borders, so common in that part of the region, are difficult to control adequately and it is easy for people to cross from one country to another without detection. Undocumented movements account for a very significant proportion of total international migration among the large countries of Southeast Asia and it is difficult to know to what extent the figures provided represent the real situation.

Thus, it is abundantly clear that the impact of the crisis on the basic patterns of migration in the region has not been marked and has been variable. There have also been differences by level of development and it is worth considering the East Asian and the Southeast Asian economies separately.

The Most Developed Economies of East Asia

Foreign residents represent a very small proportion of the total populations of the developed economies of East Asia. Numbers of migrants can be large in terms of absolute figures, as in the case of the 1.4 million in Japan, but these account for just over 1 per cent of that nation's total population. Of this not insignificant absolute number, fully 46 per cent came from South Korea, that traditional area of migration to Japan, and a further 17 per cent came from China, including Taiwan. Thus, the number of recent foreign labourers, even accepting that the data exclude quite large numbers of overstayers, represents a very small proportion of Japan's labour force. Similarly, in South Korea and in Hong Kong, foreign workers represent very small proportions of the total labour force. The overall figures are somewhat deceptive as foreign workers are often concentrated in specific neighbourhoods and are highly visible, giving the impression that they are more important overall than they really are. This distributional effect is one factor in explaining the strident public and official reactions to foreign labour in these economies, and indeed in economies in other parts of the world.

The fact that they are small in proportion does not necessarily mean that the foreign workers make an insignificant contribution to their host economies. They tend to undertake jobs that are low-paid and that local workers find undesirable, and they fill important 'niche' activities in local economies. Some foreign workers have not had their contracts renewed and are having to leave the developed economies of East Asia, but this should not necessarily be related to the economic crisis in Asia. In Taiwan, for example, structural shifts in the nature of the economy have reduced the demand for construction workers while increasing demand in other areas. Thus, it is virtually impossible to separate the effects of these long-term structural shifts in the economy from the more short-term effects of the crisis in these developed economies.

Where the crisis may have an impact on the more developed economies is in the increasing number of job-seekers from more affected parts of Asia who came without contracts to try to find work illegally. However, tight border controls characterise all the developed economies of East Asia, and illegal immigration is not a significant problem. Job-seekers will enter legally as tourists, students or trainees but then stay on after the expiration of their visa as 'overstayers'. However, even here, there is little evidence of a migration crisis, with the numbers of overstayers remaining small compared with legal foreign workers, and there is no evidence of sharp increases in their number in the recent past.

Of all the economies of Asia, Taiwan remained relatively unaffected by the crisis and is one of the perceived opportunities for governments such as Thailand's which wish to export their domestic unemployed.[4] Certainly, the number of migrants in Taiwan increased throughout the years of the crisis from 230,000 in June 1997 through 250,000 in June 1998, and accelerated to 326,515 by the end of 2000. Almost half the number of workers came from Thailand. With domestic unemployment at less than 3 per cent, or about 280,000 people, Taiwan sought initially to halt labour imports. The later acceleration in migration was accompanied by an increase in unemployment, which reached 4.4 per cent in 2001. However, many of the domestic unemployed were supervisory or technical staff who were unwilling to undertake labouring jobs, and employers in Taiwan in early 1999 estimated that there were some 200,000 vacant positions in manufacturing jobs. The importation of labour continued, with an increase of almost 40 per cent in the number of foreign workers in manufacturing from 1997 to 1998 to reach 71,000. At present, the Taiwan legislature is considering extending employment contracts from their present three years to six years and allowing the workers to change employers. It would thus appear that the labour market of Taiwan is becoming more, rather than less, open to foreigners. Taiwan, in the post-crisis period, sought to diversify its sources of recruitment to include workers from Vietnam, which was expected to supply between 5,000 and 10,000 workers by the end of 1999.

The principal issues involving migration to the most developed Asian economies related clearly to more long-term structural change rather than to anything that can be attributed directly to the crisis itself. Construction workers were replaced by those in manufacturing, for example. The critical issues in the more developed economies revolved not around the deportation of workers but around questions of the protection of migrant workers, particularly those who fell into the 'grey' area of entering as trainees, but who participated fully in the labour force, and those women who were in isolated or vulnerable positions in the service sector.

The Economies of Southeast Asia

The situation in the economies of Southeast Asia is somewhat different from that described above. In Singapore, Malaysia and Thailand, foreign workers play a much more important role, both absolutely and relatively. Singapore, with a total population of 3.7 million, has a total foreign population of 633,200 including dependants. The number of foreign workers was over 612,000 at the end of 2000, which accounted for some 30 per cent of the labour force.

The numbers of migrants in Malaysia and Thailand are much more difficult to estimate accurately owing to the large number of undocumented entrants to both countries. Immediately before the crisis, the ILO estimated that fully 1 million of the 2.5 million migrants in Malaysia were in that country illegally (ILO, 1998, p. 28). The official Malaysian figures for 1997 were much lower, at under 1.5 million legal and undocumented migrants. By 2000–2001 this figure was to have declined to around 800,000 migrants. The official figure suggests that the number of foreign workers represented just under 20 per cent of the labour force in 1997. The proportion of foreign workers in Thailand was, however, much lower, with the over one million foreign workers accounting for only about 4 per cent of the labour force in 1998. The actual number of foreign migrants in Thailand is likely to be much higher as many are accompanied by family members, particularly in border areas. For example, about 20 per cent of the migrant population of some 100,000 in Ranong Province was estimated to be made up of family members (Chantavanich et al., 2000, pp. 110–11). In 1998, Malaysian authorities estimated that 200,000 wives and children of foreign workers, mostly from Indonesia, were in the country (cited in Hugo, 2000, p. 102). These data are suggestive of the emergence of more settled migrant communities in some parts of Southeast Asia in a way that is reminiscent of the transition from guest worker to permanent resident in the Europe of the 1970s. The Asian financial crisis of 1997, however, appears to have played a more marginal role in this process than did the oil crisis from 1973 for Europe.

The implications of the large number of foreign labourers in Southeast Asian countries do have to be tempered somewhat by the fact that many of the transnational migrants belong to peoples of similar ethnic backgrounds separated by modern state boundaries. Although international boundaries in Asia are much more meaningful as a guide to nations than they are in many parts of Africa, for example, there are often large transitional areas along the borders where the populations are ethnically quite distinct from those forming the dominant 'core' nation. This situation would apply along the Thai-Myanmar border, where substantial numbers of the migrants from Myanmar to Thailand would not be ethnic Burmese but minority peoples. In Indonesia, Hugo (1998a) has identified two quite separate systems of international migration: one essentially based on Sumatra and Java towards Peninsular Malaysia and the other from Nusa Tenggara towards East Malaysia in Sabah and Sarawak. Both these flows, in different ways, have strong ethnic dimensions and are influenced by kinship ties and traditional fields of mobility. Much of the movement from Laos into the northeast of Thailand (Isan) can also be seen in this light where Lao-Isan ties were traditionally closer than those between Isan and the central Thai. Despite these caveats, labour migration is unquestionably of great relative and absolute importance in the countries of Southeast Asia.

Given the importance of foreign labour in the economies in this region, the question must be whether the observed rising levels of unemployment were to be found disproportionately among the migrants. The reverse, however, is suggested, with retrenchments felt in those sectors where foreign labour was least concentrated. In Malaysia, only 12 per cent of those retrenched during the first quarter of 1998 were foreign labourers (Pillai, 1998). In Singapore, in the final quarter of 1997, the vast majority (almost 80 per cent) of those retrenched were in the manufacturing sector, with the construction industry, a sector which employs large amounts of foreign labour, actually expanding during 1997, even if at a slower rate than previously (Hui, 1998).

In both Malaysia and Thailand, there have been loud calls to expel large numbers of foreign labourers – and unskilled foreign labour is implied here – either because they were assumed to have become unemployed or because they were seen to be taking jobs from local labour. As suggested above, the reality is somewhat different. Unskilled foreign labour was not found primarily in those sectors most affected by the crisis and there were no strong reasons to suggest that the crisis resulted in mass expulsions. First, foreign labour, as in the economies of East Asia discussed above, tends to carry out jobs that local labour is unwilling to undertake: in the plantation sector in Malaysia and in the fishing or rice-milling industries in Thailand, for example. Thus, there is a mismatch between the skills and occupations of the newly redundant local labour and those of migrant labour. Second, the presence of foreign labour exerted downward pressure on wages, which was to the benefit of local entrepreneurs. As the latter were often either local political leaders themselves or closely allied with that class, they were unlikely to implement policies not in their own best economic interest. Third, it is much easier to maintain a compliant foreign labour force, particularly if it is illegal, than to employ indigenous labour which can seek support in the local community and insist on minimum wages and other entitlements. Fourth, there was often a mismatch in the location of the local unemployed, who in Thailand were to be found primarily in Bangkok and its periphery, and the regions where foreign labour was employed, which, again in Thailand, tended to be more in peripheral parts of the country. Thus, entrepreneurs were faced with the expense of transporting the unemployed to areas where these might not wish to live, increasing discontent. Finally, the situation in the countries of origin of the majority of the migrants was often worse than in their host economies.

Governments of countries of origin of migrants may have brought political pressure on host governments not to exacerbate the economic situation in origin countries by expelling tens of thousands of workers. In the interests of regional solidarity, host governments may comply, which seems to be the case of Malaysia and its treatment of the majority of migrants from Indonesia, and Thailand's attitude toward Laotians, and possibly migrants from Myanmar.

The number of legally permitted workers in Thailand was reduced by two thirds in the aftermath of the crisis: all others were to be deported and all illegal foreign workers were supposed to have left by 4 August 1999. 'Strictly no illegals after the deadline' (headline, *Bangkok Post*, 9 July 1999). Yet, on 16 July 1999, the headline in that same national newspaper trumpeted 'Ban on foreign workers to be eased soon'. The policy was again modified to allow migrant workers from Cambodia, Laos and Myanmar who were already working in the country to register and remain in their jobs for 12 months. The deadline was fixed at the end of September 2001 and by that time some 568,000 had registered. As in Taiwan, the Thai unemployed do not wish to undertake jobs at the bottom end of the skill spectrum. Of those registered, 104,000 were in the fisheries industry, 103,000 in farming and 92,000 in domestic service (*Migration News*, 9 (6), 2002).

Nevertheless, expulsions of migrant labour did take place, particularly of illegal workers. The number of people expelled frequently reported in the press in Thailand was 300,000. Many, however, surely as part of the normal circulation of labour after they have achieved their target, and others who have failed to pay the appropriate 'tea money'. Although there is pressure on local authorities to show that something is being done to protect the integrity of Thai workers, absolute bans on foreign labour are met with resistance from Thai entrepreneurs, particularly in industries such as rice milling and fisheries which are dominated by foreign labour. There is no information about the number of migrants who may have entered the country during the period of the exodus of the 300,000, the almost certainly incorrect assumption being that there was a one-way traffic out of the country.

Malaysia has also resorted to deportations, with about 160,000 being returned to Indonesia during 1997 and 1998. However, at precisely the same time as deportations were proceeding, the recruitment of additional labour was going ahead in response to the acute labour shortages in the country. In late 1998, the government reported that employers had been given permission to import 220,000 additional foreign workers (*Migration News*, 5 (12), 1998). In February, the Malaysian Immigration Department announced that 109,425 Indonesian and Thai workers could enter the country and that temporary work permits for 380,773 foreign workers would be extended (*Migration News*, 6 (3), 1999). What occurred in Malaysia appeared to be more a drive to regularise the status of foreign workers rather than a move to reduce the numbers as such. Nevertheless, official figures do suggest (Table 3.4) that the stock of foreign workers declined from 1997 from almost 1.5 million to around 800,000 in 2000–2001. However, these figures do not sit easily with the numbers leaving Indonesia. Indonesia, the country most deeply affected by the crisis, is where a direct and longer-term impact from the financial crisis on migration can perhaps be most clearly seen. The worsening employment situation in that country increased pressures to migrate and numbers leaving both legally and illegally rose markedly after 1997 (Hugo, 2000). The numbers of workers who left legally during 1998–99 were double or triple the numbers leaving during the years immediately prior to 1997: the numbers of those going legally to Malaysia more than tripled.[5] A marked increase occurred in the number of women going overseas, mainly to the Gulf States, as a coping strategy in order to support their families at home, but there was also a rise in the numbers of both men and women going to Malaysia. The apparent contradictions in the existing data sets demonstrate just how much there is still to learn about migration in the Asian region.

The Philippines is the country of emigration *par excellence,* with almost seven million of its citizens overseas. Bohning (1998), in an analysis of the worst-case scenario, found that the impact of the crisis on the movement of workers from the Philippines was not likely to be as profound as might initially have been thought: perhaps less than 50,000 out of many hundreds of thousands deployed would return to the Philippines. Similarly, the impact of the crisis on international migration is likely to be more apparent than real in the case of Thailand. No dramatic changes in the fortunes of the perhaps half a million Thais working abroad occurred, primarily because the principal destinations in Asia for workers from Thailand (as well as for the Philippines) were not amongst those most severely affected by the crisis, namely Taiwan, Hong Kong and Singapore. Also, as suggested earlier, the workers to those destinations occupied niches in the economies that local workers were either unwilling or unable to fill.

Where the financial crisis is likely to have made the most profound impact is on the status of migrants in the region. That is, the position of foreign labourers in regional economies may have become increasingly tenuous. Levels of exploitation are likely to have increased as employers sought to take advantage of the illegal status of foreign workers in the context of the economic slowdown. Some workers may be forced to become illegal migrants after terminating their contracts, and they then become more manipulable. Hugo reported that Indonesian workers in Malaysia shifted from the formal to the informal economies as they lost jobs in the construction sector and sought a living in petty trading and the service sector in Kuala Lumpur (Hugo, 2000, p. 113). Few foreign workers will have wanted to be sent back to even more depressed economies. The opportunities for abuse, for corruption by local officials, and for criminal gangs smuggling virtual slave labour all probably increased. Thus, in the aftermath of the crisis the issues of migrant protection and migrant rights loom large, and increased illegal movements appear likely to have been a significant fall-out.

The crisis had an impact on one particular group of migrants, small in terms of absolute numbers but large in terms of its role in regional economies: the skilled migrants who were representatives of transnational corporations, both regional and global. Many were from western companies but the majority perhaps came from the Asian region itself as corporations based in Japan, South Korea, Taiwan, Hong Kong and Singapore reduced or even closed overseas plants. Such firms are among the first to respond to any economic downturn as, ultimately, they must act in the long-term interests of their principal shareholders in balancing short-term losses against the potential for more long-term gain. Plant closure or reduction in production is directly the result of the contraction of regional demand for such goods as automobiles, electronic goods and even lower-cost consumer goods such as shoes and clothes. The impact upon migration is likely to be in three areas: first, in the departure of a number of highly paid expatriates; second, in the indirect effect of this exodus of expatriates upon the demand for services for domestic servants, restaurateurs and so on, and, third, the direct impact on the workers who are laid off through cutbacks in production.

Quite clearly, some economies in the region, and particularly that of South Korea, had 'bounced back' by 2002 (*The Economist*, 6 July 2002). Although many of the underlying reasons for the Asian financial crisis have still not been addressed in some economies, growth has been restored throughout much of Southeast Asia as well as South Korea, based upon internal and intraregional demand. In other economies, a restructuring which accelerated but certainly did not cause the crisis is likely to have a longer-term impact on migration in the region than the crisis itself. Displaced workers may either switch to the urban informal sector or seek to return to the village for their survival. There are thus links between the crisis and internal migrations and between international and internal movements where returned international migrants moved back to their villages of origin. Nevertheless, the return to the village never seemed more than a short-term solution to the economic downturn, with little evidence from countries in the region showing a reversal in rural-to-urban migration.

One final group of migrants that was profoundly affected by the crisis consisted of students. The reduced purchasing power of the emerging middle classes in countries such as Malaysia and Thailand saw children in expensive private schools in North America, Europe and Australasia returning home to local schools.

Conclusion

Intense domestic political pressure in Malaysia and Thailand was exerted to have undocumented workers deported in the aftermath of the crisis. However, there was also intense, but less visible, domestic and international pressure to limit the extent of any deportations. Both political and economic considerations loomed large in a complex matrix of issues. Those favouring the expulsion of undocumented workers argued, understandably, that in a time of increasing domestic unemployment work should be provided for domestic labour rather than for foreign labour. On the opposing side, there was considerable doubt about the extent to which domestic labour could, or would, substitute for foreign labour. In the rapidly evolving free market economies of the region, local entrepreneurs did not wish to pay the higher wages that would have resulted from the limitation or reduction of foreign labour. As these same entrepreneurs tended to be closely linked to the evolving political system, attempts to limit or control the flows reflected rhetoric rather than reality.

Some of the basic reasons why it was difficult to carry out deportations were economic. Differences in desired income, skill levels, location and that amorphous concept 'tastes' meant that complete substitutability of newly unemployed labour for illegal foreign labour was not possible. Thus, the expulsion of foreign labour, legal or illegal, could have actually harmed economic performance and aggravated the crisis. Origin countries, most of which are neighbours, also did not want to see the sudden return of thousands, perhaps hundreds of thousands, of workers. All these factors gave substance to the hypothesis suggesting that the economic downturn did not have as large an impact on the international migration flows as initially expected. The principal impact may have been concentrated on internal migrants returning to the rural sector where this remained a viable option in the face of rising unemployment. Even here, however, the impact was unlikely to have been lasting. The urban informal sector almost certainly played the major role in absorbing the new unemployed, although the whole relationship between the crisis and internal migration still requires careful examination.

What appears apparent is that there has been a rise in undocumented migration both within and to destinations outside the region as Asian men, and increasingly women, search for employment overseas. Unscrupulous brokers increase their trade to take advantage of the local demand to leave, and issues of migrant protection become prominent as trafficking, human smuggling and the exploitation of the vulnerable take on greater importance (Skeldon, 2000). Even accepting the increasing pressures to emigrate from several economies, the 1997 economic crisis in Asia may have been more a catalyst for change throughout the region, reinforcing existing migration patterns, rather than generating a completely new set of circumstances.

Notes

*   This chapter is an updated (to mid-2002) and substantially modified version of an article that originally appeared in the *Asian and Pacific Population Journal*, 14 (3), 1999.
1   Data cited in *Migration News*, May and July issues, 2002.
2   Data cited in *Population Headliners*, May–June 2002.
3   Data cited in country chapters presented at the *Workshop on International Migration and Labour Market in Asia*, Tokyo, OECD and Japan Institute of Labour, 4–5 February 2002.
4   The information in this paragraph comes from the monthly issues of *Migration News*, volumes 5 and 6.
5   Unfortunately, the year 1997 itself was an exceptional year as far as recording the number of overseas contract workers was concerned, with some 300,000 undocumented workers in Malaysia regularised in that year and added to the annual total (Hugo 2000: 97).

References

Abella, M.I. (ed.) (1994), 'Turning Points in Labor Migration', *Asian and Pacific Migration Journal*, 3 (1), special issue.

Arnold, F. and Shah, N.M. (eds) (1986), *Asian Labor Migration: Pipeline to the Middle East*, Boulder: Westview.

Bohning, W.R. (1998), 'Conceptualizing and Simulating the Impact of the Asian Crisis on Filipinos' Employment Prospects Abroad', *Asian and Pacific Migration Journal*, 7 (2–3), pp. 339–67.

Castles, S. and Miller, M. (1993), *The Age of Migration: International Population Movements in the Modern World*, London: Macmillan.

Chalamwong, Y. (2002), 'Thailand', country report presented at the *Workshop on International Migration and Labour Market in Asia*, Tokyo, OECD and Japan Institute of Labour, 4–5 February.

Chantavanich, S. et al. (2000), *Cross-border Migration and HIV Vulnerability in the Thai-Myanmar Border: Sangkhlaburi and Ranong*, Bangkok, Asian Research Center for Migration, Chulalongkorn University.

Clarke, C., Peach, P. and Vertovec, S. (1990), 'Introduction: Themes in the Study of the South Asian Diaspora', in C. Clarke, C. Peach and S. Vertovec (eds), *South Asians Overseas: Migration and Ethnicity*, Cambridge: Cambridge University Press, pp. 1–29.

Feridhanusetyawan, T. (1999), 'Social Impacts of Indonesia's Economic Crisis: Employment, Income and Poverty Issues', in *Social Impacts of the Asian Economic Crisis in Thailand, Indonesia, Malaysia and the Philippines*, Bangkok, Thailand Development Research Institute (TDRI).

Findlay, A.M. (1994), *The Arab World*, London: Routledge.

Gray, R. (1999), 'The Effects of Globalisation on Labour Force and Migration in Thailand', paper presented at the Policy Seminar on the *Impact of Globalisation on Population Change and Poverty in Rural Areas*, Bangkok, ESCAP , 31 March–2 April.

Gunatilleke, G. (ed.) (1986), *Migration of Asian Workers to the Arab World*, Tokyo: The United Nations University.

Hammar, T., Brochmann, G., Tamas, K. and Faist, T. (eds) (1997), *International Migration, Immobility and Development: Multidisciplinary Perspectives*, Oxford: Berg.

Hugo, G. (1998a), 'International Migration in Eastern Indonesia', paper prepared for East Indonesia Project, mimeo.

Hugo, G. (1998b) 'Migration and mobilization in Asia', in E. Laquian, A. Laquian and T.G. McGee (eds), *The Silent Debate: Asian Immigration and Racism in Canada*, Vancouver: Institute of Asian Research, pp. 157–92.

Hugo, G. (2000), 'The Crisis and International Population Movement in Indonesia', *Asian and Pacific Migration Journal*, 9 (1), pp. 93–129.

Huguet, J. (1995), 'Data on International Migration in Asia: 1990–1994', *Asian and Pacific Migration Journal*, 4 (4), pp. 521–9.

Hui, W.-T. (1998), 'The Regional Economic Crisis and Singapore', *Asian and Pacific Migration Journal*, 7 (2-3), pp. 187–218.

Iguchi, Y. (2002), 'Japan', country report presented at the *Workshop on International Migration and Labour Market in Asia*, Tokyo, OECD and Japan Institute of Labour, 4–5 February.

ILO (1998), *The Social Impact of the Asian Financial Crisis*, Bangkok, Regional Office for Asia and the Pacific.

Martin, P.L. (1994), 'The United States: Benign Neglect toward Immigration', in W.A. Cornelius, P.L. Martin and J.F. Hollifield (eds), *Controlling Immigration: A Global Perspective*, Stanford: Stanford University Press, pp. 83–9.

NESDB (1999), 'Poverty and Inequality during the Economic Crisis in Thailand', *Indicators of Well-Being and Policy Analysis: a Newsletter of the National Economic and Social Development Board* ,3 (1).

Pan, L. (ed.) (1998), *The Encyclopaedia of the Chinese Overseas*, Singapore: Archipelago Press.

Pillai, P. (1998), 'The Impact of the Economic Crisis on Migrant Labour in Malaysia: Policy Implications', *Asian and Pacific Migration Journal*, 7 (2–3), pp. 255–80.

Skeldon, R. (2000), 'Trafficking: a Perspective from Asia', *International Migration*, 38 (3), pp. 7–30.

Zlotnik, H. (1998), 'International Migration 1965–96: an Overview', *Population and Development Review*, 24 (3), pp. 429–68.

Chapter 4

Economic Integration, Labour Market and International Migration: the Mercosur Case[1]

Neide Patarra

Mercosur Context: Confluences and Disparities

The 1991 Mercosur Trade Agreement involves a group of nations in Latin America's South Cone (Argentina, Brazil, Paraguay and Uruguay, with the latter addition of Chile and Bolivia), geographically contiguous, with similar historical and cultural dimensions, but, at the same time, with deep diversities in social and economic life.

Heirs to a Europe-originated colonial past (Portugal, in Brazil's case, and Spain, in the case of other countries), their territorial division, cultural traits, urbanisation processes, economic cycles, relations with the colonial metropolis, independence processes, relations with native populations, and the presence of African slaves (mainly in the case of Brazil), have forged similarities and diversities. In the twentieth century, this process had developed into a general effort towards the industrialisation of colonial societies, which became independent nation states in the last century.

The most evident discrepancy is the territorial extension of their geographic unities in themselves; Portuguese colonial policy created, in Brazil's case, a geographically and linguistically consolidated territory comprising 8,512 km^2 and a population reaching around 170 million people today. In the case of Spanish colonisation, territorial dismemberment delineated very small countries, like Paraguay, with 407 km^2 and with a population around 5.5 million, and Uruguay, with only 177 km^2 and a population up to 3.2 million today. Even Argentina, a country with larger territorial dimensions (2,767 km^2)[2] and a more advanced and diversified industrialisation level, which has experienced a precocious urbanisation process and was marked by a particular European influence has joined the integration process with a population up to 36 million (Table 4.1).

Those countries have arisen and consolidated through strong international immigration flows, constitutive and markers of cultural peculiarities in the area; from colonisation until approximately the first half of twentieth century, Latin America absorbed an impressive contingent of foreign migrants who, for reasons that forced them out of their homeland, or for reasons that attracted them to new lands, came with the goal of permanent settlement, to place themselves in a new social context and to participate in the construction of a new country (Pellegrino, 1995).

During the eighteenth century, there was a heavy flow of foreign migrants into the area, mostly from coloniser countries. There was also the significant arrival of Africans, who were imported as slaves, mainly in the slavocratic Brazilian economy, a fact that created, in some areas of this country, deep cultural specifities.

In the nineteenth century, Europe's sociopolitical crises and the liberation movements in Latin American countries created a new migratory flow to the region. This flow was mostly directed towards Argentina, Brazil, Uruguay and Chile, with a significant participation, mainly towards the end of the century, of Italian migrants, whose cultural, social and economic influence outlined a commonality among South Cone countries (except Paraguay).

The last great influx of European immigrants to Latin America came just after World War II, targeting Argentina, Brazil and Venezuela (Lattes and Lattes, 1996). By the 1970s, the attraction of immigration showed signs of decline, while the socioeconomic gap between these countries and the more developed ones increased. At the same time, economic crises, social disturbance and the adoption of dictatorial regimes in a number of Latin American countries, allied to the economic and social development of the so-called First World nations, provided another migratory movement, this time of Latin Americans out of Latin America (Villa, 1996).

Efforts towards industrialisation in South Cone countries have gone through particularities and hindrances that complemented the historical diversity of their social formation. To the present day, Paraguay remains a largely agrarian-based economy along traditional patterns. Uruguay, with a precocious urbanisation and high schooling level, shows an incipient industrialisation that, beside political matters, favours a high index of emigration, mainly of young people. Argentina and Brazil have showed a more structured process of industrialisation, although with a number difficulties and exhibiting strong social inequalities.

Every country involved in the economic integration process faces, simultaneously, the need to find a place on the international scene in the context of globalisation and, internally, the pressure towards the restructuring of production with internal and external debts, the downsizing of state apparatus and the deterioration of living conditions for large sectors of the population.

Economic indicators presented below reflect some of such disparities: most (US$688 billion, or 69.1 per cent) of a total gross national product (GNP) up to US$995 billion in 1997 came from Brazil, topped up with Argentina's US$281 billion, Paraguay's US$8 billion and Uruguay US$18 billion. Note that, at the same time, the per capita income varied between a maximum value of US$ 5.8 in Argentina and a minimum of US$ 1.2 in Paraguay (Table 4.1).

Table 4.1   Basic indicators

Area	Population (million and %)		Language	Regime
Brazil	8,511,963	146.8 (1991)	Portuguese	Presidentialism
Argentina	2,780,092	32.3 (1990)	Spanish	Presidentialism
Paraguay	406,752	4.5 (1990)	Spanish *guarani*	Presidentialism
Uruguay	177,508	3.1 (1990)	Spanish	Presidentialism

	Currency	Unemployment rate	GNP(US$ billion)	Per capita income (US$)
Brazil	Real	5.7%	688	3.21
Argentina	Peso	14.9%	281	5.79
Paraguay	Guarani	9.0%	8	1.25
Uruguay	Peso	11.5%	18	3.78

Source: Relatorio Anual banco do Mundial (1994) e boletim do Subgrupo de Trabalho n. 10 do MERCOSUL.

Other social indicators confirm Mercosur's countries disparities: Paraguay's urbanisation rate was 42 per cent in 1982, contrasted with Uruguay's 88.7 per cent (Table 4.2); infant mortality rates ranged, around 1990, in the same countries, from 124.2 per thousand in Paraguay to 20.6 per thousand in Uruguay (Table 4.3); life expectancy for the respective populations of those countries (Table 4.4), including significant differences by sex, as well as educational indicators underscore Brazil, the country with more consolidated industrialisation (Table 4.5). Poverty and indigence levels (Table 4.6) underline the precariousness of social indicators in Brazil, with figures that fall, in both cases, considerably below from those of the three other Mercosur's countries.

Table 4.2 Urbanisation level

Country	Urbanisation level (%)
Brazil	85.89 (1990)
Argentina	75.59 (1991)
Paraguay	42.75 (1982)
Uruguay	88.75 (1990)

Source: Fundacao IBGE, Censo Demografico de 1991 (Brazil); United Nations, *Demographic Yearbook*, 1991 and 1992 (Argentina, Paraguay and Uruguay).

Table 4.3 Total fertility rate and infant mortality rate

	Total fertility rate	Infant mortality rate
Brazil	2.88 (1990/95)	57.7 (1990–95)
Argentina	2.71 (1993)	22.9 (1993)
Paraguay	4.31 (1985/95)	38.1 (1990–95)
Uruguay	2.330 (1990)	20.1 (1993)

Source: United Nations, *Demographic Yearbook*, 1994.

By the early 1990s, the total population in the four countries was near 190 million. Population estimates for 2000 pointed to a figure of about 218 million, most of which – some 80 per cent – would be Brazilians. Tables 4.7 and 4.8, show a long-term evolution in those countries and their respective percent distribution by age groups (Table 4.8), as well as demographic growth rates (Table 4.9), in the period from the middle of the present century, with projections that enter twenty-first century's first two decades, which allow to build future alternative socioeconomic scenarios.

Population growth rate in those countries, as everywhere in Latin America, was significantly slowed down in the last decades. From the early 1960s to the late 1980s, total fertility reduced from 6 to 3.4 children per woman and life expectancy grew a mean of ten years, from 57 to 67 years. After having reached a maximum figure up to 3 per cent, present growth rates are around 1.7 per cent (CEPAL, 1993). Starting from very different levels, in 1950, Mercosur countries tend, in the projections shown, to converge toward considerably lower levels, notwithstanding the relatively higher level of Paraguay.

Table 4.4   Life expectancy at birth

Years	Male	Female
Brazil		
1980	58.95	64.68
1990	62.28	69.09
1990–95	64.04	68.68
Argentina		
1980–81	65.48	67.30
1985–90	72.70	74.00
1990–91	68.17	73.09
Paraguay		
1980–85	64.45	64.80
1985–90	68.51	69.10
1990–95	66.30	70.83
Uruguay		
1980–81	67.80	68.90
1985–90	74.30	75.30

Source: Fundacäo IBGE, *CensoDemografico de 1991* (Brazil); United Nations, *Demographic Yearbook*, 1991, 1992, 1994.

Table 4.5   Educational indicators

	Schooling level				Mean schooling years
	Illiteracy	*Basic*	*Intermediary*	*University*	
Argentina	4.7	97.2	79.4	56.9	8.7
Brazil	18.9	77.9	74.9	22.8	3.9
Paraguay	9.9	80.1	50.2	15.3	4.9
Uruguay	3.8	94.6	80.0	61.6	7.8

Source: CEPAL, 1994.

Note: School enrolment relatively to population, according to the age corresponding to schooling
       level (%).

Table 4.6   Poverty and indigence indicators

		% of total households				
		Poor			**Indigent**	
	Total	*Urban*	*Rural*	*Total*	*Urban*	*Rural*
Argentina	13	12	17	4	3	6
Brazil	43	39	56	22	–	–
Paraguay	15	10	23	3	2	8
Uruguay	39	34	53	18	13	30

Source: CEPAL, 1994.

For the purpose of the discussion about reciprocal influence between the economic integration treaty and labour market, it is important to underline the effects of those changes on the age structure of the respective populations along the time series here considered. Age pyramids in those countries (Figures 4.7 and 4.8) provide a quick visualisation of the implications of such changes; the graphs show the effects of different demographic transitions processes in each country. Argentina and Uruguay have undergone a very precocious transition process that started in the early twentieth century. Brazil and Paraguay are in similar phases of the process and are considered as moderate transition countries (intermediary fertility and mortality), though the recent fertility decline was greater in Brazil.

These changes in population age structure have important implications in terms of both the labour market configuration, and the configuration of different social policies and demand profile. In the four countries here discussed, the lower participation of younger population groups may provide an opportunity for improved school conditions and for the achievement of improved professional capability in the context of globalisation. On the other hand, also in all cases, the participation of adult age groups, that is, the population of an economically active age, is expressive. As we can see in Table 4.7, the 20–59 years age group tends toward a growing per cent participation in the total population, in addition to an increasing potential of that sector of the population to be inserted into the labour market, strengthened by a probably increasing tendency of female participation in the same market.

Besides, as we can also see in Tables 4.7 and 4.8, the participation of that part of the population aged 60 years or more is increasing, which poses the emerging question, in those countries, of the so-called 'third age', with

Table 4.7 Total population % distribution and annual demographic growth rates by age groups and median age, Mercosur countries

Countries/age groups	1950	1960	1970	1980	1990	2000	2010	2020
Uruguay								
Population (1.000)	2.239	2.538	2.808	2.914	3.094	3.274	3.453	3.61S
Total (%)	100.0	100.0	100.0	100.0	100.0	100.0	100.0	100.0
00–04 years	9.8	10.1	9.5	9.5	8.4	8.1	7.7	7.2
05–19 years	27.0	25.9	26.5	25.9	25.8	23.6	02.8	21.8
20–59 years	51.4	52.3	51.1	49.9	49.3	51.4	52.7	53.3
60 years or more	11.8	11.8	12.9	14.7	16.5	17.0	16.8	17.7
Median age	27.3	28.1	28.7	30.1	30.7	31.4	32.5	33.8
Argentina								
Population (1.000)	17.150	20.616	23.962	28.237	32.322	36.238	40.193	43.837
Total (%)	100.0	100.0	100.0	100.0	100.0	100.0	100.0	100.0
00–04 years	11.4	11.0	10.3	11.5	10.0	9.4	8.9	8.2
05–19 years	28.3	28.2	28.1	26.8	28.5	26.7	25.2	24.2
20–59 years	53.3	52.0	50.9	49.7	48.4	50.4	51.8	52.3
60 years or more	7.0	8.8	10.7	12.0	13.1	13.6	14.1	15.3
Median age	25.5	26.5	26.9	26.9	27.2	27.7	30.0	31.4

Table 4.7 con'd

Countries/age groups	1950	1960	1970	1980	1990	2000	2010	2020
Brazil								
Population (1.000)	53.444	72.594	95.847	121.286	149.042	172.777	194.002	212.350
Total (%)	100.0	100.0	100.0	100.0	100.0	100.0	100.0	100.0
00–04 years	16.9	17.3	15.2	13.8	11.8	9.5	8.5	7.6
05–19 years	35.4	35.8	37.8	35.3	32.8	29 8	25.1	22 8
20–59 years	43.5	42.0	41.6	44.8	48.3	52 4	56.3	56.3
60 years or more	4.2	4.8	5.4	6.2	7.1	8.3	10 1	13.4
Median age	18.1	17.7	17.9	20.4	22.3	25.7	28 4	32.2 -
Paraguay								
Population (1.000)	1.351	1.774	2.351	3.147	4.277	5.538	6.928	8.423
Total (%)	100.0	100.0	100.0	100.0	100.0	100.0	100.0	100.0
00-04 years	16.4	16.4	17.2	15.5	15.4	13 8	12.5	11.5
05–19 years	37.3	37.3	41.5	38 1	35.3	34 8	32 6	30.4
20–59 years	41.2	41.2	36.0	41 0	44.0	46.0	48 8	49.7
60 years or more	5.0	5.1	5.3	5.4	5.4	5.5	6.1	8.3
Median age	17.6	16.0	16.2	17.7	18.8	20.6	22.1	23.7

Source: Centro Latino Americano de Demografia, Boletin Demografico, America Latina, Proyecciones de Poblacion 1950–2025.

Table 4.8　Annual demographic growth rate, Mercosur countries

Age groups	1950–60	1960–70	Annual growth rate 1970–80	1980–90	1990–2000	2000–10	2010–20
Uruguay							
Total	1.3	1.0	0.4	0.6	0.6	0.5	0.5
00–04 years	1.5	0.4	0.4	-0.7	0.2	-0.0	-0.2
05–19 years	0.8	1.3	0.1	0.6	-0.3	0.2	0.0
20–59 years	1.4	0.8	0.1	0.5	1.0	0.8	006
60 years or more	1.3	1.9	1.7	1.7	0.9	0.4	O.0
Argentina							
Total	1.9	1.5	1.7	1.4	1.2	1.0	0.9
00–04 years	1.5	0.8	2.8	-0.0	0.5	0.5	0.0
05–19 years	1.8	1.5	1.2	2.0	0.5	0.5	0.5
20–59 years	1.6	1.3	1.4	1.1	1.6	1.3	1.0
60 years or more	4.2	3.5	2.8	2.3	1.5	1.4	1.7
Brazil							
Total	3.1	2.8	2.4	2.1	1.5	1.2	0.9
00–04 years	3.3	1.4	1.4	0.5	-0.7	0.0	-0.2
05–19 years	3.2	3.4	1.7	1.3	0.5	-0.5	-0.1
20–59 years	2.8	2.7	3.1	2.8	2.3	1.9	0.9
60 years or more	4.4	4.0	3.8	3.6	3.1	3.2	3.8
Paraguay							
Total	2.8	2.9	3.0	3.1	2.6	2.3	2.0
00–04 years	4.3	1.8	1.9	3.0	1.5	1.3	1.1
05–19 years	3.0	3.7	2.1	2.3	2.5	1.6	1.3
20–59 years	1.8	2.4	4.3	3.8	3.1	2.9	2.2
60 years or more	3.1	3.1	3.1	3.2	2.8	3.4	5.2

Source: Centro Latino Americano de Demografía, Boletin Demografico, America Latina, Proyecciones de Poblacion. 1950–2025.

Table 4.9   Argentina: foreign population definitively established, according to nationality, 1986

Nationality	Foreign population definitively established
Americans	32.543
Bolivians	6,119
Brazilians	352
Chileans	12.870
Americans (USA)	265
Paraguayans	4.721
Peruvians	465
Uruguayans	7.421
Other	330
Europeans	1.229
Spaniards	457
Italians	309
Other	463
Asians	911
Koreans	235
Chinese	343
Israelis	60
Japanese	26
Other	247
Oceanian	40
Unspecified	37

Source: INDEC, *Anuario Estadistico de la Republica Argentina – 1983–86*, from Fundação IBGE, Mercosul: sinopse estatistica, Vol. 1, Rio de Janeiro, 1993.

serious implications on the health and welfare systems, in a context marked by a declining state participation in social policies financial support.

Recent Migratory Movements

A characteristic of South Cone countries' recent international migration was the prevalence of two basic patterns: emigration to industrialised countries, especially the USA, and intraregional migration (Chakiel and Villa, 1992). In the first case, we note that migration towards industrialised countries increases as Latin American countries consolidate their educational systems and widen the middle sectors of their populations. This fact underlines the difficulties in retaining both qualified human resources and those sectors which have access to an ascending social mobility through education. Developed countries' consumer habits and lifestyles globalisation, through mass communication media, generate ambitions that could be fulfilled in the home countries and result in migratory potentiality which has significant implications for intraregional movements and for labour market changes in the context of economic integration (Pellegrino, 1996).

Even in Brazil, a country which traditionally attracts migrants and was considered, in the last few decades, a country of closed population, the estimates for the period 1980–91 pointed to a negative international migration balance up to 1.4 million people. It was the first time in its history that this country had an outmigration and the fact surprised even population experts and embarrassed several civil society agents who, having in mind values linked to the image of a reception country, saw, in the exit of young people from urban middle sectors and with intermediary schooling, a defeat for the national development project (Patarra, 1955).

The other kind of migration, intraregional migration, is not a new phenomenon in Latin America. In the regional context, there are borders that have had a particular permeability for migratory movements. Such a population mobility occurred preponderantly between regions with common historical and cultural roots. In fact, these are intraregional movements that the existence of a political border converted into international migration.

So, inequalities between countries in the process of development have caused international migratory movements that constitute, in fact, an internal migration modality in the respective countries, for those displacements mean a 'transfrontier' extension of the same social processes (Palau, 1997). More recently, because of integration and globalisation processes and the consequent opening of markets, intraregional migration gained more dynamic and expressive forms, particularly in the Latin American subregions where economic blocks are coming to the fore. In those regions, economic integration processes are in articulation, promoting economic exchanges and population movements.

In the South Cone, these movements' modalities particularly tend to change, both between and within countries. In this sense the recent economic integration and the increased communication among Mercosur's countries tend to consolidate binational spaces which present different dynamics, where migratory flow is permanent and economic activities act as integrated regional markets (Pellegrino, 1996).

In spite of that integration, inequality between countries is growing and is resulting in a greater variety of population displacements; these movements are no longer circumscribed to national border areas, but involve temporary, seasonal, circulatory and even inter -metropolitan areas inside the region.

As already noted, Argentina, Uruguay and Brazil – traditionally recipients of European (and Asian, in the case of Brazil) immigration – received the last inflows of those streams in the years following World War II. Since then, and in some cases, since the 1930s, the greater population movements constituted of redistribution processes of their own internal population and, in particular, by rural-urban migration in the urbanisation process within each national society.

Argentina remained, at least until the mid-1970s, a poular reception area for neighbouring countries' nationals (Bolivia, Chile, Paraguay and Uruguay), and, at the same time, became an expeller of population (Maguid, 1993), a tendency noticed since the 1960s, also for political reasons, which determined mass outflows that included technicians and qualified professionals.

Uruguay transformed itself into a traditional emigration country with marked outflows, including a flow to neighbouring Argentina. In the whole, the magnitude of the Uruguaian emigration process, mainly in the 1970s, decreased the country's population in absolute terms in the years 1974–75 (Niedworok and Fortuna, 1989). The configuration of the country as a population expeller is related to political questions as well as to the effects of an economic crises that last several decades and created a tendency towards the emigration of young people. Although economic indicators show signs of recuperation, feedback effects of past emigration trends involving a considerable proportion of the population still the enhance the tendency to emigrate (Palau, 1997).

Besides the recent tendency towards emigration to First World countries, as we said, Brazil comes third in the Latin American scale of importance as a Latin American population immigration reception country, although the total volume of immigrants from Mercosur countries is substantially less than that to Argentina. Brazil's state policies, which favour scientific and technological research, as well as the development of modern industry sectors, brought about specific effects on the composition and integration of streams. In the 1970s, Brazil received the most qualified Latin American migratory flows; more than 10 per cent of total immigrants were professionals and technicians, and, in the case of the flow coming from Argentina, Uruguay and Paraguay, the proportion corresponded to 25 per cent, 15 per cent and 9 per cent respectively. Similarly, the proportion of immigrants with more than 10 years of study in that country is significantly higher than that of Latin American immigrants in Argentina. During the 1970s some economic expansion resulted in the attraction of immigrants along with a considerable return of emigrants from Argentina (Palau, 1997).

More recently, Brazil has received a new type of immigrant, from other Latin American countries, mainly Peru and Bolivia, who come from poor social groups in urban areas and go straight to big cities, mainly Sao Paulo; in these centres they provide a sort of putting-out system of ready-made articles for export. No doubt this type of movement corresponds to the new restructuring phase of metropolitan economy and is gaining force; it is very difficult to estimate the number involved, since the majority are illegal immigrants, but it is estimated at around 100,000 persons in the Metropolitan Area of São Paulo alone.

The case of the emigration of Brazilians to neighbouring South Cone countries deserves special attention. To a considerable extent, that movement arose as a response to Brazil's agrarian policies during the 1970s and the 1980s. Whether explicitly for agrarian reform purposes or merely for the democratisation of access to land property and support for small-scale agrarian production, these policies produced negative side effects; favouring the development of an agrarian land market, which had as a consequence the entrance of large groups and industries into Brazil's agriculture; that policy, in fact, was prejudicial to the former family production (Sales, 1996).

Brazil's rural population displacements – mainly to Paraguay, but also to Argentina and Uruguay – were closely linked to a process of improving land value (Reydon and Plata, 1995). The movement towards those countries includes rural landowners and agricultural entrepreneurs in search of cheaper land to produce or speculate, and rural workers or small-scale producers, numerically much more noticeable and motivated by subsistence conditions, who were dispossessed in the process of agricultural modernisation and technical updating.

In the case of the displacement towards Argentina and Uruguay, probably the landowners themselves buy land on the frontiers of those countries and take with them – permanently or, in most cases, temporarily – the manpower they will use in cultivation. That type of migration, generally of illegal character, tends to result in the return of a substantial amount of that manpower at the end of the harvest, or, sometimes, each weekend (Sales, 1996), and represents a kind of 'transfrontier seasonal worker'. According to local information, Brazilians represent today up to 50 per cent of total Uruguay rice producers.

Economic Integration, Labour Market and Emerging Social Questions

The effects of the Latin American countries' financial readjusting period on economic dynamics, employment and wage levels, as well as on government

Table 4.10   Brazil: naturalised Brazilians and foreigners, by sex, according to country of birth

Country of birth	Naturalised Total	Naturalised Male	Naturalised Female	Foreigners Total	Foreigners Male	Foreigners Female
Total	198,062	118,738	79,324	912,848	481,248	431,600
America	19,006	10,576	8,430	106,872	55,575	51,297
Argentina	4,499	2,371	2,128	22,134	11,037	4,670
Bolivia	2,638	1,511	1,127	10,342	5,672	4,670
Chile	703	465	238	17,127	9,325	7,802
Colombia	262	132	100	1,228	648	580
USA	1,453	793	660	12,350	6,385	5,965
Paraguay	3,873	2,119	1,754	13,687	6,651	7,036
Uruguay	3,975	2,170	1,805	17,263	8,837	8,426
Other	1,035	608	427	9,520	5,079	4,441
Europe	131,007	77,738	53,269	627,523	331,848	265,675
Spain	17,225	9,708	7,517	81,290	42, 174	38,116
Italy	21,714	12,347	9,367	87,076	46,548	40,528
Portugal	43,846	28,944	14,902	348,815	187,780	161,035
Other	48,222	26,739	21,483	110,342	54,346	55,996
Asia	43,355	27,672	15,683	155,420	81,970	73,450
China	4,078	2,210	1,868	4,721	2,442	2,279
Korea	996	575	421	6,262	3,114	3,148
Israel	1,188	678	510	1,507	867	610
Japan	24,362	15,753	8,609	115,118	59,869	55,248
Lebanon	6,578	4,489	2,089	15,331	8,661	6,670
Syria	2,753	1,835	918	5,340	2,873	2,467
Turkey	839	496	343	922	422	500
Other	2,561	1,636	925	6,219	3,692	2,527
Africa	4,065	2,396	1,669	12,430	6,314	6,116
Oceania	104	52	52	558	275	283
Unspecified	525	304		10,045	5,266	4,779

Source: Censo Demográfico: Dados Gerais, from Fundação IBGE, *Mercosul: sinopse estatística*, Vol. 1, Rio de Janeiro, 1993.

policies performance, are an issue of debate and discussion (see, among others, Tokman, 1993; Castro, 1996; CEPAL, 1993; Tavares and Fiori, 1993; Cano, 1991; Pochman, 1996). The external debt crisis in the early 1980s actually threatened the continuity of the industrialisation process, with per capita income stagnation, labour market precariousness and public sector disability. The role of exports grew, with a mounting privatisation proceeding

Table 4.11   Migrant population of Latin American countries who settled in Brazil between 1981 and 1991, according to nationality

Country	Naturalisation	
	Naturalised	*Non-naturalised*
Argentina	5,860	2,935
Bolivia	5,657	1,516
Chile	4,824	540
Colombia	797	434
Costa Rica	101	103
Cuba	62	69
Equador	264	667
Guatemala	20	73
British Guyana	511	41
French Guyana	109	390
Haiti	34	–
Honduras	157	140
Belize	110	–
Jamaica	–	12
Mexico	181	542
Nicaragua	30	156
Panama	34	111
Paraguay	3,508	15,224
Peru	1,764	456
Dominican Republican	118	33
El Salvador	98	46
Suriname	77	118
Uruguay	2,816	884
Venezuela	487	849
Others	15	342
Total	27,634	25,681

Source: Fundaçao IBGE. Censo Demografico, 1991.

against the public sector indebtedness and inability to proceed with investing in several economic and social activities.

Despite major inflation control and major monetary stability, as well as some signs of per capita income increase, the public sector disability process persists, with insufficient social policies and enormous difficulties for regaining sustained growth. Therefore, today's context has the character of a combined

Table 4.12   Paraguay: immigrants in permanent admission, by sex, according to country of birth

Country of birth	Immigrants in permanent admission		
	Total	*Male*	*Female*
Total	4.569	2.905	1.664
America	3.106	2.148	958
Argentina	292	179	113
Bolivia	23	10	13
Brazil	2.144	1.579	565
Colombia	10	4	6
Chile	30	19	11
United States	99	63	36
Peru	250	149	101
Uruguay	53	28	25
Other countries	205	117	88
Europe	505	276	229
Germany	154	89	65
Spain	29	21	8
France	31	18	13
England	20	11	9
Italy	36	24	12
Others	235	113	122
Asia	949	474	475
Korea	726	320	406
China	129	81	48
Israel	3	3	–
Japan	24	12	12
Lebanon	61	55	6
Others	6	3	3
Africa	9	7	2

Source: Direccion General de Estadistica, Encuestas y Censos, Anuario Estadisticos del Paraguay. Extraldo de Fundação IBGE, *Mercosul: sinopse estatistica*, Vol. l, Rio de Janeiro, 1993.

result of economic opening-up, reduction of state action, labour market deregulation and state productive sector privatisation. And more, a stronger international competitiveness implies labour cost reduction and market deregulation, privileged mechanisms favouring world trade and employment expansion (Pochman, 1996). Thus measures relative to the labour world have privileged the loosening of labour rights without, on the other hand, bearing in

Table 4.13 **Uruguay: population living in the country, born abroad, by sex, according to country of birth**

Country of birth	Population living in the country		
	Total	*Male*	*Female*
Total	103,002	48,103	54,899
America	38,057	15,890	22,167
Argentina	19,669	8,432	11,237
Brazil	12,332	4,799	7,533
Other countries	6,056	2,659	3,397
Europe	62,145	30,759	31,386
Spain	31,546	15,228	16,318
Italy	14,872	7,867	7,005
Other countries	2,424	1,148	1,276
Middle East	1,999	1,017	982
Other	801	437	364

Source: Direccion General de Estadistica, Encnestas y Censos, *Anuario Estadisticos del Uruguay, Extraido de Fundacao, 1993; IBGE, Mercosul: sinopse estatistica, Vol. l,* Rio de Janeiro.

mind its effects on wage inequality, income concentration and labour market precariousness.

After the so-called Washington Consensus, Latin American countries in general tended to follow the recipe of reforms and economic adjustments presented by international agencies. The IMF has a major role as a formulator of macroeconomic policies, for monetary stability by means of downsizing public costs, trade opening, reserves formation, control of inflation and so on. The World Bank, in turn, gave the impetus to the so-called 'structural reforms' that necessarily imply market deregulation, trade and financial opening, state downsizing, public sector privatisation, and so on. In such a context, social and labour items of agreements are increasingly governed by the rules of world trade, with loss of national policies autonomy. The strong internationalisation of the economy, in turn, acts through investment and production planning nets in different world regions, with high economic rationality and competitive advantages, and contributes to weakening national states policies autonomy (Pochman, 1996).

In that scenario, the counterpart is significant changes in the social division of labour. Craftsmanship and traditional employment are quickly disappearing. There is a strong call for labour specialisation, which demands, in turn, constant qualification and higher capability of manpower. Higher level of unemployment occurs even in countries where manpower is better qualified. Manpower demand has decreased everywhere, not only in the industry stable core, but also relatively to occupations generated at secondary, contracted and subcontracted services. The rise of new forms of occupation, many of them part-time or household work, result in the intensification of the informal use of manpower, which tends to increase more than formal employment, and in a more precarious labour market (Pochman, 1996).

As we can see below, between 1989 and 1993 Argentina and Brazil's labour force decreased; in the same period, household service and the participation of minor industry are expressive and even ascending; the informal sector, in turn, represented approximately a quarter of labour force in the respective countries (Table 4.14), with a continuous growing tendency in subsequent years.

Table 4.14   Percentage distribution of labour force (1989–1993), Mercosur countries

	Argentina		Brazil		Paraguay		Uruguay	
	1989	*1993*	*1989*	*1993*	*1989*	*1993*	*1989*	*1993*
Labour force*	100.0	100.0	100.0	100.0	100.0	100.0	100.0	100.0
Occupied labour force	92.2	91.9	97.0	94.7	93.9	94.9	91.4	93.4
Formal sector	68.5	65.2	72.0	68.9	62.2	66.9	74.4	–
• public	19.6	16.8	11.3	10.0	10.9	12.2	–	–
• private	48.9	48.4	60.7	58.9	51.3	54.7	–	–
Major industries	34.1	32.4	38.1	34.5	25.1	25.2	–	–
Minor industries	14.8	16.1	22.7	24.5	26.2	29.5	–	–
• informal sector	24.0	26.6	20.2	23.4	26.6	21.5	23.8	–
Household Servants	7.5	8.2	7.7	7.7	11.2	11.6	–	–
Unoccupied	7.6	8.1	3.0	5.3	6.1	5.1	8.6	6.6

*   Except agriculture and mining.

Source: OIT, 1994.

Labour market general characteristics in the Mercosur context include the above-mentioned tendency to growing participation of women in the labour force. Actually, between 1950 and 1990, the female proportion in the total labour force grew from 20.0 per cent to 27.0 per cent in Argentina, from 15.4 per cent to 20.6 per cent in Brazil, from 21.0 per cent to 24.4 per cent in Paraguay, and from 18.7 per cent to 38.5 per cent in Uruguay (Table 4.15). For an idea on the size of this labour market at the end of the century, it is worth bearing in mind that in 2000 the estimate total labour force for all these countries is up to 90 million people, which means, respectively, 15 million, 72 million, 2 million and 1.5 million people in Argentina, Brazil, Paraguay and Uruguay and corresponds to 41.1 per cent, 43.0 per cent, 38.5 per cent and 46.9 per cent of their total population (Palau, 1997, p. 7).

Table 4.15   Evolution of the proportion of women in the total labour force between 1950 and 1990. Latin America and Mercosur countries

	1950	1960	1970	1980	1990
Latin America	21.9	19.0	21.1	25.3	28.1
Argentina	20.0	21.2	24.8	25.8	27.9
Brazil	15.4	17.8	20.4	27.0	29.6
Chile	25.2	22.0	22.2	26.0	29.4
Paraguay	21.9	21.9	21.0	25.0	24.4
Uruguay	18.7	19.4	27.1	33.5	38.5

Source: Valdes and Gomariz, 1995 (apud Abramo, 1997).

It is on that reality that the effects of the Mercosur Trade Agreement, with its characteristics, potentialities and, at the same time, limitations and difficulties, start to act. As a part of a series of previous integration agreements that go back to the 1960s, with arguable results, the Assumpción Treaty, signed in 1991, has as its main goal the enlargement, through economic integration, of today's dimensions of signatory countries' national markets, an issue that is considered essential for the insertion of that subregion into the contemporary international scenario, and to accelerate its processes of development with social equity. For this, the countries agreed on the proposal of free goods, services and productive factors trade, of a common external tax, of macroeconomic and sector policies coordination and on the harmonisation of pertinent laws (Tratado para a Construcao, 1991). Actually, the document does not include any sort of compromise or mechanism to promote or regulate the social dimension of the integration agreements (de Filippo and Franco, 1997, p. 35).

So the search for social equity, as set out in the Foreword of that document, does not bring explicit means for actions that promote compromises which would protect the social groups involved, nor the articulation of activities that would tend to promote good living conditions for those social segments more vulnerable to the globalisation process. In the years that followed the signing of the agreement, the sole dimensions relative to social relations in the context of the new geopolitical space were those attuned to a minimum of regulation and to the compatibilisation of labour relations, which actually means an attempt to concretise the proposals of economic integration with free goods trade, postponing the inevitable regulation of its counterpart, the free circulation of people.

In a meeting of the Ministers of Labour of the signatory countries that took place in Montevideo in 1991, while recognising the urge to consider labour issues, the governments agreed to adopt 'all the necessary cooperation for the reciprocal knowledge of the proper regimes linked to employment, social security, professional formation and labour individual and collective relations', thus creating the Labour Subgroup and making way for the representation of entrepreneurs and workers of the four countries (Espino, 1995).

The Assumpción Treaty created the Common Market Council, a high-level body in charge of political conduction and decision-making, integrated by the signatory countries' Ministers of Foreign Affairs and Labour, with a changing chairmanship. The Common Market Group is the executive organ, coordinated by the Ministries of Foreign Affairs, and, among other attributes, may constitute the necessary working subgroups. Ten subgroups were created for the coordination of macroeconomic and social policies. In its early elaboration, it was planned that Mercosur should establish organs for the representation of socioeconomic groups interests, the so-called Social and Political Representation Organs. Only the Mercosur Industry Council was initially created; in the meeting in Ouro Preto (1994), it was decided to incorporate that Council into the Economic and Social Consulting Forum, which means an enlargement of the latter Industrial Council to other social segments, similar to the Economic and Social Committee of European Union. The Conjunct Parliamentary Commission (CPC), a consultative and deliberating body, completes the incipient chart of possibilities in the treatment of the social questions in the Mercosur Treaty.

In this context, the trade union movement has acted in a consistent and organised way, not only regarding labour issues, but also as almost the only space for social claims (Castro, 1995, 1996). Benefiting from the trade union centres' coordination (CCSCS), created in 1987, the trade union movement have had an intensified role since the Assumpción signature. CCSCS participation in the negotiations, although of little significance on the whole for decisions, had an influence on the pace of integration towards a better knowledge about trade union organisations and the problems and possible consequences of Mercosur for the workers (Castro, 1995).

The movement's action focused on inequalities in economy and dimensions between the four countries. It denounced the vanishing of industries because of entrepreneurial rivalry, labour flexibility, national policies and the reduction of social benefits. As has been underlined, the national economic models under way increased unemployment, worsened income distribution and enlarged social marginalisation (Castro, 1995).

Trade union political action faces, among other tasks, the urge of a minimum of compatibility between labour law in the four countries; in fact, law mechanisms for contract and dismissal of workers, for the treatment of the pensions issue, for trade unions contributions and so on, are very different or vague. The definition of compatible mechanisms between the countries became undelayable, given the region's considerable migratory potential; different treatments may affect precarious and unprotected migration movements, while the desirable design of migration policies just can attenuate the negative effects of the integration process if they are faced together.

The welfare issue, in turn, is also an undelayable dimension. Mercosur countries are going through a reformulation in their policies. Argentina, Brazil and Uruguay were the first ones to adopt social security regimes, although they are also the countries with the largest deficit in this field. The increase in the number and duration of pensions – partly because of the increase in life expectancy, inflation effects and administrative difficulties – give those systems priority in current attempts for the state apparatus.

One important dimension in these reformulation processes has been the urge to reduce differences between the amount and the sources of financial resources and the levels of workers' contribution resources and the contributions levels. Another aim is to establish agreements that allow immigrant workers to enjoy, in the country of residence, rights acquired or in way of acquisition (Tokman and Wurgaft, 1995). Similarly, distinct health and education law provisions and policies must be taken into account in the Mercosur trade schedule, so as to hinder the deepening of inequalities and explicit or potential conflicts, in a subregion where people's mobility tends to become an intrinsic part of economic and social dynamics.

To summarise, in the trade union and social schedule of Mercosur there is a wide range of issues to face. The women's movement has organised two discussion forums and listed, under the perspective of gender, the urgent need to face social questions in the integration context . Different segments of civil society also will surely tend to act, in a more dynamic way, in monitoring the increasing and diverse population displacements and the disorganisation of social life in the context of integration.

Notes

1   This chapter first appeared in the *Brazilian Journal of Population Studies*, Vol. 2, 1999/ 2000, pp. 165–82.
2   Population Studies Nucleus (NEPO) and Institute of Economics, University of Campinas, Sao Paulo, Brazil.

References

Abramo, L. (1997), 'Oportunidades y nuevas experiencias de trabajo para la mujer en el contexto de la restructuracion productiva y de la integracion regional', Sao Paulo, UNIFEM (mimeo), 29–30 April.

Cano, W. (1991), *Reflexoes sobre o Brasil e a nova (des) ordem internacional*, Campinas: Unicamp.

Castro, M.S.P. (1995), 'Reflexos do Mercosul no Mercado de Trabalho', *Sao Paulo em Perspectiva*, 9 (1), January–March.

Castro, M.S.P. (1996), 'Cinco anos de Mercosul: uma tentativa de avaliaçao da açao das perspectivas sindicais', *Revista brasileira de Politica Internacional do Instituto Brasileiro de Relaçoes Internacionis*, Ano 39, No. 2.

CEPAL (1993), *Comision Economica para America Latina y el Caribe*, CELADE, Santiago de Chile: Centro Latino Americano de Demografia e Naciones Unidas, Poblacion, equiaad y transformacion productiva.

Chackiel, J. and Villa, M. (1992), *America Latina y el Caribe: Dinamica de la Poblacion y Desarrollo*, Documento de Referencia, DDR/1, Naçoes Unidas.

de Filippo, A. and Franco, R. (1997), *Aspectos sociales de la integracion*, Serie Politicas Sociales, Comision Economica para America Latina y el Caribe, Naçoes Unidas.

Fortuna, J.C., Niedworok, N. (1989), *Uruguay y la emigración de los 70*, Montevideo: CIESU-UNRISD, Ediciones de la Banda Oriental.

Lattes, A. and Lates, Z.R. (1996), 'International Migration in Latin America', in N.L. Patarra (ed.), *Emigracao e Imigracao Internacionais no Brasil contemporaneo*, Vol. 2, Campinas: FNUAP.

Maguid A. (1995), Desafios Metodol6gicos e sistema de informa,cao no Mercosul', in N.L. Patarra (ed.), *Emigracao e Imigracao Internacionais no Brasil contemporaneo*, Vol. 1, Campinas: FNUAP.

Morell, M.G.G. and Costa, L.B. (1995), 'Populacoes do Mercosul: evoluçao histörica e cenarios futuros', *Sao Paulo em Perspectiv*a, 9 (1), January–March.

Müller, G. (1995), 'Agricultura Brasilera no futuro do Mercosul', *Sao Paulo em Perspectiva*, 9 (1), January–March.

Palau, T. (1995), Migracoes Transfronteiricas entre Brasil e Paraguai: o caso dos brasiguaios', in N.L. Patarra (ed.), *Emigracao e Imigracao Internacionais no Brasil contemporaneo*, Vol. 1, Campinas: FNUAP.

Palau, T. (1997), 'Migration among Countries in MERCOSUL, Trends and Perspectives', Barcelona, IUSSP (mimeo), May 7-10.

Pattarra, N.L. (1996), 'Introducao', in N.L. Patarra (ed.), *Emigracao e Imigracao Internacionais no Brasil contemporaneo*, Vol. 2, Campinas: FNUAP.

Pattarra, N.L. and Baeninger, R. (1996), 'Migracoes internacionais recentes: o caso do Brasil', in N.L. Patarra (ed.), *Emigracao e Imigracao Internacionais no Brasil contemporaneo*, Vol. 2, Campinas: FNUAP.

Pellegrino, A. (1995), 'As migracoes no Cone Sul, com enfase no caso Uruguai', in N.L. Patarra (ed.), *Emigracao e Imigracao Internacionais no Brasil contemporaneo*, Vol. 1, Campinas: FNUAP.

Pochmam, M. (1996), 'Economia Global e os Direitos Trabalhistas na Periferia do capitalismo', in N.L. Patarra (ed.), *Emigracao e Imigracao Internacionais no Brasil contemporaneo*, Vol. 2, Campinas: FNUAP.

Reydon, B.P. and Plata, L.A. (1995), 'Migracoes e os mercados de terra agricula no Cone-Sul', in N.L. Patarra (ed.), *Emigracao e Imigracao Internacionais no Brasil contemporaneo*, Vol. 1, Campinas: FNUAP.

Sales, T. (1996), 'Migracoes de Fronteiras entre o Brasil e os Paises do Mercosul', *Revista Brasileira de Estudos Populaiconais*, 13 (1), January–June.

Sales, T.O. (1995), 'Trabalhador brasileiro no contexto das novas migracoes Internacionais', in N.L. Patarra (ed.), *Emigracao e Imigracao Internacionais no Brasil contemporaneo*, Vol. 1, Campinas: FNUAP.

Schwartz, G. (1995), 'Mercosul entre Safta e Nafta: uma reestruturacao destrutiva ou integracao Pan-americana?', *Sao Paulo em Perspectiva*, 9 (1), January–March.

Spino, A. (1995), 'Mujeres y Mercosul', Uruguay: CIEDUR (mimeo).

Tavares, M. da C. and Fiori, J.L. (1993), *(Des)ajuste Global e Modernizacao Conservadora*, Rio de Janeiro:Paz e Terra.

Tokman, V.E. and Wurgaft, J. (1995), 'Integracion Economica y Mercado de Trabajo', *Sao Paulo em Perspectiva*, 9 (1), January–March.

Tratado Para a Construção de um Mercado Comum entre a República Argentina (1991), A República Federativa do Brasil, a República do Paraguale a República Oriental do Uruguai.

Villa, M. (1996), 'Una nota acerca de la informacion sobre migracion internacional en Latinoamerica (IMILA)', in N.L. Patarra (ed.), *Emigracao e Imigracao Internacionais no Brasil contemporaneo*, Vol. 2, Campinas: FNUAP.

Chapter 5

Return Migration in Africa

Oladele O. Arowolo

Introduction

This chapter presents a regional perspective on the issue of return migration and the complex problem of reintegration back into civil society. The Africa region is the focus of the chapter, with emphasis on Sub-Saharan Africa (SSA). It has been argued that future patterns of migration in SSA will most probably be dominated by refugee and clandestine workers, and the political and economic situations giving rise to such migrants are likely to remain unstable. The changing political, economic and environmental situations that propel such migratory movements are also potent factors in return migration. Following the wars of independence and cessation of civil conflicts, many countries in the region have been facing the problem of reintegrating the returnees back into civil society (Arowolo, 1998).

In 1991, some 16 SSA countries were harbouring over 5.4 million refugees, most of them originating from Mozambique, Ethiopia, Sudan, Angola, and Somalia. Although concrete data are not yet available, the civil wars in Liberia, Sierra Leone and Guinea have added hundreds of thousands of refugees and internally displaced persons to the 1991 records. To these should be added thousands of other categories of internal and international voluntary migrants, all over the subcontinent, who find it convenient to return home at different points in time, and who also require assistance in one form or another in the process of their social and economic reintegration.

Largely because return migration is a neglected area in migration research, the development of a viable framework for addressing the complex problem of reintegration is still in its infancy. Most organised schemes for the rehabilitation of return migrants tend to be a spontaneous response to emergency situations and are largely donor driven. The focus of most of such schemes, invariably spearheaded by the UNHCR, is commonly on the repatriation process, and success is measured in terms of timely provision of physical transportation, and relocation of exiles, rather than the subsequent process of reintegrating them into civil society.

This explains in part why many projects of refugee resettlement and rehabilitation have recorded limited positive impact, and many countries continue to adopt ad hoc measures to address this growing problem. Even then, most countries do not have any provision for voluntary migrants who make their private arrangements to return home and fend for themselves. The purpose of this chapter is to raise the issue of return migration and associated problem of reintegration high on migration research agenda in SSA countries. The review work on methodology, conceptual clarification and programming strategy, however, goes beyond the African continent. This chapter presents, in the end, a programme approach to national strategies for social, economic and political reintegration of returnees.

Conceptual Issues

Return Migration

If the mobility process is conceptualised in terms of a series of behavioural phases, seven distinct movements have been identified in the literature on migration, each one corresponding to the possible migratory movement which any member of a population will fit. These behavioural phases (migratory moments) have been defined (Standing, 1984) as follows:

1   migration never considered;
2   migration considered but rejected (for definite future, or temporarily, on a contingency basis);
3   migration intended/planned, but timing and/or destination uncertain;
4   migration in process;
5   migration completed;
6   migration made, and repeated;
7   migration made, returned to area of origin or place of previous residence.

The last behavioural phase in the above list defines return migration (also see Viderkamp, 1972; Da Vanzo, 1976; Da Vanzo and Morrison, 1981). In this regard, Peek (1981) has argued, with reference to rural–urban migration, that a person who after living in an urban area returns to a different village rather than to his village of origin should not be regarded as a return migrant. However, this view is rather narrow, and its application is bound to exclude some categories of return migrants.

A variant of return migrants, for example, may be those who return to a rehabilitation centre or newly created settlements, their area of origin or previous residence having been destroyed by war, or natural disaster, or simply fallen victim of gerrymandering. In some other cases, the original home or place of residence before migration may be unknown for a variety of reasons, especially in situations involving war exiles returning to their country of origin, after 20 or more years away from home, following cessation of hostilities. Depending on their duration of stay away from home, a steam of returning migrants, sometimes referred to as 'returnees', may also include children who were born abroad and whose place of origin is technically not the place to which they now find themselves as *derivative return migrants*. The UNCHR estimated that by June 1990 when its repatriation programme in Namibia officially ended, 43,454 exiles had returned. And in the account of Simon and Preston (1993), many of the returnees had been outside Namibia for a very long time; some for up to 30 years and the majority of them had left the country as children or were born in exile.

Most of the general typologies of migration tend to omit the subject of return migration. Such classifications focus on methodological approaches (Eichenbaum, 1975); or analytical issues of personal and other relationships, social forces and types of migration (Petersen, 1958). Hugo's migration classification schema is narrowly focused on rural-urban population mobility and only on the so-called 'spontaneous movers'. However, it is useful for analysing migrant 'assimilation' to urban areas and the links between population mobility, community involvement and social networks, all of which are relevant to the study of return migration and the issue of reintegration. Because of its relevance to the concern of this paper, Hugo's schema of rural-to-urban population mobility in a Third World context is presented in Figure 5.1.

Reintegration

There are conceptual problems as well in the literature on *reintegration*, sometimes used interchangeably with *integration,* of return migrants. The Oxford Dictionary defines 'integration' as the intermixing of persons previously segregated; and 'reintegration' as the process of integrating back into society. When applied to return migrants, the two words do not mean exactly the same thing.

Preston (1993, pp. 2–4) has argued that within migratory cycles, the process of integration is one of adaptation; a process of give and take on either side as people learn to live together. At destinations this adaptation takes place between the host community and their guests, while at places of origin, it is between those who have returned and those who remained at home during their absence. The extent of integration, she argues, will depend upon a series of constantly changing contextual factors, ranging from contingencies of the physical environment, climate and pestilence, as well as social and economic circumstances.

The point is that integration is applied to the return migrant as if there was no integration experience at the point of origin prior to migration. The argument by Preston (1993) that the term 'reintegration' may be taken to imply that the social and economic environment to which people return has not changed since they left is unrealistic. There is nothing about the process of reintegration to suggest that such a process is only feasible under conditions of graveyard social and economic stability and quiet. Integration or reintegration can take place in the face of changes in the economy, society and the environment.

If it can be safely assumed that a potential migrant is a fully integrated member of his place of origin, the decision to migrate and his actual departure from his home environment should not rob him of his status as a formerly integrated member of his home base. Upon his return from a chosen place of destination, he needs to be *reintegrated* back into the original society to which he was already acculturated. This process applies to returnees from voluntary migration, and to those returning from various forms of forced movements, including people moving out of their countries and living in exile, or living in 'inxile' as a result of internal displacement.

Methodological Problems

A return migrant is a person who moved back to the area where he formerly resided (Shryock and Siegel, 1973, p. 618). It is difficult to capture all return migration in the usual sources of migration data; information is required from individual migrants on the origin and destination for at least two migration periods. This type of information can be obtained from special surveys. This explains in part why most studies of migration have ignored return migrants (Oberai, 1984, p. 165). Indeed, Molho (1986) has argued that the importance of separately identifying return migrants from the other migrant streams must depend on the relative prevalence of such migration in observed flows.

In order to define a return migrant, a reference period since return should be established, to avoid grouping all returning migrants together in a study of

Type of spontaneous mover	Characteristics of move	Commitment to city	Commitment to village
Short-term visitor	Adventitious shoppers, tourists, visitors.	None.	None.
Seasonal or shuttle migrant	Search for work to augment meagre agricultural income.	Very little financial or social investment in city. Sleep in open, group-rented room or employer-provided barracks. Social interaction almost entirely with other migrants from village. Employment in sectors.	Family of procreation remains in village. Retain all political and social roles in village. Remit bulk of income (after living expenses) to village. Traditional or day-labouring. Retain village citizenship. Almost total orientation to village.
Target migrant	Come to city for limited period (though longer than a season) to accomplish a specific purpose (e.g., reach a particular education level).	Moderate. May bring family of procreation. Seek more permanent accommodation, e.g., individually rented room. Have more interactions with settled urban population but retain close contact with fellow city. Usually employed in traditional villages in sector.	Strong links maintained with family in village through visits and letters, although some roles may be temporarily given up. Remittances remain regular and high. Usually retain village citizenship.
Short-term life cycle sojourner Stage migrant	Migrants who move to the city at one or more specific stages of life cycle.		

Working life migrant	Migrants who spend their entire working lives in the city but intend to, eventually do retire to, their home village.	High. Family of procreation always accompanies. Purchase or build individually housing, occupy employer supplied (e.g. government) housing, or rent housing on long-term basis. Often in formal sector occupations. High level of interaction with settled urban population but retain contact with fellow migrants through associations, etc. Always transfer citizenship to city. Assist new arrivals to city from home village.	Sufficient links maintained with village to ensure acceptance on eventual return. Investments in housing and land although unable to maintain most social and political roles. Periodic remittances to family. Return visits made at end of fasting months and for important life cycle ceremonies.
Permanent migrant	Migrants committed totally to exchanging a rural for an urban way of life.	Total.	None.
Undecided migrant	Migrants who have no clear intention to either stay in the city or return to the village.	Unknown.	Unknown.

Figure 5.1   Rural-to-urban population mobility in a Third World context

Source: Hugo, 1978.

reintegration. In addition, a minimum period of absence away from the usual residence should be considered. In both cases, the determination of reference period is arbitrary and may vary from one study to another, depending on the research objectives. Since information will have to be obtained directly from each return migrant and there is the additional problem of location in the field. That is why it may be easier to investigate return migrants as part of a larger migration survey carried out in (at least) origin areas: if migrants are rare, return migrants will be even rarer (Bilsborrow et al. 1984, p. 63). This, of course, raises the sampling problem of locating relatively 'rare elements' of the population (Kish, 1965).

Part of the problem of reintegration of return migrants into their places of origin may have to do with the 'intensity of circulation', an index described in the following words:

> When migrants return home after only one period of residence away, it is very 'intense'; when they make many intervening moves before returning home, they still participate in circular migration but it is a less important process.

Based on residence history data, the proposed index is computed as follows:

$$\text{Index of circular migration} = \frac{\text{Number of return moves to village x 2}}{\text{Total number of moves}} \times 100$$

At maximum intensity, the index gives a value of 100 per cent, or zero if no circular migration. Emphasis in this calculation is on the intervening moves, and there is no intrinsic importance in this.

As a refinement to this index, an index of the *velocity of circulation* has been developed. The index is calculated as follows:

Velocity of circulation = $(\bar{t}.\bar{n}/T \times M/P) \times 100$; where,

$\bar{t}$ is the average duration of time away for those who circulated;
$\bar{n}$ is the average number of absences among such migrants in the period;
T is the period, which could be a year, expressed in the same units as t days or weeks;
M is the number of those involved in circular migration;
P is the population 'at risk'.

The measure of velocity of circulation seems to be analytically more useful, as changes in residential stability of a population have implications for social and economic planning. It also provides a measure of the extent of circulation and is useful in identifying trends, as well as comparing circulation in two or more areas (Standing, 1984, p. 51). As a phenomenon, return migration has been observed to vary pro-cyclically, implying that in times of high national unemployment, return migrants tend to go home whilst the remainder of the population stay home. In essence, the balance and composition of migration flows may adjust during national downswings in favour of return migrants (Vinderkamp, 1972).

The study of reintegration, per se, relies on answers provided by return migrants in a survey, and analysis of relevant environment and community level variables associated with place of final destination. The longer the period since returned, the less likely the information supplied will be accurate and reliable. This is why a reference period of five years (those who have returned within five years prior to the survey) is suggested in the literature as a guide to selecting return migrants in a survey. Again, there is the need to determine the minimum period of absence away from the usual residence in order to define return migrants. It is suggested that that three months may be used as the minimum period (Oberai, 1984, p. 165). In both cases, the choice of reference period is arbitrary and may vary from one research to another, depending on their objectives. This, of course, sets a limit on comparability of findings on the subject in different historical and environmental settings.

Characteristics of Return Migrants

The fact that migration flow is not always unidirectional means that some outmigrants or emigrants do return to their place or country of origin. The reasons for returning varies widely but are intimately related to the objectives for migrating in the first instance. While some migrants return after achieving their objectives, others return out of frustration and failure to realise their dreams at the point of destination. Some find it most fulfilling to return home after retirement from work away from home, while others prefer to return home and work after acquiring necessary skills abroad.

Based on a study of the determinants and consequences of internal migration in India (Oberai, Prasad and Sardana, 1989), it is reported that migrants may return to their place of origin if they fail to achieve the objectives with which they outmigrated or because they cannot reconcile themselves to the social environment and way of life in the destination areas. They may also return if they went for a fixed contract period or after completing their service tenure. In addition, some successful outmigrants are reported to find it more worthwhile to return to their native home and make use of the skill/wealth acquired during their stay away. The tabulated results of their investigation of reasons for return migration in three states of India are shown in Table 5.1.

Table 5.1   Percentage distribution of return migrants (in three states of India) by reason for return 1984/85

Reasons for returning	Bihar	Kerala	Uttar Pradesh
Job terminated	21.6	47.7	3.2
Retirement	11.4	0.0	34.1
Job transfer	1.4	27.7	4.9
Strike, etc.	23.2	0.0	0.0
Did not like place/job	19.4	5.5	15.7
Illness	7.1	0.0	4.3
To set up business in place of origin	0.0	19.1	0.0
Needed back in family	11.8	0.0	23.7
Followed family	3.8	0.0	3.8
Others	0.0	0.0	6.4
All	100.0	100.0	100.0
Sample size (N)	(211)	(220)	(185)

Source: Oberai, Prasad, Sardana, 1989, Table 3.13, p. 42.

In her study of selected towns in Nigeria, Sierra Leone and Zimbabwe, Margaret Peil (1995) reported a variety of factors accounting for return migration especially among the elderly and retired persons. Based on her analysis, she concludes that Africans generally prefer to return to their place of origin, on retirement or before, rather than leaving for good and settling permanently in the host location. This preference has to do with some economic and social factors; returning home may mean retaining or regaining land rights and as such an opportunity to support themselves by farming.

However, returning migrants under normal circumstances often want to be sure of their personal safety, accommodation and social recognition upon return to their place of origin. For an illustration, with the hope of returning home eventually, a typical pioneer Nigerian migrant within Nigeria or outside would like to 'invest' at home, or 'register' his/her presence at home while away. This objective is best achieved by owning a modern house back home, regardless of the economic justification for such an investment.

In many cases, retired out-migrants invest a substantial proportion of their lump sum pension benefits to achieve this cherished objective. Indeed, out-migrants that are yet to make their presence felt in this manner while away can hardly lay any claim to success in their venture away from home. Such a migrant, in local parlance, is 'yet to arrive'! That is why a traveller through Nigeria may come across the anomaly of a few ultra-modern houses in the midst of rural-type dwellings in a remote rural location. For most of the time such houses are unoccupied, except for the security person(s) and occasionally at festive seasons by their owners, once in a while or if at all. However, such modern houses seem to offer hope, the hope that in future a migrant family may move in, to fulfil the initial pre-migration expectation to be together again.

However, there are exceptions such as the Hausa migrants in northern Nigeria who often sell their land when they leave and thus have no reason to return (Hill, 1972). Also, it is reported that in Tanzania, those who are not members of the village cooperative under the land collectivisation system will have nothing to return to and thus plan a permanent stay away from home village (Peil, 1995).

It has also been observed that return migration may be precipitated by certain circumstances related to retirement, as with the majority of southern Nigerians and Ghanaians in the past (Caldwell, 1969). As Peil puts it, many people consider themselves old when they go home, or they retire from an urban job when conditions seem ripe for the return home. In addition, becoming a widow may precipitate a woman's return home in the middle or old age, but they are more likely than men to prefer remaining in a town away from home.

For those who have been forced to live in exile or otherwise displaced, as a result of struggle for independence or autonomy, the issue changes from return migration to voluntary (or forced) repatriation. Judged by the numbers of persons involved and the complexity of problems created in the process of reintegration, repatriation is perhaps the most challenging problem faced by many African countries that have been plagued by civil wars, ethnic hostilities or secessionist struggles during the past three decades or so.

In almost all cases of repatriation, the reason for returning to place or country of origin is because peace has, or is perceived to have, returned and conditions are conducive to reintegration. And for those who are forced to return, they have no option, particularly if the host country can no longer retain them. It is estimated that by 1991, some 16 Sub-Saharan African countries harboured over 5.4 million refugees and asylum seekers in need of protection and/or assistance. Their distribution is shown in Table 5.2.

According to the report of the US Committee for Refugees (1991), 1.4 million refugees originated from Mozambique, 1.1m from Ethiopia, and close to 0.5 million each from Angola, Sudan and Somalia (see details in Table 5.3). The statistics exclude thousands of refugees from Namibia (estimated at 50,000 in 1991, out of which 43,454 had returned by 30 June 1990, soon after independence), South Africa, and some other African countries for which there are no hard data. It is reported (Adepoju, 1995) that among countries in the world with the highest proportion of refugees to local population in 1992, 8 were in Sub-Saharan Africa (Swaziland, Malawi, Somalia, Sudan, Zambia, Zimbabwe, Burundi and Ethiopia). These figures indicate the magnitude of the potential problem of reintegration faced by the countries from which these millions of refugees originated.

When the unknown but large numbers of regular internal and international return migrants are added to the volume of those being repatriated, there is hardly any African country that can afford to ignore the seriousness of the potential problem of reintegration. Failure to achieve reintegration soon after return may again lead to internal strife, political agitation and civil war, with its predictable negative consequences on the economy and society.

The concluded war between NATO and Yugoslavia over ethnic cleansing of Kosovo Albanians, fought in the full glare of the Central News Network (CNN) and watched literally by the whole world, presents a formidable challenge to research in the field of return migration. While the war was on, the whole world was kept informed about almost every artillery fired in the front. The process of displacement of ethnic Albanians from Kosovo was monitored meticulously and numbers were calculated to facilitate the resettlement of refugees at their organised and well-supervised points of destination. When the war ended, the whole world knew who won and how the challenge had moved from war to resettlement of refugees. Later, only brief attention was focused, by the media, on internally displaced people. And since the war ended, media attention moved away from the process of return of the refugees. As for their reintegration into the different home communities, it is not a subject of interest to the media. Only future research can uncover the social, economic and political obstacles faced by returning refugees, and the success of the various strategies employed in their reintegration.

Now that the formerly displaced Albanians are being assisted to return home, little is known about the strategies for resettlement and reintegration. In

Table 5.2   Refugees and asylum seekers in need of protection and/or assistance in Sub-Saharan African (SSA) countries[1]

Country	1988	1989	1991[2]
Angola	95,700	26,500	11,900
Burundi	76,000	90,200	90,700
Djibouti	2,000	4,650	67,400
Ethiopia	700,500	740,000	783,000
Kenya	10,600	15,500	14,400
Malawi	630.000	812,000	909,000
Rwanda	20,600	20,500	21,500
Somalia	365,000	350,000	358,500
South Africa	180,000	201,000	201,000
Sudan	693,600	694,300	726,500
Swaziland	70,700	71,700	47,200
Tanzania	266,200	266,200	266,200
Uganda	125,500	170,500	156,000
Zaire	325,700	338,800	370,900
Zambia	149,000	131,700	133,950
Zimbabwe	171,500	185,500	186,000
Total SSA	4,055,260	4,338,400	4,571,350
Total Africa	4,088,260	4,524,800	5,443,450

Notes

1   Table refers to countries with 10,000 or more refugees in 1991.
2   As of December 1990.

Source: United States Committee for Refugees (USCR), 1988, 1989, 1991.

situations as we have in Africa where such conflicts do not enjoy the privilege of CNN and Western media coverage, it is not surprising that there is practically no information at the country level on returnees. Yet their return and effective integration into the original society can go a long way in resolving internal political crisis, restoring peace and stability, and rejuvenating the economy. In the Africa subregion, return migration and the issue of reintegration is a virgin area of research enterprise.

Table 5.3   Principal sources of refugees in Sub-Saharan African countries, 1988–1991

Country	1988	1989	1991
Mozambique	1,147,000[2]	1,354,000	1,427,500
Ethiopia[1]	1,101,200[2]	1,035,900	1,060,300[2]
Angola	395,700	438,000	435,700
Sudan	355,000	435,100	499,100
Somalia[1]	350,000	388,600	454,600[2]
Rwanda	217,800	233,000[2]	203,900
Burundi	186,600	186,500[2]	186,200
Western Sahara	165,000	165,000[2]	165,000[2]
Chad	41,300	–	34,400
Zaire	53,200	50,400	50,700

Notes

1   Changes in certain populations in early 1991.
2   Indicates that sources vary significantly in number reported.

Source: United States Committee for Refugees (USCR), 1988, 1989, 1991.

Internally Displaced Persons

Largely because of political sensitivity, the focus of the international community has been almost exclusively on international refugees, asylum seekers and other categories of cross border migrants who need assistance to return home. When the stream of returning international migrants (or refugees) is potentially large, media attention excites the international community even more.

However, little or no attention is given to internally displaced persons yearning to return home as soon as the circumstances that caused their displacement change for the better. Ironically, it is usually for political reasons that governments discourage focus of media attention on the problem of internally displaced people in their country. And for the same reason, hard data are difficult to find from government official sources, except in planned resettlement schemes following official acquisition of land, or for political reasons. Even then, such planned resettlement schemes are known better for their poor performance in the Africa region (Rahmato, 1989).

For example, it still remains a mystery, except for media speculations, how many people were displaced internally in Kenya between 1993 and 1996 when ethnic conflicts in the Rift Valley and neighbouring Districts were most pronounced. The phenomenal growth of the population of Nairobi and peri-urban areas, spurred by the influx of hundreds of thousands of displaced population, is a classic example of internal displacement of population: a large population of rural origin, suddenly displaced and immediately 'urbanised', or rather 'urban placed'. When will they return? Or are they ever expected to return to their confiscated rural homes and landed property? Yet, if the Government is willing to solve the chronic problem of urban congestion, crime and ravaging poverty, the return of millions of displaced rural people from Nairobi Metropolis to the Rift Valley and other rural areas of origin may be the answer.

Elsewhere in the subcontinent, the situation is even worse. The civil wars in Somalia, Liberia, Sierra Leone, Sudan, Uganda, Rwanda, Burundi, Angola and the Democratic Republic of Congo have together generated millions of internally displaced people whose fate is unknown. To the extent that these wars have been on for about two decades in Sudan and Angola and evidence of skirmishes is there in almost all of these other countries, the generation of internally displaced population in SSA is now a growing phenomenon. It is possible that the numbers involved may even be much larger than the estimate of 5.4 million refugees/asylum seekers for SSA in 1991 (see Table 5.2 above). Oucho (1996) has reviewed the complex social, economic and political factors inducing the outflow of refugees from Sudan and displacement of population in the country and came to the sad conclusion that the end of refugees crisis and the related problem of population displacements in the country was not in sight in the foreseeable future.

Reintegration Strategies

Within the context of voluntary migration study, return migration has for long remained invisible. This is largely because return migration tends to be a private, individual or family affair. However, over the past three decades, the increased scale of international return migration has made it conspicuous, and the growing problems of reintegration have in many cases led governments and agencies to intervene (Preston, 1993, pp. 2–5).

Intervention strategies include pre-return or on-arrival orientation to prepare for changes and difficulties to be encountered; provision of financial and investment advice for those hoping to start business or acquire property (Athokorala, 1986); provision of information about qualification and skill recognition for labour market entry; language training for children born abroad and their preparation for entering the school system at 'home' (Dumon, 1976).

In spite of such support strategies, many return migrants still face acute problems of reintegration, ranging from joblessness and social maladjustment to boredom and frustration. In cases of accompanying foreign dependants, they tend to encounter on the one hand problem of adaptation between themselves and their relation, and on the other hand between themselves and the community. In such situation, both foreign wives and children are reported to have experienced loss of identity and trauma (Gmelch, 1980).

Both the host country and the country of origin often jointly plan the return of refugees to their home country, invariably with the assistance of international agencies. However, reintegration of returning refugees is even more challenging because their return, although often planned and orchestrated, tend to be dramatic and chaotic. Unlike voluntary migration, construction of frameworks for analysing the integration of refugees into their country of origin is recent and poorly developed. Part of the problem is that while the total numbers involved tend to be large, the numbers of people who return independently are far in excess of those who take part in organised schemes (Rogge, 1991).

Some governments have utilised policy and legal instruments as a strategy for achieving the integration of returning migrants, particularly refugees. For example, it is reported that Zimbabwe issued several Acts of Parliament in support of the country's scheme to reintegrate an estimated 300,000 people who had left the country to seek refuge abroad during the prolonged war of independence which ended in 1980. But implementation of these Acts met with different kinds of problems, including resistance from the civil service establishment, poor information and inadequate commitment of the government itself to ensure compliance by the public (Makanya, 1992).

It is against this background that the economic and social aspects of reintegration are discussed in the sections that follow, with a view to providing a coherent framework for successful reintegration of different categories of returnees (migrants, refugees and displaced persons) under different social, political, economic and environmental situations.

Economic Aspects of Reintegration

Any programme of economic reintegration of returnees, to be successful, must be based on a careful analysis of their background characteristics: age, sex, education/skills acquired, reasons for leaving, host country or place of residence, type of work done while away, family characteristics, amount of money repatriated, access to property at home, and so on. All these will determine the individual/personal needs for economic integration or reintegration. In addition, the absorptive capacity of local economy must be placed against the potential demand by returnees for employment. If information is lacking, or of poor quality, on either the returnees or the local economic environment, planning for a smooth reintegration could be rendered difficult.

Among most returnees in general, 'homecoming' tends to generate a revolution of rising expectations. This is more so if the repatriation programme coincides with long awaited political independence in the country of origin. In the case of Namibia, the problem was compounded by the resettlement strategy adopted; large numbers of returnees were repatriated to their rural homes, thereby generating pressure on the fragile economic and environmental resource base. And given their location in scattered rural settlements throughout the region, they were effectively isolated from major towns and from potential job markets ((Tapscott and Mulongeni, 1990). In addition, most returnees came back from exile with very limited funds and lacked the initial investments for seeds and tools to start farming ((Tamas, 1992). In essence, the general lack of development activity at the place of destination can pose a major constraint to the economic reintegration of return migrants in general.

The single most important impediment to the full reintegration of returnees into the civil society is perhaps their inability to secure wage employment. Unable or unwilling to work on the farms, many return migrants rely on the education and experience acquired while away from home to get appropriate wage employment back at home. But most of them are often disappointed by the negative impulses from the labour market. The reasons for this are many and may be summed up as follows:

- where unemployment is already high and problematic, returning migrants in search of jobs barely exacerbate the problem;
- with a poorly developed labour market information system in most African countries, and lack of experience in looking for jobs, many returning migrants, particularly repatriated refugees, simply do not know how or where to get a job;

- back at home, the returning migrants have to submit their qualifications to the scrutiny of professional bodies or official institutions; and in many cases, the process has served to reinforce the prejudices and biases of potential employers in different sectors of the economy;
- depending on the host countries while in exile, many returnees may find language to be a serious impediment to their re-entry into the wage employment, as inability to communicate effectively with prospective employers could be a justification for rejection;
- for some returnees, the skills they possess may not match existing job opportunities at their home location.

Social Aspects of Reintegration

If a returning migrant effectively overcomes the problem of economic reintegration, the social dimension of the process is equally critical to full reintegration. Apart from the background characteristics of the returning migrants and the community level variables referred to already, social reintegration of returnees calls for an understanding of their cultural environment as well, both at their point of destination as migrants and their home base.

Adjustment to life at the migrants' place of destination invariably calls for change in life styles and of living conditions. In cases of voluntary migration, inability to achieve full acculturation at the place of destination may lead to frustration and eventual return. But having acquired a new lifestyle, as in the case of rural-to-urban migrant who has become 'urbanised', return migration means that the old or traditional way of life must now be relearned upon return.

The process can be smooth or rough depending on the combination of factors; namely, duration of stay away from home, age at the time of departure, extent of assimilation of foreign culture and nature and intensity of links with home while away (see Figure 5.1). In addition, the receptivity of family and friends who stayed behind and the personal disposition of the returnee could be vital to social reintegration.

The demographic situation of returnees may also present a barrier to social reintegration. In the case of Namibian returnees in the wake of independence in 1990, many returnee families were too large to be absorbed into the households of their parents or relations. In such situations reintegration was impeded because families were either broken up and members distributed among the extended family or, alternatively they were isolated and compelled to start up with whatever resources they had (Tapscott and Mulongeni, 1990).

Some returnees also face an identity crisis, which often lead to personality disorders or trauma. For example, post-traumatic stress has been found among numerous returnees, as well as those who stayed behind, following Namibia's protracted war of independence. Among the returnees, the effects of this stress have manifested themselves in a number of ways including depression, alcoholism, suicide and various other misdemeanours or antisocial behaviour (Tapscott and Mulongeni, 1990). Given such state of emotional and psychological stress, social reintegration is inhibited.

Social integration of returning migrants may also be constrained by disability conditions, particularly if the official strategy makes no provision for special cases of disabled persons. In the absence of counselling services, it is even more problematic for the family members and relations at home to relate to one of them who had been away and is now back but blind, deaf, mentally handicapped, or sick.

Political Aspects of Reintegration

The politics of returning migrants and their reintegration into civil society can be confounding. At the political level, the issue may boil down to: who may return? Even if those who want to return are known, the process of actual return (logistics of transportation, receipt of grants and benefits, and so on) may be the roll call of those who have connections with the high and mighty in political circles. Tamas (1992) observed some examples of criticism from various directions in Namibia about returnees receiving too much attention at the expense of other needy groups in the society.

Much may also depend upon the sociopolitical climate in the local environment hosting returnees. As noted by Rogge (1991):

> the receptiveness of the local population also affects the nature of responses returnees encounter. If local chiefs, for example, are supportive of the returnees, then an array of response strategies will be available from within the community. If there is no support, or if local people are hostile to the returnees, then the re-integration process will be seriously impeded.

Refugees and asylum seekers tend to be politically active, and their potentials for political activism upon return is predictably a cause for concern in political circles. There is therefore the sharp division between those who were in exile and those who 'compromised' and remained at home, such as people involved in liberation struggle in countries like South Africa, Namibia, and so on. Equipped with political experience, returnees tend to make a significant input into the political system upon return (Gasarasi, 1991).

Conclusions and Recommendations

Programme Response to Different Aspects of Reintegration

A programme approach is proposed here as a viable strategy for achieving the social and economic reintegration of all categories of return migrants (returning refugees, displaced persons, or voluntary migrants) into civil society. Most organised schemes for rehabilitation of return migrants tend to be a spontaneous response to emergency situations and are largely donor driven. The focus of most of such schemes is on the repatriation process, and success is measured in terms of timely provision of physical transportation, and relocation of exiles, rather than the subsequent process of reintegrating them into civil society.

As noted by Tamas (1992), former exiles who have returned to their country of origin are no longer refugees, and thus no longer the formal responsibility of the UNHCR. Shortly after relocation, some government agencies or special disaster committees may be established to organise reception for returnees as well as provide assistance with basic accommodation, food rations, agricultural kits, tracing of relatives and provision of educational and medical services. But without any longer term planning, such ad hoc committees soon run out of steam and may wind up before most of the returnees get started with their reintegration process.

In the programme approach being proposed here, the process of reintegration should start with a comprehensive study of the social, economic and demographic conditions of the returnees and the environment to which they returned. Bilsborrow et al. (1984) provide guidelines for such studies, including sampling, questionnaire design and analysis. The report of such an investigation should form the basis for the design of the reintegration programme.

Based on the available evidence, the major elements of a reintegration programme should include the following:

- employment creation and the promotion of employment opportunities;
- awareness creation on political development and social change;

- provision of education, vocational training, health services and welfare support;
- counselling and career guidance;
- provision of pension and other welfare support;
- rehabilitation of disabled persons.

These six elements appear to address the major social, political and economic problems of reintegration in most situations. The dimensions of the problems may vary, depending on the peculiarity of the situation being addressed. This should in no way affect the feasibility of the framework proposed in this chapter.

Following the identification of the major elements of the programme, attention should focus on the institutional mechanism for programme management; the creation of responsible agency or agencies of the government and development of clear and comprehensive terms of reference for their operation. The issue of returnees should not be confined to the mass movement of returning refugees, a phenomenon that tends to be rather episodic. Rather, the concept should be broadened to include the less visible streams of returning voluntary migrants who also require assistance to achieve reintegration into society. Given such an understanding, the organisational structure being proposed here is not an ad hoc affair, but rather an institutionalised mechanism for addressing the problems of reintegration as they occur.

Based on the six programme elements identified above, the management structure should be based in the National Planning Ministry of Government, supported by a number of Standing Committees corresponding to the number of major programme issues identified. By implication, each Standing Committee is a specialised body comprising experts and administrators with a professional orientation in the assigned problem area.

The successful operation of the programme, or indeed any programme of Government, calls for commitment and political will. Of course, resources for the operational aspects of the programme should be provided adequately and in time. In order to justify any further input into the running of the programme, management should have built in mechanisms for continuous programme monitoring and periodic evaluation. Through such a process, the government can, at any point in time, determine the extent to which the various investments in the programme are together yielding the desired results.

Such a process will most likely inspire donor confidence, and given government commitment, programme activities should be sustainable. The ultimate impact of a fully reintegrated stream of returnees on the society is that homecoming would no longer be a nightmare for potential returnees, and their reintegration will boost the economy through their contributions. The social, economic and political gains of such an achievement are too obvious to warrant any further elaboration.

Research

Return migration has been a poor area of research interest for too long. The quantity of research reports on return migration suggests that return migration is probably a neglected area of migration research. In the past, such neglect was probably justified because return migration was largely an individual or family affair. And where large numbers of people were displaced as part of an official planning process, resettlement programmes, even if inadequate, were designed to provide solution to the problem of integration.

Migration research can no longer continue to ignore the refugee phenomenon; the numbers involved are large, and continue to grow almost at the increasing pace of economic migration. To the issue of refugees must be added the problem of internally displaced persons. The numbers involved are invariably obscured, but the magnitude is almost the same as refugees who are noticed only because of international official recognition.

References

Adepoju, A. (1995), 'Emigration Dynamics in Developing Countries', *International Migration Quarterly Review*, 23 (3/4).

Arowolo, O.O. (1998), 'Return Migration and Economic and Social Aspects of Reintegration', paper presented at the Regional Meeting on International Migration in Africa at the Threshold of the Twenty-first Century, organised by UNESCO, Dakar and the Central Statistics Office, Gaborone, Botswana, 2–5 June.

Athokorala, P. (1986), *Sri Lanka's Experience with International Contract Migration and Reintegration of Return Migrants*, Geneva: ILO.

Bilsborrow, R.E., Oberai, A.S. and Standing, G. (eds) (1984), *Migration Surveys in Low-Income Countries*, Geneva: published for the ILO by Groom Helm, London and Sydney.

Caldwell, J.C. (1969), *African Rural-Urban Migration: the Movement to Ghana's Towns*, Canberra: Australian National University.

Da Vanzo, J. (1976), 'Differences Between Return and Non-return migration: an Econometric Analysis', *International Migration Review*, 10, pp. 13–27.

Da Vanzo, J. and Morrison, P. (1981), 'Return and Other Sequences of Migration in the United States', *Demography*, 10, pp. 85–101.

Dumon, N. (1976), 'The Situation of Children of Migrants and their Adaptation and Integration in the Host Society and their Situation in the Country of Origin', *International Migration*, 17 (1–2), pp. 59–75.

Eichenbaum, J (1975), 'A Matrix of Human Movement', *International Migration*, 13 (1/2) pp. 21–41.

Gmelch, G. (1980), 'Return Migration', *Annual Review of Anthropology*, 9, pp. 135–59.

Hugo, G.J. (1978), *New Conceptual Approaches to Migration in the Context of Urbanization*, paper presented at the Conference of IUSSP Committee on Urbanisation and Population Redistribution, Bellagio, Italy.

Kish, L. (1965), *Survey Sampling*, New York: Wiley.

Makanya, S.T. (1992), 'Lessons from Elsewhere: Integration Strategies in Independent Zimbabwe', in R. Preston (ed.) (1993), *The Integration of Returned Exiles, Former Combatants and War-affected Namibians*, Windhoek: Namibian Institute for Social and Economic Research.

Molho, I. (1986), 'Theories of Migration: a Review', *Scottish Journal of Political Economy*, 33 (4), pp. 396–419.

Oberai, A.S. (1984), 'Identification of Migrants and Collection of Demographic and Social Information in Migration Surveys', in R.E. Bilsborrow, A.S. Oberai and G. Standing (eds) (1984), *Migration Surveys in Low-Income Countries*, Geneva: published for the ILO by Groom Helm, London and Sydney.

Oberai, A.S., Prasad, P.H. and Sardana, M.G. (1989), *Determinants and Consequences of Internal Migration in India*, Delhi: Oxford University Press.

Oucho, J.O. (1996), 'Refugees and Displacements in Sub-Saharan Africa: Instability due to Ethnic and Political Conflicts and Ecological Causes', in A. Adepoju and T. Hammar (eds), *International Migration in and from Africa: Dimensions, Challenges and Prospects*, Dakar: Senegal.

Peek, P. (1981), *A Typology of Migrants: some Methodological Aspects*, Geneva: ILO, World Employment Programme research working paper.

Peil, M. (1995), 'Ghanaians Abroad', *African Affairs*, 94 (376), pp. 345–67.

Petersen, W. (1958), 'A General Typology of Migration', *American Sociological Review*, 23 (2), pp. 256–65.

Preston, R. (ed.) (1993), *The Integration of Returned Exiles, Former Combatants and Other War-affected Namibians*, Windhoek: Namibian Institute for Social and Economic Research.

Preston, R. (1993a), 'Studying Integration', in R. Preston (ed.) (1993), *The Integration of Returned Exiles, Former Combatants and War-affected Namibians*, Windhoek: Namibian Institute for Social and Economic Research.

Rahmato, D. (1989), 'Rural Resettlement in Post-revolutionary Ethiopia – Problems and Prospects', in ONCCP, *Conference on Population Issues in Ethiopia's National Development: Report of Conference Proceedings*, Vol II, pp. 668–747.

Rogge, J.R. (1991) 'Repatriation of Refugees: a Not so Simple "Optimum" Solution', UNRISD, paper presented at the Synposium on Social and Economic Aspects of Mass Voluntary Return Migration, Harare, Zimbabwe, 12–14 March.

Shryock, H.S., Siegel, J.S. et al. (1973), *The Methods and Materials of Demography*, Washington DC: US Bureau of the Census.

Simon, D. and Preston, R. (1993), 'Return to the Promised Land: the Repatriation and Resettlement of Namibian Refugees 1989–1990', in R. Black and V. Robinson (eds), *Geography and Refugees: Patterns and Processes of Change*, Belhaven Press.

Standing, G. (1984), 'Conceptualising Territorial Mobility", in R.E. Bilsborrow, A.S. Oberai and G. Standing (eds) (1984), *Migration Surveys in Low-Income Countries*, Geneva: published for the ILO by Groom Helm, London and Sydney.

Stein, B.N. (1992), *Policy Changes regarding Repatriation in the 1990s: Is 1992 the Year for Voluntary Repatriation?*: Michigan: Michigan State University.

Tamas, K. (1992), *After Return; Repatriated Exiles in Independent Namibia*, Windhoek, NISER Discussion Paper No. 15.

Tapscott, C. and Mulongeni, B. (1990), *An Evaluation of the Welfare and Future Prospects of Repatriated Namibians in Northern Namibia*, Windhoek, NISER Research Report 3.

US Committee for Refugees (1991), Washington DC: Immigration and Refugee Service of America.

Viderkamp, J. (1972), 'Return Migration: Its Significance and Behavior', *Western Economic Journal*, 10 (4), December, pp. 460–65.

Chapter 6

Migration Theory and Migratory Realities: a Gendered Perspective?

Annie Phizacklea

Introduction

In the early 1980s Mirjana Morokvasic drew attention to the ways in which migration theory to that date had been largely gender blind, (Morokvasic, 1983). Writing nearly 20 years later four commentators concluded that: 'over the last fifteen years feminists have highlighted the heterogeneity of women's position within the migration stream, their presence in the labour market, their contribution to welfare and their increasing political activities. Yet, the migration of women continues to receive little attention in mainstream literature and migration theorists have not adequately taken on board the significance of gender in understanding migration to-day' (Kofman et al., 2000, p. 3). It is not the aim of this chapter to give a detailed account of contemporary migration flows in a gendered way, but initially to provide a critique of some of the assumptions in migration theory over time and in the second section to test some of the propositions that emerge from this by examining the findings of a study carried out by Anderson and Phizacklea of migrant women domestic workers in London.[1]

The chapter focuses largely on what might be termed 'mid-level' units and institutions that facilitate migration, these include households, social networks and a large number of institutions that broker migratory flows such as employment agencies, 'fixers' and traffickers. Writing in 1993, Massey et al. argue that a full understanding of contemporary migratory processes cannot be achieved by focusing on a single level of analysis (Massey et al., 1993). Again this chapter is somewhat guilty of doing this and its scope must be judged within that context. Readers who want a summary of the 'bigger picture' of contemporary migration theory might want to look at Chapter 1 by Arango in this book and, for a gendered commentary, Phizacklea (1999).

A final cautionary note about the scope of this chapter is that, while the theoretical critique has global implications, many of the examples relate to

Asian migration as the domestic worker case study relates to a predominantly Asian workforce with Filipinas constituting the largest nationality grouping.

The Feminisation of Labour Migration: True or False?

In the 1998 edition of the *Age of Migration*, Castles and Miller argue that one of the general tendencies in migration movements around the world which is likely to play a major role in the next 20 years is the feminisation of migration: 'women play an increasing role in all regions and in all types of migration … since the 1960s women have played a major role in labour migration' (Castles and Miller, 1998, p. 9). However some migration specialists challenge what they refer to as the 'conventional wisdom' that female labour migration has outnumbered male since 1974 (Zlotnik, 1995, p. 229). The argument being that 'the fact remains that the majority of women who migrate internationally do not do so for work purposes. That is especially the case of women migrating legally from developing to developed countries' (ibid., p. 230).

On the basis of official entry data Zlotnik is correct; apart from professionals with scarce skills, it has been very difficult for anyone to migrate legally for employment purposes from the developing to the developed world since 1974. But we need to get behind the official figures as well as unpack them in three ways. First, if we examine the gender composition of regularisation programmes (the decision by nation states to regularise the immigration status of people who for one reason or another are 'undocumented') over the last ten years then we can conclude that indeed women do constitute a significant proportion of labour migrants in transnational movements. Elsewhere there are figures to indicate the substantial numbers of women who have been regularised under such programmes (Phizacklea, 1999; DeLaet, 1999). Second, the 1999 OECD report states 'Immigration for family reasons continues to predominate …' (OECD, 1999, p. 17). We have argued elsewhere that we should not draw conclusions about motives for migration from the status of the individual migrant on entry: 'Thus treating those who enter through family reunion merely as dependants renders invisible their independent contribution' (Kofman et al., 2000, p. 199). Third, if we focus on labour migrants we see that the feminisation of labour migration is heavily concentrated in Asia, so that for instance 64 per cent of migrants from the Philippines are women and 75 per cent from Sri Lanka, Asian women are also more likely to migrate to developed countries (Lim and Oishi, 1996; Skeldon, 1999). Commenting on numbers, Lim and Oishi argue that: 'The important point concerning the above data is that they refer to legal labor migration and only to that part which is officially recorded as overseas employment migration ... When undocumented or illegal flows are also considered, both the numbers and proportions of women are likely to be higher' (ibid., p. 87).

The Ungendered Labour Migrant

Much has been made of the inadequacies of neo classical economic accounts of migration which cast the migrant as a rational decision-maker who sets off to work in the country best suited to the maximisation of their human capital. As challenged by Castles and Miller (1998, p. 22): 'the idea of individual migrants who make free choices which not only "maximise their well-being" but also 'lead to an equilibrium in the marketplace' [Borjas, 1989, p. 482] is so far from historical reality that it has little explanatory value'. Suffice it to say here that by the early 1980s not only had migration theory fallen into a kind of theoretical impasse between structural accounts (which tended to view migrants whether male or female as being drawn into and thrown out of, advanced industrial labour markets according to the needs of capital) and rational decision-making accounts, it remained largely gender blind as well.

Some saw the solution to this impasse in the development of migration systems theory (see Castles and Miller, 1998 for a summary of this approach and the literature). Migration systems theory may be regarded as an improvement in that it 'connects' the different 'levels' of the migratory process but it does not necessarily provide us with an account that is less mechanical.

Thus this approach suggests that an understanding of any migratory movement necessitates our incorporation of macro-structural factors with micro-level structures, such as the family, social networks, the huge number of intermediaries now involved in the 'business' of migration and the individual migrant's motivations and understandings. At the macro level we would want to look at the processes of globalisation, the free movement of capital, the revolution in communication technologies and the linkages between sending and receiving societies at a time of increasingly restrictionist attitudes towards the entry of labour, refugees and asylum seekers in states at the 'core'. These macro factors will influence and interact with intermediary institutions such as informal social networks and more institutionalised agents such as recruiters, brokers and 'fixers'. They in turn interact with households and the individuals which make up that household.

Households and Migration

Writing in 1989, Monica Boyd indicated that 'current migration patterns and new conceptualisations of migration underlie more recent interest in the role of family, friendship and community based networks' (Boyd, 1989, p. 641). Thus during the 1980s, attention in the study of migration began to shift attention to the role of intermediary institutions in the migratory process particularly the role of households and social networks. Initially these accounts simply shifted the household into a position of effective decision-making unit rather than the individual (Stark's work, 1984 and 1999, is an example of this).

Certainly households are an important unit of analysis in mediating between individual migrants and the larger structural context, but we also need an analytical shift which recognises that households are deeply implicated in gendered ideologies and practices. That recognition is missing in accounts such as Stark's. Rather it is assumed that households represent shared income, resources and goals and that household-wide decisions are made about migration (see for instance Wood, 1982; Selby and Murphy, 1982). Goss and Lindquist have pointed out that this conception of the household is

> unlikely to be applied uncritically to Western societies and is consistent with the ideological tendency in social sciences to romanticise peasant and community in the Third World. Somehow, members of Third World households, not burdened by the individualism of Western societies, resolve to cooperate willingly and completely, each according to their capacities, to collectively lift the burden of their poverty (Goss and Lindquist, 1995, p. 328).

More recent accounts provide evidence to support this critique. In her research on Mexican migration, Hondagneu-Sotelo shows that men who migrated ahead of wives and children did so quite autonomously with little regard for the rest of the family's views on this decision. Rather than the women who were left behind viewing this decision as based on a recognition of family need, they were in fact fearful that they might be abandoned altogether. As male remittances rarely met household consumption expenditure in Mexico, many women effectively became sole heads of households. The result was an increased desire by women to move North in order that husbands resume at least partial social and economic responsibility for family welfare (Hondagneu-Sotelo, 1994, p. 95).

Other accounts acknowledge the gendered power relations which households represent, for instance in their book the *Age of Migration* (1998)

Castles and Miller cite Hugo's research on Asian migration (1995) which shows that migration decisions are usually made not by individuals but by families. In their words: 'In situations of rapid change, a family may decide to send one or more members to work in another region or country, in order to maximise income and survival chances. In many cases, migration decisions are made by elder (especially the men) and younger people and women are expected to obey patriarchal authority. The family may decide to send young women to the city or overseas, because the labour of the young men is less dispensable on the farm. Young women are also often seen as more reliable in sending remittances. Such motivations correspond with increasing international demand for female labour as factory workers for precision assembly or as domestic servants, contributing to a growing feminisation of migration' (Castles and Miller, 1998, p. 25). The problem here is that there is a tendency to fall back into the trap of casting women 'as unburdened by the individualism of Western societies' and passively deferring to patriarchal authority for the benefit of the household.

The second section of this paper examines empirical data which point to the complexity of the decision-making process within households, as we shall see women migrants may not be deferring, in an altruistic way, to patriarchal authority, they may in fact regard migration as a way of escaping from a society that sanctions that authority, as well as increasing their own economic power within it. Thirty years ago Morokvasic recognised this in her research on Yugoslav women migrants where their migration represented not simply an enforced response to material hardship but also a calculated response to escape a society where patriarchy was an institutionalised and repressive force (Morokvasic, 1983). All sorts of negotiations go on within households and beyond them, societies and gender relations are not static and there is a general recognition of this sociologically as it applies to Western societies but non-western societies are not locked into some kind of 'traditional gender' time warp either. Skrobanek et al. conclude from their research in Thailand that parents tacitly accept their daughter's involvement in sex work as long as she is sending money home: 'Parents may wield less power over their daughters decisions and choices. This contrasts with the not-too-distant past, when parents were the decision-makers in all things ... Now a family with several daughters is considered lucky' (Skrobanek et al., 1997, p. 74). What these examples illustrate is the diverse and shifting nature of gendered relations within households and their role in the migratory decision.

Reference to this empirical work presumably falls foul of Portes' view that:

A cautionary note must be introduced here about analyses that concentrate exclusively on the individual motivations of household members and the conflict of interests between them. This has often become the centre of gender-focused research' and he goes on to warn against: 'making respondents' definitions of the situation the ultimate test for theoretical propositions (Portes, 1997, p. 816).

Portes does not make reference to the reason why a growing number of scholars have been keen to give women as well as men a voice, a voice which before was never heard and which is often at odds with the overriding assumption in much of the literature, that women simply follow men in the migration process or get packed off by parents to work abroad because they are more reliable remittance senders than their brothers. In the latter part of this chapter the household strategy model will be explored with reference to the in-depth interviews that we conducted with migrant domestic workers in London.

But ultimately the migratory decision will be effected, facilitated and perpetuated by the existence of a range of other extra household institutions and processes one being the formation of migrant networks, the other the proliferation of migration 'brokers' who have assumed a predominant role in Asian overseas labour migration.

Migrant Networks and Beyond

According to Massey et al. (1993, p. 448), migrant networks are:

> sets of interpersonal ties that connect migrants, former migrants and nonmigrants in origin and destination areas through ties of kinship, friendship and shared community origin. They increase the likelihood of international movement because they lower the costs and risks of movement and increase the expected net returns to migration. Network connections constitute a form of social capital that people can draw upon to gain access to foreign employment.

Basically what they are saying is that the 'pioneers' in any migratory flow shoulder higher costs and risks in their migratory project than those who follow. Letters, phone calls, visits to home will provide information on job availability, the prospect of accommodation in at least the initial period, all factors which lower the costs and risks for those that follow. But this somewhat benign economic analysis of how networks can facilitate migration is tempered by many sociological accounts which paint a far less benign picture, particularly in the face of restrictionist immigration policies. Baxter and Raw, writing on the Chinese fast food industry, argue that in the UK reliance on Chinese sponsors already established, became a codified condition of emigration under the 1962 Commonwealth Immigrants Act resulting in:

> Total reliance on Chinese employment channels put workers completely at the mercy of their employers. Long hours of split shift work, flexible duties and lack of statutory entitlements..all too frequently accompanied tied housing and arbitrary management (Baxter and Raw, 1988, p. 65).

For those who enter without papers and who 'vanish' into the ethnic economy, the prospects are even bleaker.

But network theory took a 'new' turn with the literature now referred to as 'transnationalism' and defined in the path breaking and richly textured study *Nations Unbound* 'as the process by which immigrants forge and sustain multi-stranded social relations that link together their societies of origin and settlement' (Basch et al., 1994, p. 6). The authors' concern was to break with a migration literature permeated with binaries:

> The migration literature describes the country of settlement as the 'host', but such a term, though compact and convenient, carries the often unwarranted connotations that the immigrant is both 'welcome' and a 'visitor'. Transmigrants take actions, make decisions, and develop subjectivities and identities embedded in networks of relationships that connect them simultaneously to two or more nation-states (ibid., p. 7).

The literature and debate around the concept subsequently proliferated with Portes arguing that transnationalism allows people to lead political, economic and social 'dual lives' through the creation of 'dense' cross border networks (Portes, 1997, p. 812). According to Vertovec, while these long distance networks preceded the nation state, contemporary transnational networks mark a new departure because they 'function in real time while being spread around the world' (Vertovec, 1999, p. 447). Portes also emphasises the importance of the 'newly acquired command of communication technologies' by individuals within such networks and that 'Participants are often bilingual, move easily between different cultures, frequently maintain homes in two countries, and pursue economic, political and cultural interests that require their presence in both' (Portes, 1997, p. 814). In fact in a later article, Portes, Guarnizo and Landolt argue that what makes 'transnationalism' a completely new phenomena are the 'high intensity of exchanges, the new modes of transacting, and the multiplication of activities that require cross-border travel and contacts on a sustained basis' (Portes et al., 1999, p. 219).

Portes et al. admit that:

> if technological innovations represent a necessary condition for the rise of grass-roots transnationalism, it follows that the greater access of an immigrant group to space-and time-compressing technology, the greater the frequency and scope of this sort of activity. Immigrant communities with greater average economic resources and human capital (education and social skills) should register higher levels of transnationalism because of their superior access to the infrastructure that makes these activities possible (ibid., p. 222).

It is an admission that such individuals had already a 'class' advantage. Bhachu's study of South Asian migrants in Britain emphasises the heterogeneity of class and caste positionings of these migrants. In the case of the 'thrice' migrants, from India to East Africa, from East Africa to Britain and then in the 1980s and 1990s their further move to countries such as US, Canada and Australia means that they possess: 'powerful communication networks, which are facilitated by the ease of global communications. Their command of Western bureaucrat skills and the English language has given them considerable expertise at reproducing their cultural bases and community infrastructures in a range of countries. Such a scenario is in complete contrast to that of the less 'culturally and ethnically skilled' direct migrants, who are often characterised by home orientation and the 'myth of return' (Bhachu, 1995, p. 224). The resort to transnationalism 'from below' as a method of countering and subverting the logic of transnational capital may not be a strategy open to all. We cannot compare the fortnightly phone call and the desperately small amounts of money remitted by poor Sri Lankan migrant domestic workers in the Gulf States to the transnational business deals of cosmopolitan entrepreneurs, without recourse to a class and gendered analysis. To state this as obvious, is not to return to the structural 'straight-jacket' of the neo-Marxist political economy accounts, it is simply to say that while all of these transactions are transnational, the actors involved have very different points of departure or degrees of autonomy over the nature of those transnational transactions.

Roberts et al. are perceptive in noting that theories of transnational migration emerged in large part as a critique of:

> overly structural approaches, and attempted to introduce the actor back into theoretical migration discussions. Countering a tendency to see migration as created by the push and pull of economic factors with migrants conceived as

mainly as passive subjects, coerced by states and marginalised by markets, work on transnational migration attempts to impute migrants with decision-making capabilities influencing their outcomes (Roberts et al., 1999, p. 253).

This criticism echoes the standpoint of virtually all currently working in the field of migration that are keen to restore an analytically coherent view (rather than prolong the phoney war) of the relationship between structure and agency. It is a particularly important consideration in moving away from a tendency, particularly in the case of migrant women, to portray them as victims being tossed around in the turbulent seas of international capitalism. The processes described by Portes and others are important features of contemporary global migratory patterns and the economic, political and cultural ethnoscapes that they represent. The question remains as to whether social scientist's current preoccupation with this supposedly 'new' phenomenon warrants another theoretical rupture of the kind we seem to go through every five to ten years.

It is important that the term 'transnational' should be used to refer to a whole spectrum of transactions and processes that migrants maintain between 'home' (as in 'where I was born') and 'home' (where I am now). These transactions may not take the form of building businesses which link the two (though as we shall see in the case study material it may do) or 'political and cultural interests that require their presence in both' (Portes, 1997, p. 814). In fact they are much more modest forms of transnationality, such as buying a phone card for the weekly chat (you buy the phone card that you can afford that week); possibly explaining that you will not be sending so much money back this month because you lost your job and with it, your accommodation, but they are no less transnational in form. Thus the role of networks in migration theory (in one form or another) continues to play a key role in the literature, but there are other factors at work, which despite their key importance have been largely ignored in the literature. These key actors are the 'brokers' of overseas employment. Lim and Oishi argue that the growth of an immigration 'industry' in Asia has 'greatly facilitated female migration, both legal and illegal' (Lim and Oishi, 1996, p. 90) and Goss and Lindquist found few returning migrants to the Philippines who did not report having found work abroad without a broker (Goss and Lindquist, 1995, p. 340). In addition they show that the more institutionalised the system becomes, the more fraudulent and corrupt it becomes with agents painting a 'rosy picture' of international labour migration. Within the context of this discussion, the findings of a case study of domestic workers in London carried out between 1998 and 2001 will be considered.

The Politics of Belonging

Anderson and Phizacklea undertook research with migrant domestic workers in London who were undergoing a process of regularisation of their visa status. On 23 July 1998 the UK government announced that it intended to regularise the position of migrant domestic workers who entered under certain immigration conditions and who had become overstayers due to no fault of their own. Specifically those conditions related to a concession introduced by the Thatcher government in 1980, which allowed foreign employers to bring in their domestic workers with them, but which tied those workers irrevocably to those same employers, they had no immigration or employment status of their own. The system was widely abused with one agency alone handling over 4,000 reported cases of imprisonment, physical and sexual abuse as well as widespread under and non-payment of workers by their employers. Workers usual means of redress was simply to run away from the abusive employer, which immediately alters the conditions under which they were admitted and many through no fault of their own became overstayers. In short they joined the ranks of undocumented workers in the UK.

In 1979 the Commission for Filipino Migrant workers was set up to support Filipino migrants in the UK, many of whom were domestic workers (Anderson, 1993, p. 59). The Commission increasingly gave support to domestics of many different nationalities who had left or wanted to leave abusive employers. While the Commission could provide support it became increasingly clear that immigration law as it applies to domestic workers who enter the country with foreign employers had to be changed. The domestic workers forged alliances with many other diverse groups, including trade unions, lawyers and other immigrant groups, to form Kalayaan. Kalayaan campaigned vigorously for ten years for the law to be changed and their efforts were rewarded in the policy change of 1998, proving yet again that even the seemingly powerless have the capacity to mobilise resources and 'carve out spaces of control'.

The campaign is obviously of huge importance at a very practical level, the consequences will lead to a significant improvement in the day-to-day lives of the women in question. But there are interesting theoretical lessons to be learnt from the success of this campaigning coalition. They relate to the theoretical move from what we might term 'the politics of universalism' to the 'politics of difference'.

There is no intention here to give an in-depth account of the research that we carried out between 1998 and 2001 relating to the regularisation process of undocumented migrant domestic workers in London. Nevertheless it is appropriate that we provide a methodological background to the research and a summary of the findings of the quantitative analysis of the data. The project negotiated access to the workers through a support group for domestic workers. We produced a sociodemographic profile of 2,837 workers who had registered with Kalayaan in the ten years up until the announcement of the regularisation process in July 1998. In addition we designed and compiled an additional database of 1,246 domestic workers who applied for regularisation between July 1998 and 1999. Both databases provide us with details of the workers themselves, of their children and their employers (92 per cent of the workers registered were women, predominantly from South-East Asia and of the 214 men registered half are from India). We analysed both databases using SPSS. We interviewed 57 workers in depth before regularisation and 23 after (we had intended to re-interview all the original 57 once they obtained their papers but the regularisation process proved cumbersome and unexpectedly protracted, many of our original interviewees remained undocumented by the final year of the project). The in-depth interviews were complemented by 18 life stories and we conducted six group interviews involving another 150 workers. We collected questionnaire data on earnings and remittances from another 136 domestic workers. At all times we explained the purpose of the research to the workers and fed back preliminary results at the regular Kalayaan Sunday meetings as well as the group discussions. In one workshop we presented a broad outline of migration theories with a particular focus on household strategy theories and invited the workers' responses. The response was enthusiastic and hugely insightful. The workers also decided to write and perform their own play, which is designed to be interventionist from an audience perspective.

Some of our main findings challenge a number of 'conventional wisdoms' in the literature on migration:

Motivations for Migration

Seventy-two per cent of those interviewed in depth had children and only one of these mentioned their children's welfare, particularly their education as a prime motivator for migration:

> So I want it was not a choice. We did not have enough to support us. We are on a farm, it is very small and I have all my children. I wanted to support my children to school; I wanted them to go to high school, which I was not able to do. It was me that decided, but my family were happy, my parents and my

husband. Because they know if I go away I can support all of them, not just my children, but my mother, all that. My husband applied also, but he had no luck. For me I can read a little, write a little, speak a little English. I'm very excited to go abroad at first, but after one week away I was sad because I missed my children (Filipina, 2 years in London, 4 children).

I started working abroad when my children went to school. We needed the money for their education. I was in Dubai for 4 years and Kuwait for five years. It began when my sister was working in Dubai and she called me to say she had an employer for me. Everyone was very happy, my husband and my parents were pleased, and I wanted to go for the money, although I was sad to leave my children. My husband could not work abroad because he gets sick if the weather changes, and besides, he has a small shop at home that he runs and he cannot leave. So I pay to put my children in a very expensive school, and they are still there. I am still paying for my children's education (Indian, 1 year in London, 2 children).

When husbands are mentioned in this context, it reveals a picture of either their not being able to provide for the family either because they did not earn enough, were unemployed or had difficulties finding work abroad or their behaviour became a motivating factor to leave. In the latter case excessive drinking or 'womanising' were mentioned:

I left school at 15 and I worked as a domestic worker before I got married. My husband had no work, he beat me, he's no use, he drinks. A friend found a family who needed a domestic and I came with them to England. I did discuss it with my parents and sister, I just wanted to contribute financially and my employers paid for the ticket (Indian, 12 years in London, 2 children in India cared for by sister).

My husband was a truck driver and a womaniser, he contributed little to the family and I decided that I'd be better off on my own, if I went to work abroad I could support my children. My mother-in-law lived close by and cousins as well, my mother in law was prepared to take responsibility for the care of the children. I attended high school until I was 14 years of age.

Having made up my mind to leave I went to an employment agency which was used by many others to find work in the Gulf. I had to pay 500,000 rupees to the agency to arrange the job and I sold my sewing machine to help finance my trip, I financed my trip my myself. My youngest child was only 6 months old when I left for Saudi Arabia. The agency insisted that my husband signed a document saying that he was prepared for me to go abroad but he was more than happy to do that because my leaving gave him even greater freedom.

My main reason for leaving to work abroad was financial, I could provide my children with better opportunities but I also knew that I was better off alone, so the decision was for me as well as the children. My mother did not want me to go but my mother-in-law had agreed to take responsibility for the children. I went to work for a Prince in Saudi Arabia and I looked after the children from birth. It hurt me so much that as they grew up they showed me no respect, they even spat at me (Indonesian, left 13 years ago, 24 months in London, 2 children in Indonesia).

Failing or failed marriages and the shame that goes with that state of affairs are rarely mentioned in the literature as motivators for migration and yet they were often threaded into explanations for leaving.

Household Decision-making

The notion that households not individuals are the effective decision-making unit regarding migration and that somehow members of households sit down around the kitchen table and make rational decisions about who is best placed to migrate does not represent the reality for the majority of the sample, in particular the Filipinas:

Then I decided to go abroad. I read about the agencies in the newspapers – I wanted to change my life. I didn't tell my uncle or brother, because they wouldn't have let me. I didn't really tell my aunt anything, just that I had had an interview for a job. I was nearly 17 when I got to the agency. I wanted to ask about going abroad. They said, if you know how to dance, you can go to Japan. I wanted to go to Saudi, Qatar, or Kuwait. They interviewed me in the Arabic language, and I understood it because I had graduated in Grade 6 Arabic language. The agency processed everything and told me that I was going to Qatar (Filipina, 6 years in London, 1 child).

I didn't have a plan to go abroad before – only when my friend came and told me that they were in need of a dressmaker. I wasn't very serious to go abroad. It was my friend's idea. But I had the ambition to earn dollars. I wanted to earn more money. What we were earning was not enough, especially when my children were starting college. My husband didn't want me to go, but I said, I've already applied, you can't do anything about it (Filipina, 9 years in London, 3 children).

Women from India were more likely than other nationalities to have made the decision to migrate in consultation with their families:

> I come from Hyderabad, my husband died 7 years ago, so we went to live with my brother. I did not go to school, I worked on a rice plantation with other families and earned 10 rupees a day. I did not want to leave India but as I had no money and my brother has only one hand we decided that I would work abroad and he would look after the children. I paid a lot of money to an agency to get work in Saudi Arabia, I paid them 50,000 rupees which meant selling my house. I saw the advertisement for the agency in a newspaper (Indian, 3 years in London, 2 children).

Some of the African women, who were more likely to be single at the time of departure, indicated that parents had encouraged them to leave:

> The family I was working for in Accra were going to the UK for business and brought me with them. They suggested it. I told my mother that I didn't want to go with them but she said go, there's nothing for you to do in Ghana. I really was reluctant because they weren't paying me in Ghana, but they reassured me that I would be paid in the UK and that they'd be staying here for 4 years. I didn't feel I had much choice and they paid for my passport and air ticket. After 15 months in London they hadn't paid me, no clothes, no day off, not allowed out, nothing, just physical abuse. So I ran away (Ghanaian, 7 years in London, 1 child born in London).

To reiterate, few describe the process as one which fits comfortably within the household strategy model of migration.

Social Networks versus Employment Brokers

Only three of the Filipinas (who also constitute the bulk of the sample) interviewed in depth had not used an employment agency for overseas work placement, confirming the level of institutionalisation of migration in Asia and particularly the Philippines:

> I go to a recruiter. Everything is charged to them. I have to pay pocket money and fare to Manila, and then everything is charged to them and they deduct from future salary. It is nine months salary. They pay your departure tax, even a new dress for you to start, shoes, placement fees, passport. They know that you have two year contract, and you have two years to pay them in, you can decide which of the nine months you will pay. But it is a very bad system. Even if you know before you join them that you must pay them that much and then before you depart you sign a contract with them. We know what is the problem, but we want to go abroad. It's very difficult to stay in Manila while

you arrange your paper, because you have no job there and it's expensive. But we only get 15 months salary for two years work, that is why we always want to extend the contract (Filipina, 2 years in London, no children).

I lived in the country in a big family, 6 sisters and one brother, we are a poor family. I went to school until I was 16 years, but I didn't have any qualifications, as there was no one to look after me I went to work in the Middle East. Somebody told me about an agency in Sri Lanka that could find you work abroad. I did discuss it with my family. I had to take out a loan to cover the airfare, but I've re-paid it (Sri Lankan, 3 years in London, no children).

My parents had to pay for my education so when my father got sick I had to stop going to school. I went to work as live in domestic worker for a rich family in Manila where I met my husband. I got married but my husband earns very little as a labourer. I did not want my children to be like me working every day so I borrowed money and went to an agency that a friend knew about and we went together. I had to pay for my flight and pay the agency another 12,000 pesos for the arrangements and the passport etc. The agency told me that the salary would be $250 a month when in fact it was only $115. My husband didn't want me to go abroad but I insisted, the children were 15, 13 and 10 when I left to work in Dubai (Filipina, 18 months in London, 3 children).

But others used social networks, often female family members or friends who provided information about employment prospects abroad:

I didn't use an agency. I went direct hire, through the friend of my mothers. That was my first and my last employer in Hong Kong. My mother-in-law was OK for caring for the children. They said, well you can't look after the children and provide for their education. My employer paid for my airfare (Filipina, 4 years in London, 3 children).

A related factor was that many (27) based their migratory decision on flimsy information about destinations, working, living conditions and pay. Interviewees who had poor information before leaving usually found themselves in unsatisfactory jobs abroad, whereas those (25) who had an agency recommended to them or who had a recommendation through a social network found themselves in more reasonable circumstances. Given that over half did not make their decision on accurate information does not support the neo-classical economic model of migration which predicts that individuals make rational choices about migration based on accurate information thereby maximising the net returns of migration.

Transnationals?

Earlier in this chapter it was argued that we need to incorporate a class and gender transparency into the debate around transnationals and transnationalism. Few of the women (or men for that matter) that we interviewed were in a position to lead dual lives through the creation of dense cross border networks, not least because as 'overstayers' and therefore undocumented workers they could not even leave the country. Many had been away from home for many years as 93 per cent had been working abroad before coming to the UK. The pre-regularisation interviews have a common thread: fear. There is not a single interviewee who does not mention fear of being apprehended and deported: 'Before I always feel scared, sick. Someone can tell you at any time, I will deport you.'

No one we interviewed had ever dreamt the day they left home that they would end up as an overstayer due to no fault of their own, they left to bring a better life to their children in most cases and in some cases for themselves. But throughout all these years they have remitted money to those that they trust will spend the money on their children's or siblings well being, in particular their education (69 per cent put education at the top of their list) they have kept in touch by phone and letters and they have forged new relationships with compatriots in London. The remittance questionnaires (completed by 136 of the workers) indicated that all were remitting money at regular intervals. Over half were remitting money at least once a month and a quarter between two and three month intervals.

But there are a few who have acted as transnationals in what is suggested as the more limited usage, that is, acting as entrepreneurs, but as we shall see from this quote that their freedom for manoeuvre is wholly dependent upon their immigration status and national regulations:

> My town mate went to Hong Kong. I heard that life there was nice, and I said to my Mum, and she wanted me away from my boyfriend for a while, so she said it was a good idea. I was there for seven years. I did business there – wholesale retailing. I bought clothes and beauty goods in Hong Kong and forwarded them to Manila and Canada. I was working as a live-in, so I had no expenses, and my salary was my own, so every day off I went shopping. Then I put all the goods in a tea chest to the Philippines, or a package to Canada – because a tea chest to there is too expensive, and sent it to my friends. Per package, not including the tea chest cost about HK dollars 1,000. I would make HK dollars 300 on each load, about a third profit. I don't know how much my friend made because that is up to her, it depends on how much she

sells it for, but my return is guaranteed. The friend in Manila sold it in … The other in Canada was a friend I met in Hong Kong. We arranged it before she left HK for Canada, with what I should get etc. I did it for about three years. But here it is too difficult, everything is taxed, and life is a higher standard here. Life in Hong Kong was more flexible, but here you have to rent rooms etc. There isn't enough left over to set up a business … When I get business in Hong Kong, my mum got the money from that and built a piggery with it. She was very happy … Then they say they are coming to England. I want to stay in Hong Kong, because I have my business there, but they said, you'll have much more in England. They told me I would have two days off, education, I'll send you to your aunties in Canada, every year you will have a holiday – enticing me to come here.

But then when I get here they give me no day off, just brings me to church and collects me from there and that's it. They bring me to friends, I do ironing and babysitting, when she goes out with her friend I babysit for both their children and it's too much seven children. And I find out her friend is paying her money for me, so she is making a business with me, because she is not giving me that money. And she's paying £30 a week. I met a Filipina in Church. I have no money to send in Philippines. I asked the boss why, where are your promises? She said, here is different to Hong Kong – your contract in Hong Kong is not valid in this country. She said, if you run away I'm going to call the police. She locked me up. Because I planned to run away. She treated me bad, shouting. She was never like that in Hong Kong. Because in Hong Kong the Labour Department and Immigration Department can go to her if I have a problem, and she would have to answer to them, that's the law. Here I don't know where I can run to help. Why I can't make my complaint in this country? This system is very difficult. I feel rejected and rebellious. It's like a challenge. If your not strong enough you feel nothing. But I'm staying here (Filipina, 7 years in London, no children (she had left this employer and thereby became an 'overstayer' at the time of interview, she had 4 different jobs as a domestic)).

Conclusion

In this chapter we have looked critically at the way in which the household is reified in many accounts of migration and why a gendered 'unpacking' of the institution allows us to retain it as a central unit without its reification. We have also seen that while social networks may be critical for an understanding of some migrations they play a less central role for women in certain parts of the world, for instance Southeast Asia, where migration has become institutionalised from the state down. While there is a history of migration within and from Asia there is now considerable evidence to show that for women at least, intermediaries such as employment agencies and brokers may be of more critical significance in facilitating, even institutionalising transnational migration.

As undocumented workers these migrants had no freedom to cross borders legally, many have been trapped in London for years and while most are bi-lingual they hardly fit the model where 'participants are often bilingual, move easily between cultures, frequently maintain homes in two countries and pursue economic, political and cultural interests that require their presence in both' (Portes, 1997, p. 814). Nevertheless however modest their transnational practices, they are no less clear cut, even if the priorities of those practices shift over time.

Some attempt has been made here to indicate where the main weaknesses lie in extant theorising from a gendered perspective and the case study of domestic workers hopefully indicates how the importance of moving between different levels of analysis is important if a more adequate account of the factors stimulating and facilitating migration is to be given. Perhaps more importantly this case study indicates that despite the harrowing conditions experienced by many women in the maid's industry worldwide their migration represents an attempt to bring a better life to themselves and their families in the face of prodigious external constraint. It is in fact in the migration setting that the importance of social networks becomes clear, in the case of the campaign to alter the 1980 concession and to regularise the immigration status of those who entered under it. Without the solidarity that was generated across ethnic, religious and class lines amongst domestic workers themselves there would have been little chance of success.

Note

1   This project was undertaken within the 'Transnational Communities' initiative of the ESRC in the UK.

References

Anderson, B. (1993), *Britain's Secret Slaves*, London: Anti-Slavery International.
Anderson, B. (1997), *Labour Exchange: Patterns of Migration in Asia*, London: Catholic Institute of International Relations.
Anderson, B. (2000), *Doing the Dirty Work: The Global Politics of Domestic Labour*, London: Zed Press.

Basch, L., Glick Schiller, N. and Szanton Blanc, C. (1994), *Nations Unbound*, Langhorne, PA: Gordon and Breach.

Baxter, S. and Raw, G. (1988), 'Fast Food, Fettered Work: Chinese Women in the Ethnic Catering Industry', in S. Westwood and P. Bhachu (eds), *Enterprising Women: Ethnicity, Economy and Gender Relations*, London: Routledge.

Bhachu, P. (1995), 'New Cultural Forms and Transnational South Asian Women: Culture, Class, and Consumption among British Asian Women in the Diaspora', in P. van der Veer (ed.), *Nation and Migration: The Politics of Space in the South Asian Diaspora*, Philadelphia: University of Pennsylvania Press, pp. 198–222.

Boyd, M. (1989), 'Family and Personal Networks in International Migration: Recent Developments and New Agendas', *International Migration Review*, 23 (3), pp. 638–70.

Castles, S. and Miller, M. (1998), *The Age of Migration*, London: Macmillan.

Cohen, R. (ed.) (1996), *Theories of Migration*, Cheltenham: Edward Elgar.

DeLaet, D. (1999), 'Introduction: the Invisibility of Women in Scholarship on International Migration', in G. Kelson and D. DeLaet (eds), *Gender and Immigration*, Basingstoke: Macmillan, pp. 1–20.

Evans, M. (1997), *Introducing Contemporary Feminist Theory*, Cambridge: Polity Press.

Fawcett, J.T. and Arnold, F. (1987), 'Explaining Diversity: Asian and Pacific Immigration Systems', in J.T. Arnold and B.V. Carino (eds), *Pacific Bridges: the New Immigration from Asia and the Pacific Islands*, New York: Centre for Migration Studies.

Goss, J. and Lindquist, B. (1995), 'Conceptualising International Labor Migration: a Structuration Perspective', *International Migration Review*, 29 (2), pp. 317–51.

Guarnizo, L.E., Sanchez, A.I. and Roach, E.M (1999), 'Mistrust, Fragmented Solidarity and Transnational Migration: Colombians in New York City and Los Angeles, *Ethnic and Racial Studies*, 22 (2), March, pp. 368–95.

Harding, S. (ed.) (1987), *Feminism and Methodology*, Milton Keynes: Open University Press.

Hondagneu-Sotelo, P. (1994), *Gendered Transitions*, Berkeley: California University Press.

Hugo, G. (1995), 'Illegal International Migration in Asia', in R. Cohen (ed), *The Cambridge Survey of World Migration*, Cambridge: Cambridge University Press, pp. 397–402.

Kofman, E., Phizacklea, A., Raghuram, P. and Sales, R. (2000), *Gender and International Migration in Europe: Employment, Welfare and Politics*, Routledge. London.

Lim, L.L and Oishi, N. (1996), 'International Labour Migration of Asian Women: Distinctive Characteristics and Policy Concerns', *Asian and Pacific Migration Journal*, 5 (1), pp. 85–116.

Massey, D.S., Arango, J., Hugo, G., Kouaouci, A., Pellegrino, A. and Taylor, J.E. (1993), 'Theories of International Migration: A Review and Appraisal', *Population and Development Review*, 19 (3), pp. 431–66.

Morokvasic, M. (1983), 'Beyond the Reductionist Outlook', in A Phizacklea (ed.), *One Way Ticket*, London: Routledge.

Phizacklea, A. (1983), 'In the Front Line', in A. Phizacklea (ed.), *One Way Ticket*, London: Routledge.

Portes, A. (1997), 'Immigration Theory for a New Century: Some Problems and Opportunities', *International Migration Review*, 31 (4), pp. 799–825.

Portes, A. (1999), 'Conclusion: Towards a New World – the Origins and Effects of Transnational Activities', *Ethnic and Racial Studies*, 22 (2), pp. 463–77.

Portes, A., Guarnizo, L. and Landolt, P. (1999), 'The Study of Transnational Communities: Pitfalls and Promise of an Emergent Field', *Ethnic and Racial Studies*, 22 (2), pp. 217–37.

Roberts, B., Frank, R. and Lozano-Ascensio, F. (1999), 'Transnational Migrant Communities and Mexican Migration to the US', *Ethnic and Racial Studies*, 22 (2), pp. 238–266.

Selby, H. and Murphy, A. (1982), *The Mexican Urban Household and the Decision to Migrate to the US*, ISHI Occasional Papers in Social Change, No. 4, Philadelphia: Institute for the Study of Human Issues.

Skeldon, R. (1999), *Migration of Women in the Context of Globalisation in the Asian and Pacific Region*, Women in Development Discussion Paper Series No. 2, Social Development Division of the ESCAP Secretariat, United Nations.

Skrobanek, S., Boonpakdi, N. and Janthakeero, C. (1997), *The Traffic in Women. Human Realities of the International Sex Trade*, London and New York: Zed Books Ltd.

Stanley, L. and Wise, A. (1983), *Breaking Out: Feminist Conciousness and Feminist Research*, London: Routledge.

Stark, O. (1984), 'Migration Decision-making: a Review Article', *Journal of Development Economics*, 14, pp. 251–9.

Stark, O. (1999), *Altruism and Beyond*, Cambridge: Cambridge University Press.

Vertovec, S. (1999), 'Conceiving and Researching Transnationalism', *Ethnic and Racial Studies*, 22 (2), pp. 447–62.

Wood, C.H. (1982), 'Equilibrium and Historical Structural Perspectives on Migration', *International Migration Review*, 16 (2), pp. 298–319.

Yuval-Davis, N. (1997), *Gender and Nation*, London: Sage.

Zlotnik, H. (1995), 'The South-to-North Migration of Women', *International Migration Review*, 29 (1), pp. 229–54.

PART II
SETTLEMENT AND ETHNIC RELATIONS

Chapter 7

Between Exile and Ethnicity

Danièle Joly

Introduction

It is not easy to determine what differentiates refugees from other migrants and no definite agreement has been reached on this point. However, it appears that when all the variables have been examined, what remains is that refugees had to leave as a result of factors which in the last analysis were not primarily economic and they did not make a decision with primarily positive connotations. What all refugees have in common is that they left their country of origin because a dramatic change jeopardised the life they were leading, although this change need not always be sudden. If things had continued as before the change, they would have stayed. This brings us back to the involuntary character of refugee movements as expounded by Kunz (1973) and Zolberg et al. (1989).

This chapter seeks to establish refugees in their country of exile/settlement as social types distinct from labour migrants. It looks at the notion of ethnic groups and their strategies as a theoretical tool for an understanding of refugees. The refugees' positioning within the structure of conflict of their country of origin is posited as a determining factor of their modes of settlement. What is important is not only the structure of conflict within which populations are caught up and which causes them to become refugees but also the actor's own consciousness of the pressure brought upon them through these conflicts and their positioning vis-à-vis the conflict. It is possible to find two large categories:

- refugees who nurtured a collective project in the land of origin and took it with them in the land of exile: Odyssean refugees;
- refugees who did not partake of a collective project oriented towards the homeland or who have forsaken it: Rubicon refugees.

Modes of Settlement: Ethnicity and Ethnic Groups

My focus is on refugees in their country of exile/reception. In this area, social scientists generally failed to establish a major distinction resting on the causes and motivations of migration, between refugees and labour migrants. All are treated as immigrants into a new country and place of settlement and studies of them look at their modes of integration, their social organisation, their communities/associations and many other aspects relating to political participation, children's education, maintenance of culture and religion and so on. There is an abundant literature on all these issues which it is not my purpose to review here. It is not the case that refugees have not been studied; the lacuna lies in the fact that they have not been treated per se, in their own right. For instance the old classic study of 'immigrants' integration in Israel by Eisenstadt (1954) in fact includes a large proportion of refugees. Closer to home, the book on 'immigrant' associations by Rex et al. (1987) in reality considers several national groups which comprise *de facto* refugees: many of the Cypriots in the UK, Portuguese in France, Kurds in Germany and so on. Until recently what this literature rarely considered was whether and how the refugee situation influenced their modes of settlement and in particular what social group they constituted as refugees, what strategies and trajectory they followed.[1]

The truth of the matter is that it is not always easy to concretely identify those who are refugees and those who are economic migrants for the purposes of fieldwork; in the first place the dividing line can be tenuous and we are not speaking of watertight categories as the discussion on the causes and motivation of refugee movements illustrates with notions of 'poles' and 'degrees' of refugeeness (Richmond, 1988; Zolberg et al., 1989). Secondly many migration flows contain both economic migrants and refugees from the same place of origin arriving in the same country of destination. Thirdly refugees are not at all a homogeneous lot and they are not easily identifiable as they come from various countries of origin, for various reasons and under different legal statuses, including that of labour migrant. Finally we are looking at processes and not at a static situation so that it makes their study more elusive: for instance it is possible that the refugees social relations differ markedly from those of labour migrants in the early stages of settlement while they might become similar under certain circumstances, after years of stay in the society of reception or where the 'second generation' is concerned. At any rate refugees are migrants, and within the context of this chapter *in-migrants*, though possibly one special case of immigrants. Consequently one does not start in a vacuum; methodologically one can make use of the knowledge accumulated on labour migrants comparing and contrasting refugees to the former, but it will be necessary also to compare refugee to refugee in order to bring out the different social types amongst the latter. Assimilation, separation and integration are the main options available in processes of settlement. Within the latter one possibility is the formation of ethnic groups: this is what I shall examine in the first instance as a potential tool for positioning refugees' settlement.

Primordial and Situational Definitions

If we accept that ethnic groups can be found outside primitive societies, who can they refer to? What we are looking at are ethnic groups that may arise as a consequence of migration and are not territorially rooted and based. According to Yinger (1986, p. 23), the term 'ethnic group' has expanded its meaning to embrace a great diversity of categories, such as

> a sub-societal group that clearly shares a common descent and cultural background ... persons sharing a former citizenship although diverse culturally ... pan-cultural groups of persons of widely different cultural and societal backgrounds who, however, can be identified as 'similar' on the basis of language, race or religion, mixed with broadly similar statuses.

This definition undoubtedly enhances the relevance of the concept for the immigrant groups we are considering in Western Europe. A series of varying criteria are advanced by social scientists to define ethnic groups (Geertz, 1963; Gordon, 1978; Yinger, 1986; Rex, 1995; Drury, 1995, to cite only a few).

The paradigm has shifted from primordial assumptions of ethnicity to a situational interpretation. Primordialists like Geertz (1963) stressed the 'attachment' based on kinship, common residence, language, religion and custom. The 'warmth' of emotional links (affective ties) is emphasised together with the cultural content. For situationists the cultural 'content' plays little role since what is paramount is the socially constructed 'boundary', the distinction between 'us and them' (Barth, 1969). One important consequence of this approach is that ethnicity and ethnic groups cannot exist on their own. They arise against or in contrast with others, other minority ethnic groups and/or the majority group in a 'system of ethnicities' (Yinger, 1986). Moreover, for situationists, another important tenet of ethnicity is that it is situational and constitutes a 'resource' in the competition for resources (Khan, 1977; Wallman,

1986); ethnicity is used and activated for economic/political or other ends, so that the markers called upon to establish the distinction between 'us and them' may change according to need (Wallman, 1986). In Wallman's view although the markers most often used are territoriality, history, language, economic considerations and symbolic identifications, there is no logical limit to their numbers. None of these are intrinsically ethnic but can become 'converted into ethnicity' (ibid., p. 230). This implies a distinctly instrumental connotation.

Gemeinschaft or Gesellschaft?

The discussion above introduces an ambiguity as to what kind of groups are ethnic groups: the warmth of the relationship described by the primordialists implies a notion of community while the instrumentalism of the situationists implies associations for a purpose (within the arena of *Gesellschaft*). Wieviorka (1994) associates them with tradition (community) while Glazer and Moynihan (1975) equate them with interest groups. Rex (1986) even hesitates to call them groups at all, because he sees that the representative aspect might be lacking and he refers to them as quasi groups. However, if one examines the modes of social organisation of immigrants/ethnic minorities, one finds that this dichotomy between *Gesellschaft* (modern society with its associations) and *Gemeinschaft* (community) is difficult to sustain. In the case of ethnic minority groups, they are not necessarily exclusive of each other but rather complementary. Associations may precede community as in the case of Sparkbrook Pakistanis (Rex and Moore, 1967) but they do not disappear when a community is established. On the contrary, the more complete the community, more numerous and thriving the associations (Joly, 1996). The latter do not either serve purely instrumental purposes but also provide moral, social and emotional support (ibid.). The mobilisation of ethnic groups in conflict with the rest of society follows distinctly modern patterns with a purpose while their internal mode of social organisation and relations are those of community. Even organisations which existed in the society of origin, such as mosques, assume different additional characteristics in the society of reception, with regard to their methods, functions and role and their internal structures (Joly, 1987). They act as interest groups in the society of reception but they are also characterised by warm and close social relations invested with emotional and moral significance.

Ethnic Mobilisation

However, the violent conflicts involving ethnic groups which one can sometimes witness lead us to consider more closely the question of ethnic mobilisation. In the first place it is necessary to distinguish between ethnicity and ethnic mobilisation. Although ethnic mobilisation is a frequent occurrence, does an ethnic group have to be 'mobilised' to constitute an ethnic group? Clearly the answer to this question rests on what is meant by 'mobilised'. If being conscious of oneself and conducting activities as a group means being mobilised, then ethnic mobilisation is concomitant with ethnicity. However, it is generally accepted that ethnic mobilisation goes beyond this level of action; it presupposes acting together in the competition for resources, political purposes and gains.

> Ethnic mobilisation can be defined as a process in which members of an ethnic group, in specific and relevant situations: first, develop heightened levels of group consciousness vis-à-vis other groups; second, employ cultural criteria or other symbols of their unity... to sharpen the boundaries between themselves and others; third, prepare, organise and consolidate their resources in order to take action and fourth, take action, usually of a political kind, in order to defend, promote and/or create collective as opposed to individual goals (Drury, 1994, p. 15).

There are varying views as to what factors and circumstances lead to ethnic mobilisation. One widely accepted explanation for the mobilisation of ethnic groups is that they feel excluded from sharing equally opportunities and resources (Bonacich, 1972; Wieviorka, 1994). Another position is that mobilisation by ethnic groups occurs when they have become socially and economically mobile because they feel the need to defend their gains against competitors, particularly during a recession (Olzac and Nagel, 1986). These two explanations may seem contradictory but they can be analysed as complementary if they are understood within the framework of a class system wherein groups mobilise, to acquire access to resources and opportunities, which they do not have or to defend such access which they have to some extent acquired and which they fear losing. A third explanation, the resource mobilisation theory, focuses on levels of group cohesiveness and organisational strength (Jenkins, 1983). Two major aspects of ethnic mobilisation are strengthened by the resource mobilisation theory; a good organisational base with leaders, associations, and organisational skills are conducive to more effective action while ethnic group consciousness is 'heightened' if there exist dense networks, associations and activities; but the multiplicity of leaders runs the risk of fragmenting the community.

Structure and Actors, Categorisation and Self-definition

A number of questions have to be discussed. Can an ethnic group exist as an objective reality or does it require consciousness of itself as a *sine qua non?* Is it comparable to a class in a partially objective manner, in the way that Marx (1973, pp. 238–9) analyses classes as determined by their relations to the means of production:

> The small peasant proprietors form an immense mass, the members of which live in the same situation but do not enter into manifold relationships with each other. Their mode of operation isolates them instead of bringing them into mutual intercourse. This isolation is strengthened by the wretched state of France's means of communication and by the poverty of the peasants. Their place of operation, the smallholding, permits no division of labour in its cultivation, no application of science and therefore no diversity of development, variety of talent, or wealth of social relationships. Each individual peasant family is almost self-sufficient; it directly produces the greater part of its own consumption and therefore obtains its means of life more through exchange with nature than through intercourse with society. The smallholding, the peasant, and the family; next door, another smallholding, another peasant, and another family. A bunch of these makes up a village, and a bunch of villages makes up a department. Thus the great mass of the French nation is formed by the simple addition of isomorphous magnitudes, much as potatoes in a sack form a sack of potatoes. In so far as millions of families live under economic conditions of existence that separate their mode of life, their interests and their cultural formation from those of the other classes and bring them into conflict with those classes, they form a class.

Despite the seemingly 'objective' character of the primordialist interpretation of ethnicity (i.e. what 'givens' the members of the group are born into), both primordialists and situationists appear to share the view that the actors concerned have to be aware of themselves as an ethnic group, either in the form of 'emotional attachment' or 'resource mobilisation'. One the main criteria often quoted in the definition of an ethnic group is also that its members must be involved in collective activity: according to Yinger (1986, p. 22):

> An ethnie exists in the full sense when three conditions are present: a segment of a larger society is seen by others to be different in some combination of the

following characteristics – language, religion, race and ancestral homeland with its related culture; the members also perceive themselves in that way; and they participate in shared activities built around their (real or mythical) common origin and culture.

These two prerequisites, consciousness of self and collective activity, give a central role to the social actors involved (Jenkins, 1986, p. 176). However, one issue remains unclear. Are those 'shared activities' actually carried out collectively, with the consciousness of acting in the name of the group and as a group, or do they include any practices, including individual practices partaking of specific cultural codes?

On the other hand, the situational approach gives scope for an enhanced influence of structural factors in the formation of ethnic groups. Could this make them a function of the structural set-up of the reception society, that is, whether or not the institutions of the latter provide a space for recognition, negotiation and potential gains which would generate a basis for group formation? In this sense can the Anglo-Saxon world be said to 'create' ethnic groups through the potential advantages awarded to them and the seeking out of community 'representatives'? In societies where there is no official nor public recognition of ethnic groups as in France, for example, political mobilisation as an ethnic group does not yield obvious benefits. In such society ethnic groups, if there were such, traditionally confined their ethnicity to the private domain. This, however, did not preclude a dense network of community associations and activities as a group in the private arenas of life (Hily and Poinard, 1987: Campani et al., 1987).

Most definitions of the ethnic group comprise perception from outside and from inside. The former is generally referred to as 'categorisation' (Jenkins, 1997). One must ask what happens when the categorisation from outside does not match the perception from inside. This is bound up with the power relations which the class system entails as the ethnic groups we are concerned with are placed in a situation of exploitation and subordination in the lower echelons of the class structure. It is difficult to claim rather mechanically that the structural situation of people and groups automatically leads to consciousness. But the mobilisation of ethnic groups is related also to the structural disadvantage in which they are placed and the discriminatory ideology and practices concomitant with it. It is thus possible that the discrimination accompanying ascription from outside or categorisation by the dominant group might lead to new forms of solidarity and consciousness as a group; it is not inconceivable but also not inevitable that the latter might then develop and mobilise as an ethnic group.

Private and Public Ethnicity

One must be careful not to confuse ethnicity and ethnic mobilisation. Indeed, according to Barth himself, ethnicity constitutes a resource in a way of differentiating oneself from others but not necessarily for engagement in political action (Barth, 1969). One needs to introduce the notion of private and public into this debate. Ethnicity may remain private while ethnic mobilisation itself is necessarily a public manifestation of ethnicity. The mobilisation of these populations does not have to assume an ethnic character but may lead to ethnic mobilisation when the ascription from outside and other structural factors (discrimination, rejection, resource allocation) prompts a group to turn some of its characteristics into ethnic markers. However, this is not inevitable. For instance, in the UK and the USA it appears that the institutional legitimation of ethnicity concomitant with concrete advantages attached to it has led to private ethnicities becoming public and even to the creation of 'imagined' ethnicities engaged in ethnic mobilisation. In France, on the other hand, while discrimination and racism may sometimes entail the affirmation of ethnico-religious identity, it usually generates action on another basis as anti-racists or 'immigrants' (de Rudder et al., 1994). The long-absent and then-limited legitimation of ethnic associations caused these to become an instrumental tool for the purposes of individual advancement and not group projects (Withol de Wenden, 1994), while the groups who were not discriminated against restricted their ethnicity to the private sphere (Lapeyronnie, 1993). The strategies adopted by immigrants are strongly influenced by the agenda of action and the political culture written in the reception society, and secondarily in the society of origin. In societies where ethnicity and ethnic minorities find a channel pre-existing in the structure of that society, they will be more likely to develop and become public. In societies where historically these channels were not open and where the logic of action was more solely one of class, ethnicity is less prominent. When the minority populations concerned were themselves raised in former colonial societies which inherited the same mode of functioning, they may have acquired these even prior to migration. These migrant workers are at the same time members of the working class and potential members of an ethnic group. They may orientate their group identification and collective action as members of the working class (as in the French model), as members of an ethnic minority group (the American model), or as both (often the British model). In most situations both identifications coexist and either of them may become more or less salient according to the circumstances but one generally takes precedence on a more stable basis for group formation, forms of actions and mobilisation. Currently ethnic groups and ethnic mobilisation are acquiring greater salience as the crisis of Western European societies jeopardises their habitual modes of functioning with the demise of both universalist national and social grand projects (Wieviorka, 1994).

The Relationship with Integration

The question is often posed rather simplistically as to whether ethnic groups help or hamper the integration of their members into majority society. It would be more appropriate to ask about the dialectical relationship between integration and the formation of ethnic groups as these interact dynamically. Indeed, the opportunities or incentives for integration and the forms of integration available will have an impact not only on the salience of ethnicity and the formation of an ethnic group but also on its role in the integration process. Lapeyronnie (1993, p. 30) sees ethnicity as an intrinsic part of the integration process: 'l'affirmation d'une identité italienne particulière est construite dans le rapport entretenu avec le pays d'accueil' ('the affirmation of a specific Italian identity is constructed through the relationship with the reception country' – my translation). It is also conceivable that segregation and discrimination measures lead to enclosure of the ethnic group (de Rudder et al., 1994). This may bring about an affirmation of specificity in order to assert a space of dignity (Lapeyronnie, 1993). More often some form of ethnic mobilisation will arise not only to protect the group but also to gain opportunities and resources in the majority society. In terms of the modes of settlement of ethnic minorities, it is clear that the ethnic group when it occurs generally contributes both to a greater interaction with the reception society and a preservation of itself as a community/ies. It entertains a project of self perpetuation but usually not as a segregated entity on the margins of society; on the contrary, it is fighting for a place in the society of settlement complete with rights on a par with autochthones and the right to preserve its difference: these are the dual objectives in its collective action. It has become a prevalent view that the ethnic group helps integration rather than hampers it (Ballis Lal, 1986). Wirth (1928) had argued long ago that it provides a secure environment from which to venture into the big wide world of the reception society. On the other hand, ethnic groups may even be deliberately used by the governing bodies as a means of control (Schierup, 1994). At any rate in almost all cases ethnic mobilisation is a positive declaration of engagement with the reception society; this is true even in the case of violent confrontation.

Ethnicisation and the Deconstruction of Ethnicities

The debate on ethnicity and ethnic group has thrown up new questions. In the nineties the field of ethnic and migration research has been characterised by two distinct trends which translate parallel phenomena in contemporary societies. On the one hand an emphasis was placed on a re-ethnification or re-ethnicisation of society (Friedman, 1997), and on the other hand this view was criticised or complemented from a variety of vantage points. New concepts have also been developed to account for processes taking place among migrant groups, such as hybridity and transnational communities.

Ethnification

It is posited that nation states are undergoing a process of ethnification which includes indigenisation, regionalisation, localisation of identification, and both the ethnification of migrants and nationals (Friedman, 1997). This is deemed to be expressed through a return to roots and to fixed identifications. Indigenous peoples throughout the world are stating new claims to territory and culture conveyed via nationally- and internationally-based organisations. It is also reflected through UN declarations and an increased recognition by states. With regard to migrants, one increasingly notices the apparent formation of ethnic groups/ethnic communities in the country of reception. Ethnic groups and ethnic processes of group identification are seen to have occupied the space left by the disintegration of national institutions and class-based forms of organisation (Wieviorka, 1992). It is argued that this process is augmented by universal deregulation and the unqualified priority awarded to market competition (Z. Bauman, 1997).

It is even posited that images of ethnic communities such as *Gemeinschaft* underpin research designs on immigrants revealing an ethnicised theoretical bias (Caglar, 1997). Ethnicity has also been increasingly portrayed as a resource whilst an exclusive emphasis on ethnicity in this manner was sometimes criticised for indirectly 'blaming the victim' (Jenkins, 1997). In a process of ethnic mobilisation, minority groups are shown to negotiate with the majority society to put forward their interests through their associations (Candappa and Joly, 1994; Rex and Drury, 1994). Abundant research on ethnic groups provides evidence of their mode of social organisation (Rex et al., 1987). Moreover, from the mid-1970s to today, what is noticeable is a growing ethnification of public social arenas, and identity politics (Friedman, 1997; Joly, 1996). This enhances the propensity among community leaders to represent culture as a monolithic body of lifestyles and convictions which the whole group shares in (G. Bauman, 1997) and which enables them to state claims to recognition and rights. However, this may pose a problem to those who might not choose to identify themselves in this way such as people from those communities born in countries of reception who wish to be able to partake of both heritages. In much of Europe and certainly in all the Anglo-Saxon world, multiculturalist policies have entailed an institutionalisation of culture and ethnicity in the public space; but this also implies that only those specific groups and identities will be publicly acknowledged and granted rights/advantages (Caglar, 1997). In a more universalist light, some social scientists have interpreted the increasing salience of ethnicity as a broadening of democratic rights: cultural rights are advanced as pertaining to the realm of democratic rights with a 'cultural democracy' elaborating on political and social democracy (Touraine, 1997).

The dominant discourse is said to ethnicise further more groups of immigrant origin through equating culture, community and ethnic identity; as a consequence, ethnicity runs the risk of becoming 'naturalised' (G. Bauman, 1997). Within majority society this means that racists may use differences as bases for irreconcilable and or threatening cultural distinctiveness: they soon reach the conclusion that those groups must be kept at a distance, segregated or expelled (Wieviorka, 1997). Extreme right organisations tend to emphasise difference to stress pure national identity and culture in order to reinforce the in-group.

In countries where the dominant discourse and the official position of the state continue to deny the acceptability of diverse ethnic identities within the national polity and the city, this has been challenged by a position defending their entitlement to recognition within the scope of difference and equality (Touraine, 1997). However, in societies where multicultural policies have been implemented, the 'essentialism' attributed to the notion of ethnic groups and ethnicity has been questioned. Is there space for a middle way?

Hybridisation and Creolisation

One important school of thought has seized upon what they consider an essentialist tendency in research focusing on ethnic groups and ethnicity as objects. The study of ethnicity is then pursued through a criticism of its reification and through discussions on hybrid, shifting or diasporic identities (Hall, 1990; Brah, 1991). In a critique of the notion of cultures as homogeneous, bounded, reified wholes, a number of concepts are advanced such as hyphenated, hybrid and creolised identities. The complexities of synchretic cultures among youth of immigrant origin is also explained as liminality and rhizomes, in terms of the transformation of symbols, identities or public roles (Back, 1996). All refer to the mixture of cultures particularly as applied to people of immigrant origin, born and brought up in their parents' country of reception. The bell is said to toll for the innocent essential black subject, to be replaced by a positive conception of the ethnicity of the margin, and a cultural diaspora-sation through a process of hybridisation, 'cut-and-mix' (Hall, 1992). These concepts are often perceived as a challenge to the nation state (Friedman, 1997). They are supposed to destabilise or subvert hierarchies imposed on differences (Caglar, 1997). The enemy is what is 'bounded' and thus essentialist (Friedman, 1997). Hybridisation dons a normative dimension and is construed as a politically correct solution.

However, a number of questions must be addressed to the advocates of hybridisation and anti-essentialism. Are all notions of ethnic groups and ethnicity condemned to essentialism? Would this entail the evacuation of ethnicity and ethnic group as analytical categories? What of ethnicity as a situationalist resource in the Barthian model? Barth deconstructed culture through his 'situational' analysis of ethnicity, which he divested of its essentialism (Barth, 1969). Is there not an incompatibility between the supposed essentialism of ethnicity and its often exercised instrumental use? How can ethnicity as a basis for collective action be analysed within the framework of hybridisation? How do these hybrid cultures relate to forms of organisation and action which develop in the course of political action (Rex, 1997)? Even the political correctness of hybridisation and related concepts founder on the mobilisation of ethnicity and ethnic groups for the purpose of political action. Moreover, it is also doubtful whether hybridisation and creolisation adequately challenge essentialism: it has been pointed out that the notion of mixture assumes the prior existence of bounded pure 'essentialist' cultures (Friedman, 1997).

A more serious interrogation bears on the capacity of creolisation to defy hierarchies and oppression; in some cases it might represent the opposite as in Central America where the mestizo concept was used as a tool of colonialism, the 'hybrids' being associated with the elite ruling over the Indians (ibid.). Finally, the celebration of cultural diversity and hybridity often overlooks discrimination and exclusion based both on ethnicity and class; it fails to effectively challenge the discrimination which ethnic groups suffer. It has been argued that hybrid identities are generally the attributes of a particular class, the intelligentsia 'who can afford a cosmopolitan identity' (ibid.). One could add that the intellectuals who advocate such concepts seem to propose not an analysis of society but a subjective description of their own situation posited as an analytical category for other groups in society. Such an approach more or less corresponds to Honoré de Balzac's word about the novel, a 'mirror' passing along the way; it focuses on a mere reflection of social reality and does not go beyond apparent fragmentation and disintegration. Sociologists in this field would do better to dig below the surface, the underpinning structures and social interactions which give rise to particular formulations of ethnicities or other forms of group identifications.

Within the modern framework of the nation state, hybridity has been advanced as a challenge to the dominant norm which imposes fixed categories. It is a fact that 'hybrids' within the British colonial regime (in India, for example) were often perceived as a threat to the established order and its ideology of racial superiority: offspring of mixed parentage were thus considered a subversive element. However, the same school of thought which posits hybridity as a counter-norm also suggests that it is becoming the prevailing characteristic of contemporary society as enhanced through globalisation. In this case, can hybridity keep its pertinence as a norm and counter-norm at the same time? It is counterposed to the essentialism of ethnic categories which is deemed to be conservative and conformist. However, social reality is more complex: what can be observed is a two-pronged process. The demise of the nation state and its homogenous assimilationist model (as in France) may lead to an ethnicisation with some dimension of resistance and subversion through the mobilisation of ethnic groups who challenge the dominant norm. On the other hand, another process may take place through which youths question both the monolithic model of the nation state and that of the ethnic group. They adopt a critical distance vis-à-vis both, and rely on one code to criticise the other, respectively. One is no longer faced with a binary opposition along the lines of assimilation-resistance, but what is happening is that young people may make use of a variety of registers. This capacity to manipulate a plurality of codes and to adopt a critical attitude vis-à-vis different registers seems to match mechanisms evidenced by current theories on socialisation. Those theories challenge functionalist approaches on actors' integrated models and stress the plurality of the subject as well as the increasing importance of their capacity to reflect on and criticise social norms (Verhoeven, 1997, pp. 209–22). What needs to be asked is whether the social individual is capable of such analytical reflection and can muster the use of several registers. To what extent does this happen and does it constitute a significant trend? Does there still exist a collective mobilisation among those groups and on what basis?

Transnational Communities

Another school of social scientists broaches the issue from the vantage point of international migration. These theories take on board the role of the social actors involved, i.e. the migrants. Theories on the individual motivations of migration do not help much to analyse its social effects. One can gain a better insight through what Massey et al. (1993) point out as the collective decision-making unit and its objective but also the distinction which they establish between what causes the initiation of migration and what causes its perpetuation. This analysis shows that migration decisions are made by larger units than the individual, such as households or extended families with a view not solely to maximising total income but also to diversifying sources of income as an insurance against a variety of risks. Migration is thereafter perpetuated as migrants create transnational networks which constitute social capital. These theories will also have wide-ranging implications for the analysis of effects of migration on both sending and receiving countries.

Another explanation pertains to notions of relative deprivation whereby status and income improvements in the country of origin are sought relative to other families involved in migration. This logic is sustainable only if links are maintained between the migrants, former migrants and non-migrants in origin and destination areas. Network theory analysing ties of kinship, friendship and shared community of origin is thereafter used to account for the perpetuation of migration as a self-sustaining diffusion process (Massey et al., 1993). It has been stated that contemporary international migration is no longer simply the case of a place of origin and a place of arrival as was traditionally assumed (Pries, 1999). What is becoming apparent is that this migration is not irrevocable and that links with the sending countries are not severed even after a long period of settlement (Faist, 1999). New theories of migration propose that migration flows assume a new and unique quality while new transnational realities are developing in and through international migration networks.

As a consequence it is argued that qualitatively new social groups are being established in new social fields in the shape of deterritorialised social spaces (Pries, 1999). To explain the factors for the creation and maintenance of transnational social spaces, theories of social capital (Bourdieu, quoted by Pries, 1999) and cumulative causation are called upon. Migrants' networks are identified as a form of social capital (Massey et al., 1993). Within this framework there is a space for both the agency of collectivities and the economic/political structural constraints underpinning them (Goldring, 1999).

Four initial reasons are advanced to account for the formation of transnational communities: the family reproduction in the face of economic and or political insecurity, social exclusion in the countries of origin, racialised exclusion in countries of reception, active relations between home states and transmigrants (Basch et al., 1994). Moreover, it seems that the importance of status claims in relation to the country of origin reinforces transnational communities, through their investing in their location of origin and their project to reorient regimes of stratification (Goldring, 1999). Migrants are simultaneously involved in the country of origin and of reception (Basch et al,. 1994) so that a triangular relationship exists (Faist, 1999). The neoliberal organisation of the global economy seems to give states an impetus to create new categories of citizenship facilitating dual belonging (Smith, 1999). What is also emphasised is the end of an equation between social space and territorial space: a deterritorialisation of groups takes place (Caglar, 1997).

A trend appears to develop whereby ethnic minority groups create transnational communities through an original mobilisation of identity and community resources which enable them to multiply economic and social advantages through their networks. A continuous interaction takes place between their community in the country of origin, the community in the first country of settlement and ramifications of these communities in other countries of settlement. Three stages are identified by Faist (1999): 1) remittances being sent by labour migrants; 2) the birth and growth of ethnic businesses in reception countries; 3) transnational production, distribution and sales. A number of factors are said to make this possible and necessary: economic and/or political exclusion in the society of origin, racialised exclusion in the country of reception (Basch et al., 1994), compounded with the declining legitimacy of cultural assimilation, and the extension of 'multicultural' rights (Goldring, 1999) which are seized upon by the migrants through their social capital. This development is apparently enhanced by the global penetration of the neoliberal model (Smith, 1999) but may enable them to cope better than autochthonous populations of the same socioeconomic level. Others have argued that the migrants' situation as strangers and outsiders at the same time as insiders (Simmel, 1964), gave them a heightened critical and analytical view of society and that this enabled them to pursue original individual and group strategies.

Social capital is locally based, a 'local asset' and functions as a transmission belt for other forms of capital. Transnational social spaces are said to emerge when persons in distinct places are connected via social and symbolic ties enabling the transfer of various forms of capital; it is grounded in at least two local contexts and has the capacity to link across borders and even continents (Faist, 1999). Local assets are thus transformed into international assets through transnational locally based community networks. Two types of transnationalisation are possible: economic and political transnational communities, namely labour migrants and refugees, both evolving through different phases. But in both cases, a process of cumulative causation is observed to explain youth cultures:

> In sum, the feedback processes involving cumulative causation concern a declining legitimacy of cultural assimilation as a shared vision, the extension of 'multicultural' rights, the denial of political rights and the experiences of cultural discrimination and socio-economic exclusion and the translation of cultural and political conflicts from Turkey to Germany and back have contributed to an increasing transnationalisation (Faist, 1999, p. 61).

According to Faist, one is not dealing with a youth subculture with lumpen dimensions and connotations of disintegration. His theoretical approach challenges the notions of disintegration and hybridity, proposing instead a concept of cultural cumulative causation (through an interactive feedback process) and of transnationalised segmented cultural spaces. This accounts for cultural elements from both the sending and receiving countries finding entry in the cultural repertoire whereby a dichotomy appears between the public and private sphere and where multiple ethnic, cultural and religious cleavages exist within the group of migrant origin (Faist, 1999).

Refugees in the Reception Society

Economic migrants can prepare themselves psychologically and materially for the move because they were able to plan it. The vast majority of refugees did not have a chance to do so and this adds to the often precipitous and traumatic circumstances of their flight, sometimes also fraught with experiences of detention camps, severe persecution, prison, torture and fear of death. Following from this many, although not all, refugees are dispersed at the whim of fate so that the discrepancy between their society of origin and of reception is likely to be greater unless they are able to remain in the vicinity of their country of origin. This sometimes was compounded by the legal restrictions governing entry in reception societies to prevent or reduce the possibility of chain migration. Refugees display differentiated attitudes to settlement in the country of reception: sometimes there is a greater willingness to adapt to the new society as fast as possible, sometimes there may be a long-drawn resistance to change and attachment to the past. Similarly refugees can display a very passive and resigned attitude alongside great daring.

Most of the research concerning refugees considers them either in their land of origin and in flight or in the land of reception. The twain do not meet and it appears that one is dealing with two completely discrete situations. I will argue that such an approach makes it impossible to progress in the understanding of the refugee situation. Although the past informs the present in any migration, the overriding importance of the past to determine and understand refugee settlement is unique. It is therefore imperative to establish the correlation between the circumstances preceding and following exile (and what may happen in between).

Kunz (1981) is the only one who clearly attempts to do so. He divides refugee populations into: majority identified refugees who identify with the nation but not with the government and are convinced that their opposition to events is shared by the majority of their compatriots; secondly, alienated refugees (usually from minority groups) who are ambivalent or embittered in their attitude towards their former compatriots either because of events immediately preceding the situation causing flight or because of past discrimination. Concerning the refugees' attitude towards displacement Kunz classifies them as 'reactive fate groups' or 'purpose groups' which include self-fulfilling groups and revolutionary activists. To identify a majority identified refugee, Kunz postulates three types of characteristics: home-related characteristics such as inexperience in handling minority or marginality situations and compensatory activities resulting from guilt or emotional attachment to the homeland, treating resettlement as a transient phase; transit-related characteristics including the effect of displacement and the effects of midway to nowhere; and host-related factors. However Kunz' typology does not account adequately for groups who technically speaking may not be majority identified but nonetheless display more of the characteristics of majority identified refugees rather than those of alienated refugees. The Kurds are a case in point, who certainly do not identify with their respective states Iraq, Iran, Turkey and Syria, but demonstrate a strong attachment to their Kurdish homeland and identity. Kunz also fails to examine in details the refugee's strategies and modes of settlement as related to his typology. My study contributes to filling these gaps, within the framework of the refugees' relationship to the 'structure of conflict' in the homeland and the reception society (see below).

With this in mind I attempt to determine the parameters which have to be considered in a study of refugées in the land of exile. I will first look at the position of refugees in their society of origin to understand their characteristics in the society of reception. Adopting the view expressed by Zolberg et al. (1989) that refugees, past and present, are a result of social conflict I propose to analyse refugee populations within the structure of conflict which led them to flee and preceded the crisis prompting departure. However, what is important is not only the refugees' objective position but also their subjective relation towards these conflicts, the actors' consciousness and commitment. Did they exist as a group prior to exile or is it the common experience of exile that created them as a group; did they have a collective consciousness and project prior to exile? Is there a collective project of return? Did they regain their position as social and political actors in the society of reception and how?

Let us now examine the diversity of refugees resulting from different conflicts. Zolberg et al.'s typology of conflicts causing refugee movements is a useful starting point (Zolberg et al., 1989). Colonial conflicts and national liberation movements give rise to three kinds of refugee groups. Prior to decolonisation, there are national liberation militants and their followers. After the retreat of colonial powers, two groups may get out: former settlers if they were forced to leave, and natives having collaborated with the colonial power, but also a mixed parentage population. The settlers and their offspring are in a refugee-like situation but enjoy more emotional and ontological security as their destination is certain and assured. The disintegration of empires or federalised states and the formation of nation states follow a similar pattern. But in many cases ethnic and religious conflicts have arisen in their wake; in such situations refugees may originate from three main groups. Ethnic or religious minorities with a defined territorial base; ethnic and religious minorities without a well-defined territorial base such as gypsies (this may include tribes and castes); and ethnic and religious groups whose close or far ancestry came from another land. Social movements followed by a counter-revolutionary dictatorship may entail the flight of militants and sympathisers involved in the movement which could be based on several classes and social strata. Social revolution gives rise to the exile of previous ruling groups in society. So-called communist regimes have provoked the exit of individual dissidents as from Eastern Europe and from larger masses of people as those running away from Pol Pot in Cambodia. Civil wars and generalised violence may entail the flight of a motley collection of victims. Finally, some wars may provoke the exile of specific groups such as conscientious objectors and war resisters.

If one looks at refugees' position in the society of origin as a determining factor towards different modes of settlement it is possible to find two large categories (see Table 7.1). One category of refugees are those who had a collective project of society in the land of origin and take it with them in their land of exile. The most common ones are national and/or social projects, but might also be religious projects. This category could include some individuals from any of the groups presented above and none of the groups will fit this description a hundred per cent as there are differentiated degrees of commitment to the projects involved. However, as an ideal type, one can posit that on the whole this category includes the following: social movements against a dictatorship, national liberation militants against the colonial power, territorially based national and ethnic groups and some religious groups.

The second category includes those who did not have a collective project in the land of origin or those who have forsaken it. It includes settlers in independent colonies which have gained independence, those natives who collaborated with the colonial power, non-indigenous religious or ethnic groups, victims of genocide and victims of generalised violence. War resisters, draft-dodgers, opponents of social revolutions or communist regimes may come under the first or second category depending on whether or not they are committed individually or as a group to a collective project. The society of reference constitutes one main parameter in the refugees' process of settlement: society of origin and society of reception will have differentiated impacts according to the types considered.

In this inquiry one needs to ask whether refugees form groups in their society of exile and what kind of groups these are; what is the basis of group formation which their situation as refugees provide, how they relate to one another amongst themselves and to others. What is the refugees modes of social organisation and, if one accepts that group formation represents potentiality for collective action (Rex, 1986, p. 89), what is the meaning and what are the nature and characteristics of such collective action.

The two broad categories proposed represent two types which will display differentiated patterns of adaptation in the land of exile and settlement (see Table 7.2). However, even the two main categories are not static as particular groups and individuals from any group may change category because of a number of factors. We shall now turn to the characteristics of the two main types.

Table 7.1   Refugee types and causes of exile

	Odyssean refugees	Rubicon refugees
Colonial conflicts National liberation movements/collapses of empire Formation of nation states	National liberation activists Ethnic national/religious minorities with a territorial base	Former settlers identified with coloniser Native collaborators
	Ethnic/religious minorities <----------- without a territorial base ------------>	
		Ethnic/religious minorities of foreign origin
Counter-revolutionary dictatorships	Social movement and activists against the regime	
Communist regimes		Dissidents
Social revolutions		Former ruling elites
Civil wars/generalised violence	<---------- Victims --------->	
Wars	<------- War-resisters ------->	

Odyssean refugees[2]

Within the framework of this paper the term refers to actors who were not just victims of the structure of conflict in their country of origin but were positively committed to the political struggle and to a project of society in their homeland; they also brought this project with them into exile so that they are committed to a collective project in the homeland despite the defeat they have suffered; in some circumstances they may have adhered to such project in exile. Return is their objective with the aim of continuing the project. Are not included those who have abandoned their political commitment.

Referring to the modes of settlement as examined for labour migrants, for these refugees assimilation is the most unlikely strategy because they do not consider their stay as long term and have no motivation to settle in the

Table 7.2 Refugee types in the country of exile

	Homeland project		No return	
	Unstable regime in country of origin	*Stabilised regime in country of origin*	*Minority group in country of origin*	*Not minority group in country of origin*
Boundary Us/them	Us: those oppressed by homeland regime Them: homeland regime and allies	(See previous column)	Us: minority group Them: wider society (or internal cleavages to minority group)	Along cleavages in majority society or possibly same as minority group (see previous column)
Social organisation	Political associations	Social and cultural projects support committees (for homeland) Political associations	Associations (economic social cultural pressure groups) Communities	Social organisation of reception country or see previous column
Goals and meaning of action	To regain position as social and political actors in homeland	1 Regain position as social and political actors in homeland 2 Organise life in reception society	1 Improve conditions of settlement 2 Maintain group identity	Settlement, integration, assimilation or see previous column
Factors of change shaping the groups	Viability of homeland, project and what impacts on it	1 Viability of homeland project 2 Circumstances in reception society	General social, political economic conjuncture in reception society Attitudes and policies towards refugees	Conjuncture in reception society or see previous column

reception society. They do not merge with the host society but definitely form groups. As their political project is tied up with a specific country of origin they tend to form groups along national/ethnic lines. One could infer from this that they form ethnic groups like labour migrants and I found it a useful approach to compare and contrast the refugee groups with the latter.

The Boundary

The boundaries and the lines of exclusion/inclusion are central criteria to define the group. Ethnic groups establish their boundary here and now with the majority society and/or with other ethnic groups in the society of reception. In space and time they primarily define themselves vis-à-vis the society of reception: they are here to stay. This does not exclude an interest in the country of origin and a myth of return but their organisations, their projects and objectives primarily relate to the society of reception. In contrast with those, Odyssean refugees perceive themselves as here temporarily; they are oriented towards the past and the homeland. For them the process of boundary definition follows a different pattern to that of ethnic groups particularly in the determination of who belongs and who is excluded. For Odyssean refugees *us* includes not necessarily all nationals of the same origin but all who were engaged in the same political struggle. If we are dealing with a national/ethnic minority in the homeland *us* includes all those who belong to it and do not support the regime oppressing it; in this case the minority/ethnic group boundaries are determined by criteria and perceptions of difference in contrast with the majority in the country of origin. This would apply to Kurds who are a national minority in Turkey, Iraq and Iran. Any one supporting the regime which forced them to flee cannot possibly find a place in the group. *Us* is also the people left behind who share in the same commitment; these refugees consider themselves as an extension of the people in the homeland fighting the regime. *Them* is the regime and its supporters in the country of origin, and outside. For instance, in the case of the Chileans, all those who were out of the country because they had fallen foul of the dictatorship were in principle included. Any individual who happened to be out of Chile for reasons of work or study was looked upon with suspicion and kept at a distance unless s/he could demonstrate a clear anti-dictatorship involvement.

There may exist additional boundary lines among the exile group according to the political organisation they belong to or support. *Us* in this case may be all members of the communist party (and its allies) and *them* those who pertain to other political organisations (Socialist, Radical and so on), *us*, all who support the KDP and *them*, PUK followers (Kurdish organisations in Iraq). These cleavages follow those which obtain in the country of origin and alliances are made or unmade at the same rhythm in the homeland and in exile, group inclusion and exclusion being determined by it. These cleavages are particularly significant when different 'vintages' (Kunz, 1973) of refugees represent political projects and organisations hostile to each other, thrown into exile at different periods according to the upheavals in the country of origin. But in all cases, the homeland purpose refugees do not position themselves vis-à-vis the majority society or other ethnic groups in the host society but vis-à-vis the structure of conflict in the land of origin. This is where their boundary and identification lie. The actors' self-definition is primary and rarely lends itself to categorisation by the majority society in the land of exile. If the majority society and its institutions categorise them as ethnic groups, the homeland purpose refugees tend to reject it or do not understand what this is all about as this concept remains alien to them. The Kurds are a case in point: when asked whether they considered themselves as an ethnic minority in Britain several informants protested vehemently; arguing that they were not a minority, that they were a national group of 20 million, that the oppressive regime constantly tried to underplay their numbers and so on (Wahlbeck, 1999). The modes of functioning of British society tends to categorise foreign groups as ethnic minority groups and interacts with them on that basis, in the granting of resources and the formulation of policies. Kurds are automatically slotted into that category but their answer to the question demonstrates that they formulate their group identifications in relation to conflict and cleavages in the country ties of origin. The determination vis-à-vis the regime is paramount so that non-Kurds are included in the in-group along the lines of political alliances against the dictatorship: that is, Kurds and Arabs from Iraq who belong to alien political formation and ideological bases. This is perhaps the strongest indicator that they cannot possibly constitute an ethnic group in the host society as their own consciousness excludes this possibility. In the case of indigenous peoples such as the Mapuches from Chile, this notion of becoming an ethnic minority is even more inconceivable; they have a double group identification, both determined by their relationship to the structure of conflict in the homeland. They define themselves in relations to the dictatorship which savagely targeted them, and they form Mapuche Comites with transnational structures in exile, linked to more of the homeland. On this basis, these comites may organise activities in common with 'Chilean' organisations. However, they also define themselves as 'Mapuches' and interact cautiously with 'Chilean' organisations/individuals on account of the ancestial prejudice and racism penetrating Chilean majority society since the colonisation of the South Croates.

The Social Organisation of the Refugees

The society of reference for this type of refugee is clearly and squarely the society of origin. They define themselves and their group identification within the structure of conflict of homeland society and its cleavages. Their social status itself is determined along the same basis according to the political or religious leadership role, past and present vis-à-vis homeland engagement and the social status which they had back home.

They consider themselves an extension, a continuation of their homeland groups outside their country of origin. Odyssean refugees are often organised as associations, that is, political associations. They form dense transnational networks which are formally structured and share programme and strategies. They were generally organised into political parties and movements prior to exile and reconstitute these as soon and as far as possible in the country of reception. The political parties proper are organically linked to the homeland parties and form sections and cells in exile with the same organisational rules; sometimes governments in exile. A specific section of the party may be thus added as that of a supplementary region (Exterior Committee). It implies organisational links with the interior but also with other branches in other countries of exile, transnational networks Trade-union sections of the homeland trade-union may also be formed. International networks are thus created and reinforced, which spread with the forced dispersion of refugees in several countries of exile. The separate identity of these organisations has been recognised by the parties of the host society which, even when they share the same ideological programme, do not propose an organic absorption into their ranks. This is not the case where labour migrants are concerned.

The homeland political parties often initiate and/or take part in other kinds of associations such as support committees, cultural groups, campaigns of denunciation to further the political objectives of supporting the struggle against the regime back home. In the early stages of exile the major groups which centralise all activities are the homeland parties and the broad campaigns based in the society of reception either launched by members of the host society or in collaboration with them. Here again, The objective of conflict in the country of origin which motivated the flight continues to determine the refugees' mode of social organisation: refugees who were persecuted for religious reasons such as Tibetan Buddhists, regroup around their religious belief and practices, and in campaigns against China.

As the duration of exile extends a variety of support committees are set up with a cultural, educational, advice character either under the auspices of the parties or independently of them. The collective activities they are engaged in are variegated. They include internal organisational meetings, public meetings, demonstrations, cultural performances, educational encounters, symbolic celebrations of key anniversaries. Despite the associational character of all these groups, they, like the labour migrants' associations often share in some of the characteristics of communities such as the closeness and warmth of relationships, the many faceted aspects of life within them, the moral and social control they exercise; other orientations appear illegitimate (Bolzman, n.d.). But these are features of those organisations which were not solely acquired in exile; they had formulated and were promoting a project of society in the country of origin and in several cases this involved an all encompassing project covering education, sports, leisure, cultural manifestations, neighbourhood issues, as well as social, economic and political objectives and so on. Even the kinship system is intertwined in this process; for instance in Chilean neighbourhoods entire families tend to belong to the same party; among Kurds this is even more noticeable as the organisations themselves are rooted among particular clans. Everyday life interactions are also based on other kinds of activities, which find their source in the society of origin: region/locality of origin social status and sphere of employment, religious belonging, shared experience in the exile trajectory, such as prison, transit in another country reception centre on arrival and so on. However the dispersion of exile makes regrouping with such richness of interaction difficult. And in most cases what is formed is a fragmented community /communities along the lines of political cleavages.

Goals and Meaning of Action

As seen above ethnic groups are formed and mobilise primarily in connection with their long-term stay in the reception society. The latter may actually sponsor or promote the formation of ethnic groups. These groups may perceive the need to create institutions enabling them to improve their conditions of settlement; through a community space for cultural, religious and social activities, through pressure group activities for an equal/better share of opportunities and resources. The means and the ends coincide as interaction with and participation in the majority society aim to achieve a place in this very society. The meaning of their action is to be found in their interaction within the structure of conflict of the reception society. Of course they also maintain links with their society of origin but these take a secondary position in their life project.

As for the Odyssean refugees the collective actions they get involved in find their meaning primarily in relation to the structure of conflict in the society of origin. It is particularly clear where the internal workings of their political organisations are concerned and with activities such as the very symbolic celebrations of key anniversaries. But it is still the case with regard to the multiple support committees which support a project back home through making it known and raising funds for it. Activities such as cultural representations and festive gatherings may seem to resemble those of ethnic groups but this is only the case if one stops short at appearances. These committees and activities generally raise funding for a project back home which is invested with a subversive agenda. A cultural manifestation and project for instance assume a political meaning in the homeland if the nature of that culture, its very existence, its ideological content constitute a culture of resistance and challenge the regime; the same may be true of language and religion. Social projects are also perceived in that way by the actors in exile when the people involved are deprived and oppressed by the regime in the homeland. In this case, support for those projects has a clear political meaning and not only expresses humanitarian purposes as any humanitarian Third World aid programme.

This does not entail that homeland purpose refugees do not interact with the reception society; in fact there may exist an intensive level of interaction as they participate in campaigns to denounce the regime in the homelands. They interact with politicians and political organisations of the host society, trade-unions, human rights and humanitarian organisations, churches or other religious institutions, the media, local authorities and so on. But this interaction is not phrased within the structure of conflict of the reception society. The meaning of this action is again to be found within the structure of conflict in the homeland as its goals are to muster forces against its regime. The Society of reception is considered according to its relevance to the return project. Interaction is relevant to engagement with homeland society and to challenging the regime responsible for exile. As such links have been established with a great variety of organisations such as trade unions and political parties of the reception society but also churches, temples, refugee agencies, NGOs and other refugees ad minority group associations with whom they may share affinities of interest. The ends (oriented towards the country of origin) and the means (interaction with the society of reception) do not coincide. The actors (homeland purpose refugees) do not mobilise to make a place for themselves in the reception society but to restore or create it in the society of origin.

Factors of Change

What we have been dealing with is the ideal type of homeland project. In practice the group is never completely homogeneous as the degree of political commitment may vary amongst its members. Children, partners and parents who followed the militant into exile may only share his/her convictions in a passive way; moreover other types of refugees may have been mixed in. But the group still retains its identity if there is a sufficient number of committed activists and if the project seems viable. Again the main factors which are likely to influence the identity of the group are those bearing upon the situation in the country of origin and their implication for the duration of exile. I have already indicated above that there tends to be a kind of periodicisation in the forms of organisation and actions of the group leading to subtypes.

In the initial period if the conjuncture back home is in turmoil and has not stabilised, exile is envisaged as a very short episode and all energies are tensed towards the goal of overthrowing the regime and returning. As the regime in the homeland stabilises, this is perceived as a consolidation and an indication that exile will last longer than initially expected. Although one is not here to stay, one is here for a while more. A subgroup is formed with a double orientation. This is when the forms of organisations and activities become diversified and this may result into a dual orientation of the action: that pursuing the political project in the homeland and a secondary one pertaining to everyday issues in the society of reception, some of which are addressed to the 'second generation'. However the former remains prioritised for the future while the latter services the temporary present. What will enhance one or the other of these actions will be fluctuations in the conjuncture of the homeland which may be influenced by international events, the fortunes of the resistance movement inside, the perceived viability of the project and 'defeatability' of the homeland regime or its durability. But it is not time and the duration of exile as such which are determining as demonstrated by the case of some refugee groups which persisted over several generations: it is the viability of the political project kept alive by the possibility of its victory, or the reverse. The structure of the society of reception plays a secondary role for this group: it may help to further the political project or hamper it but cannot eliminate it. In some countries the refugee group may have reconstituted a near to complete society in exile if a sympathetic government made it possible, and particularly if they are close to their country of origin or if the refugees were segregated in camps and a kind of separation was established. In most cases some measure of integration was rendered necessary by the motions of living and functioning in the reception society while participation was actively taken up for supporting the project back home.

When exile draws to an end with a change of regime and the possibility of returning, the strategies of this group may become diversified and lead to return, assimilation, or integration and ethnic group formation. This is when the structure of conflict of the reception society becomes preponderant in influencing the paths followed for those who stayed. This is when community associations (across party lines) may be created for community activities. If an ethnic group is formed, negotiations will take place with the society of reception to make a place for the group in this very society, through interest groups and ethnic mobilisation. Bolzman (n.d.) quoted how for the first time, residents' associations were formed, representative of all the Chileans in the same canton, in Switzerland, after the end of exile; how for the first time the refugees associations promoted citizens and social rights in the society of reception (Bolzman, n.d.).

Rubicon Refugees

The relationship of these refugees to the society of origin stands at the opposite pole to that of Odyssean refugees. They have turned their back on it and do not retain a commitment towards it although they may be concerned with the fate of their kin and others from the same group left behind and still have an attachment to their culture of origin. Return for the purpose of settling back home is not envisaged within the framework of options for the future and exile is perceived as definitive. This may mean a greater propensity to have a positive attitude towards the society of reception and perhaps a greater availability to make a fresh start and to innovate. On the other hand, the involuntary character of the migration invested the move with a negative character which may have adverse effects on settlement.

These refugees have severed their link with their country of origin; they cannot go back and they do not intend to go back. However the strategies followed and their itineraries will be influenced although not determined (as was the case for homeland purpose refugees) by their position within the structure of their society of origin. One major line of differentiation will be whether they existed as a minority group in the society of origin (particularly an ethnic and/or religious minority) or were general victims of violence, human rights violations and so on.

For Rubicon refugees assimilation is a possible option particularly if they did not exist as a group prior to exile and if the structure of the reception society encourages it. In this, they differ markedly from the political refugees but also in the fact that they frequently form ethnic groups in the society of settlement. Let us examine how these are articulated.

The Boundary

Refugees who existed as a minority group in the society of origin tend to take their boundary with them into the country of settlement but do not establish it any longer in relation to the majority society in the homeland. The central immediate change affects the composition of *them* which becomes the majority society in the country of reception. *Us* may remain the minority group which was thrown into exile but may also undergo variations. For instance if there exists a minority group of the same national/ethnico/religious origin *us* may include these in contrast with the autochtonous population. More rarely it includes refugee nationals of the same state. Ultimately the inclusive/exclusive categories are subject to multiple variations according to circumstances and needs so that different markers may be turned into ethnic markers accordingly, as was the case for labour migrants. Refugees who were not a minority prior to exile may follow the same patterns but the group formation is likely to take longer in their case; in addition they are more prone to become divided amongst themselves and set up supplementary boundaries within the original population of refugees. Potential dividing lines are heightened by the competition within the group. But in all the circumstances the main frontier of exclusion/inclusion is established in relation to the society of reception.

In some cases one must mention a significant additional dimension for the mapping of these groups' identity; when substantial groups of the same origin have become settled in different geographical locations around the world, the inclusive category may embrace the minority group within and without one specific country of settlement as the whole discussion on diasporas indicate (Clifford, 1994; Ma Mung, 1994). This possibility is all the more marked where refugees are concerned as the dispersion they generally underwent and the prohibition of return to the country of origin create the material bases for a diaspora and make its consciousness more probable.

Social Organisation

The modes of organisation of the Rubicon refugees are similar to the patterns followed by labour migrants. They may create a dense network of institutions and communities which provide emotional and material support, warmth and moral control. Like labour migrants, they also set up a variety of associations to service the community; for the purpose of furthering entrepreneurship, service delivery, the nurturing of culture and religion, looking after the young generation and so on. Kinship networks are intertwined with these associations which may negotiate and compete for resources and opportunities through ethnic mobilisation. The refugees existing as a minority before exile tend to be faster and more efficient than economic migrants in this process if they had acted collectively as a minority group in their society of origin. This is partly the result of their experience and know-how about functioning as a minority group (Bonacich, 1938). The refugees altogether often have an additional advantage on labour migrants as the causes and motivations of the flight, as well as its mechanisms, frequently lead to the arrival of skilled and educated people in European and other Western industrialised societies, and also of individuals who had prior experience of associations. More human resources are therefore available to them. However, they may not so easily constitute a group in the reception society as conflicts in the society of origin may hamper the formation of groups as was the case fore Bosnian who back home found it difficult to identify one single other as alliances changed and varied according to their particular geographical location of origin.

For some Bosnian Muslims, Serbs were responsible for persecution, for others those were the Croats. Islam represented a tenuous, mostly private marker which did not seem to be the cementing feature of society in Bosnia Herzegovina. Islam which is the category as a consequence of which they had to flee their homeland, does not necessarily constitute a strong basis of group identification, particularly when they encounter Muslim groups of other national origin (much as Pakistanis in the UK).

It may also happen that no real group formation occurs when the commonality of the refugees situation and their position within the society of reception does not provide a space for the defence of their interest. For instance, Bosnians who were given the status of temporary protection were thus deprived of developing a positive motivation and a project in the society of reception. When this was compounded by the release of state subsidies, passivity was encouraged.

Other modes of social organisation developed based on the reconstitution of replacement family networks, nonetheless took place mostly in the realm of leisure activities socialisation and traditional fetes and holidays. Women tend to be more proactive in this domain.

The organisation of formal associations, imposed by the society of reception according to a model which is alien to the refugees' traditions and where their interest does not make it necessary to constitute one does not prove particularly successful (Kelly) Moreover, there may be more fragmentation among the refugees particularly those of non-minority origin, sometimes exacerbated by the resources and settlement mechanisms placed at their disposal by the reception society. Moreover, as noted above, obstacles to chain migration make it more difficult to reconstitute communities, and large scale networks in the society of reception (Gold, 1992). Instead, what might develop are international networks whereby communities become 'extraterritorialised' through the diaspora. The social organisation is often based on practices and customs brought over from the country of origin transplanted with modifications. For instance, for the Vietnamese, kinship ties are prominent and underpin much of their social interaction, whenever it is possible to reconstitute those networks, which often extend across borders. According to Ma Mung (1994) the diaspora is characterised by:

- its spacial configuration due to the multipolarity of the migration;
- the interpolarity of social relationships;
- uprootedness from its original territory and the impossibility of returning (mythical or real);
- the awareness of this situation which may lead to a 'culture of diaspora' turning it into an asset.

Goals and Meaning

The Rubicon refugees' relationship to the society of origin is important in so far as they do not look back on it. Return is not considered as an option so that they have little choice but to settle for good. In this, they differ from the Odyssean refugees whose find a meaning to their action in homeland parameters without any positive relationship with the land of reception, but also with economic migrants. The latter, in Europe, generally came with a positive motivation to improve themselves economically and intended to return home thereafter (myth of return). They came as single men joined by their families years later; only then did these populations reconstitute communities and a full array of associations as the consciousness that they were here to stay developed. For Rubicon refugees, here to stay starts with arrival; exile is perceived as definitive. They have burnt their bridges (or these have been burnt for them) with the society of origin. Their project for the future begins here and now. As a consequence, the purpose of their organisations is primarily to assist their settlement. The meaning of their action as a group is to engage with the majority society to compete for resources and opportunities but also to insure the maintenance of the group as the dislocation of their world (before exile) creates a greater need for some form of solidarity and cultural closeness. This is the dual collective goal of this refugee population as implemented through its advice centres, educational support groups, religious institutions, business associations, Saturday schools and mother tongue classes for children. The Vietnamese illustrate this situation, as they formed association to service the needs and interests in their settlement project, to 'facilitate their successful integration' (Joly, 1996) as some leaders of association stated. At the same time, they maintain their group's cultural practices through organising the celebration of their traditional festivals, the maintenance of their food culture, the teaching of their mother tongue. Ethnic mobilisation to further these goals occurs when the structure of the reception society makes a space for its achievements. For minorities which have a diasporic dimension international networks will be harnessed to further the interests of the group in countries of settlement. These constitute the best ideal type of the stranger as analysed by Simmel (1964): objective to and free from country of origin but also of arrival. However, Rubicon refugees who have lost their identification with the society of origin may also take longer before they find a new meaning in their society of settlement, for lack of a positive motivation and the potential despondency associated with it.

Factors Shaping the Groups

To a certain extent, Rubicon refugees are more than any other subject to the influence of the reception society. The outcome of their group formation will be largely determined by host-related factors. If the institutions of the society of settlement gives recognition to ethnic groups and grants advantages on this basis, it is likely that ethnic mobilisation will occur. This can also result in the greater fragmentation of this population within which different groups compete for resources. However, ascription from outside and the discrimination or advantages deriving from it are likely to prompt the formation of new groups while the settlement industry may lead to divisions and fragmentation within groups as it creates a scope for exacerbated competition for resources. This accentuates the diversity and divisions characteristic of a refugee group (political affiliation, religion, gender, age, class, level of education). As a consequence, this may result in what Gold (1992) called 'a third pattern of adaptation in which distinct localised networks play a central role' (p. 229), alongside the two poles of community-wide mobilisation and assimilation. One important factor influencing the groups is whether they are defined as refugees by host societies or not. It has important implications for groups self-definition and patterns of adaptation. The legal status of the refugees, and particularly the rights associated with it have an impact on the forms of organisation and their thrust. The policies of the reception society vis-à-vis immigrants and refugees also have an impact. Where benefits cater for most aspects of material life, the groups organise to meet cultural and social needs. This is exemplified by the Kurds in Finland and Britain (Wahlbeck, 1999). Where these benefits are reduced or absent associations service all aspects of everyday life such as business, housing, education, and a multiplicity of others. If no space is made for ethnic 'bargaining', ethnicity when it leads to a group formation will remain private and be used as a channel of internal solidarity for the purpose of business, support, cultural and social interaction. Differences in status deepen the divisions between refugees and labour migrants of the same origin and may create divisions among the refugee group. Whether the group is or is not defined as refugees by the host society has important implications for the group's self-definition and process of settlement. And altogether the attitudes of the wider society are preponderant. One negative outcome is possible although less frequent. The fact that the refugees did not have a positive motivation in their flight and had not formulated a definite plan for the future runs the risk of causing a move towards separation and withdrawal. Discrimination on the part of the reception society and lack of opportunities may be compounded by long-term dependency on the state. The two factors combined may bring about a double marginalisation, from the society of origin and of reception. One case in point is that of the *harkis* from Algeria in France (Arab-Berber collaborators with the French army during the Algerian war of independence). Bosnians are a case in point who had lost the hope that it would be possible to live in their society of origin ever again because of the conflict had torn it apart beyond recognition. They were thus not animated by a return project. At the same time the policy of temporary status implemented in the society of reception impeded them from formulating a positive project of settlement. They lived in the temporality of exile without having a positive return project. their main interaction was with the society of reception and this could have motivated initiatives to defend the groups interest. But it is precisely the fact that the society of reception was over-riding, which made its negative premisses more significant.

Conclusion[3]

We have established that the refugees' pattern of group formation and social interaction with the society of reception must be examined in relation to their position within and vis-à-vis the structure of conflict in the society of origin. Two main types are thus identified which follow differing paths and strategies. The structure of the reception society influences these respective types in a differentiated manner.

Odyssean refugees organise and act collectively according to the cleavages which existed before exile and in relation to the homeland society. The construction, maintenance and reproduction of their social organisation will be determined and modified according to factors which affect the political project vis-à-vis the society of origin. Rubicon refugees, on the other hand, organise themselves primarily in interaction with and through the influence of the structure of conflict in the society of reception. In this they resemble labour migrants, and their patterns of group formation, sometimes in the shape of ethnic group and ethnic mobilisation.

Despite their divisions, their suspicions (because of past persecutions) and the fragmentation of their communities with reduced transplanted networks, both types of refugees form some kind of group or groups and regroup geographically. Their purpose is to re-establish themselves as actors, either in the society of reception (Rubicon refugees) and/or in the society of origin (Odyssean refugees) or possibly in the diasporic community to find meaning and support in their communities, in order to rebuild the social world shattered by exile.

Notes

1   Naturally there exists some literature on the refugees per se but it remains disproportionately little. Moreover it must be noted that throughout this chapter the term refugee is not used according to legal definitions but in a broad sociological sense.
2   See the subtitle of Vasquez and Araujo (1990), *Exils latino-américains: la malédiction d'Ulysse* (my emphasis).
3   Part of the latter section of this chapter was published in Joly, 2002.

References

Back, L. (1996), *New Ethnicities and Urban Culture*, London: UCL.

Ballis Lal, B. (1986), 'The "Chicago School" of American Sociology, Symbolic Interactionism, and Race Relations Theory', in J. Rex and D. Mason (eds), *Theories of Race and Ethnic Relations*, Cambridge: Cambridge University Press, pp. 280–98.

Barth, F. (1969), *Ethnic Groups and Boundaries*, London: Allen & Unwin.

Basch, L. Glick Schiller, N. and Szanton Blanc, C. (1994), *Nations Unbound, Transnational Projects, Post-colonial Predicaments, and Deterritorialised Nation-states*, Langhorne, PA: Gordon and Breach.

Bauman, G. (1997), 'The Making and Unmaking of Strangers', in P. Werbner and T. Modood (eds), *Debating Cultural Hybridity*, London and New Jersey: Zed Books, pp. 29–46.

Bauman, Z. (1997), 'Dominant and Demotic Discourses of Culture: their Relevance to Multi-ethnic Alliances', in P. Werbner and T. Modood (eds), *Debating Cultural Hybridity*, London and New Jersey: Zed Books, pp. 193–209.

Bolzman, C. (n.d.), 'Stages and Modes of Incorporation of Exiles in Switzerland: the Example of Chilean Refugees'.

Bonacich, E. (1938), 'A Theory of Ethnic Antagonism: the Split Labour Market', *American Sociological Review*, 38 (October), pp. 583–94.

Brah, A. (1991), 'Difference, Diversity, Differentiation', *International Review of Sociology*, New Series 2, pp. 53–72.

Caglar, A.S. (1997), 'Hyphenated Identities and the Limits of "Culture"', in T. Modood and P. Werbner (eds), *The Politics of Multiculturalism in the New Europe*, London and New York: Zed Books, pp. 169–86.

Campani, G., Catani, M. and Pallida, S. (1987), 'Italian Immigrant Associations in France', in J. Rex, D. Joly and C. Wilpert (eds), *Immigrant Associations in Europe*, Aldershot: Gower.

Candappa, M. and Joly, D. (1994), 'Local Authorities, Ethnic Minorities and "Pluralist Integration"', Monographs in Ethnic Relations No. 7, CRER, University of Warwick.

Clifford, J. (1994), 'Diasporas', *Cultural Anthropology*, 9 (3), pp. 302–38.

Commission for Racial Equality (1985), *Ethnic Minorities in Britain: Statistical Information on the Pattern of Settlement*, London: CRE.

de Rudder, V. and Goodwin, P. (1993/4), 'Theories et débat sur le racisme en Grande-Bretagne', *L'homme et la société*, Paris: L'Harmattan.

Drury, B. (1995), 'Ethnic Mobilisation: Some Theoretical Considerations', in J. Rex and B. Drury (eds), *Ethnic Mobilisation in a Multicultural Europe*, Aldershot: Avebury, pp. 13–22.

Eisenstadt, S.N. (1954), *The Absorption of Immigrants*, London: Routledge and Kegan Paul.

Faist, T. (1999), 'Developing Transnational Social Spaces: the Turkish-German Example', in L. Pries (ed.), *Migration and Transnational Social Spaces*, Tyne and Wear: Athenaeum Press, pp. 36–73.

Friedman, J. (1997), 'Global Crises, the Struggle for Cultural Identity and Intellectual Porkbarrelling: Cosmopolitans versus Locals, Ethnics and Nationals in an Era of De-hegemonisation', in P. Werbner and T. Modood (eds), *Debating Cultural Hybridity*, London and New Jersey: Zed Books, pp. 58–70.

Geertz, C. (1963), *Old Societies and New States – The Quest for Modernity in Asia and Africa*, Glencoe Illinois: Free Press.

Glazer, N. and Moynihan, D. (eds) (1975), *Ethnicity: Theory and Experience*, Cambridge, MA: Harvard University Press.

Gold, S.J. (1992), *Refugee Communities*, London: Sage.

Goldring, L. (1999), 'Power and Status in Transnational Social Spaces', in L. Pries (ed.), *Migration and Transnational Social Spaces*, Tyne and Wear: Athenaeum Press, pp. 162–87.

Gordon, M.M. (1978), *Human Nature, Class and Ethnicity*, Oxford: Oxford University Press.

Hall, S. (1990), 'Cultural Identity and Diaspora', in J. Rutherford (ed.), *Identity, Community, Culture, Difference*, London: Laurence and Wishart.

Hall, S. (1992), 'New Ethnicities', in J. Donald and A. Rattansi (eds), *'Race', Culture and Difference*, London: Sage.

Hily, M.-A. and Poinard, M. (1987), 'Portuguese Associations in France', in J. Rex, D. Joly and C. Wilpert (eds), *Immigrant Associations in Europe*, Aldershot: Gower.

Jenkins, J.C. (1983), 'Resource Mobilisation Theory and the Study of Social Movements', *Annual Review of Sociology*, pp. 527–53.

Jenkins, R. (1986), 'Social Anthropological Models of Inter-ethnic Relations', in J. Rex and D. Mason (eds), *Theories of Race and Ethnic Relations*, Cambridge, Cambridge University Press, pp. 170–86.

Jenkins, R. (1997), *Rethinking Ethnicity*, London: Sage.

Joly, D. (1987a), 'Associations amongst the Pakistani Population in Britain', in J. Rex, D. Joly and C. Wilpert (eds), *Immigrant Associations in Europe*, Aldershot: Gower, pp. 62–85.

Joly, D. (1987b), 'Mosques and Islam as a Minority Religion', Committee on the Comparative Study of Muslim Societies, Conference on Muslims under Non-Muslim Rule, Delhi, 14–19 December.

Joly, D. (1996), *Britannia's Crescent: Making a Place for Muslims in British Society*, Aldershot: Avebury.

Joly, D. (2002)'Odyssean and Rubicon Refugees: Towards a Typology of Refugees in the Land of Exile', *International Migration*, 40 (6), pp. 3–25.

Kelly, L. (2002), 'Programme, Policies, People: the Interaction between British Social Policies and Bosnian Refugees', PhD thesis, University of Warwick.

Khan, S.V. (1977), 'The Pakistanis: Mirpuri Villagers at Home and in Bradford', in J. Watson (ed.), *Between Two Cultures*, Oxford: Basil Blackwell, pp. 57–89.

Kunz, E. (1981), 'Exile and Resettlement: Refugee Theory', *International Migration Review*, 15 (1–2), pp. 42–51.

Kunz, E.F. (1973), 'The Refugee in Flight: Kinetic Models and Forms of Displacement', *International Migration Review*, 7 (2), pp. 125–46.

Lapeyronnie, D. (1993), *L'individu et les minorités La France et la Grande-Bretagne face à leurs immigrés*, Paris: PUF.

Ma Mung, E. (1994), 'Groundlessness and Utopia: the Chinese Diaspora and Territory', paper presented at international conference 'The Last Half-century of Chinese Overseas (1945–1994)', 19–21 December, University of Hong Kong.

Marx, K. (1973), *Surveys from Exile*, ed. and intro. by D. Fernbach, Harmondsworth: Penguin Books.

Massey, D.S., Arango, J., Hugo, G., Kouaouci, A., Pellegrino, A. and Taylor, J.E. (1993), 'Theories of International Migration: A Review and Appraisal', *Population and Development Review*, 19 (3), pp. 431–66.

Olzak, S. and Nagel, Y. (eds) (1986), *Competitive Ethnic Relations*, London: Academic Press.

Rex, J. (1986), *Race and Ethnicity*, Milton Keynes: Open University Press.

Rex, J. and Moore, R. (1967), *Race, Community and Conflict: a Study of Sparkbrook*, London: Oxford University Press.

Rex, J., Joly, D. and Wilpert, C. (eds) (1987), *Immigrant Associations in Europe*, Aldershot: Gower.

Richmond, A.H. (1988), 'Sociological Theories of International Migration: the Case of Refugees', *Current Sociology*, 36 (2), pp. 7–25.

Schierup, C.-U. (1994) 'Multi-culturalism and Ethnic Mobilisation: Some Theoretical Considerations', in J. Rex and B. Drury (eds), *Ethnic Mobilisation in a Multi-cultural Europe*, Aldershot: Avebury.

Simmel, G. (1964), *The Sociology of George Simmel*, ed. K.H. Wolff, New York: Free Press.

Smith, A. (1986), *The Ethnic Origins of Nations*, Oxford: Blackwell.

Smith, R. (1999), 'Reflections on Migration, the State and the Construction, Durability and Newness of Transnational Life', in L. Pries (ed.), *Migration and Transnational Social Spaces*, Tyne and Wear: Athenaeum Press, pp. 162–87.

Touraine, A. (1997), *Pouverons-nous vivre ensemble? Egaux et differents*, Paris: Fayard.

Vasquez, A. and Araujo, A.M. (1990), *Exils latino-américains: la malédiction d'Ulysse*, Paris: L'Harmattan.

Verhoeven, M. (1997), *Les mutations de l'ordre scolaire, régulation et socialisation dans quatre établissements contrastés*, Louvain-la-Neuve: Academia-Bruylant.

Wahlbeck, O. (1999), *Kurdish Diasporas: A Comparative Study of Kurdish Refugee Communities*, Basingstoke: Macmillan.

Wallman, S. (1986), 'Ethnicity and the Boundary Process in Context', in J. Rex and D. Mason (eds), *Theories of Race and Ethnic Relation*, Cambridge: Cambridge University Press.

Wieviorka, M. (1992), *La France raciste*, Paris: Seuil.

Wieviorka, M. (1994), 'Ethnicity as action', in J. Rex and B. Drury (eds), *Ethnic Mobilisation in a Multicultural Europe*, Aldershot: Avebury, pp. 23–9.

Wirth, L. (1928), *The Ghetto*, Chicago.

Withol de Wenden, C. (1994), 'Changes in the Franco-Maghrebian Association Movement', in J. Rex and Drury, B. (eds), *Ethnic Mobilisation in a Multicultural Europe*, Aldershot: Avebury, pp. 106–15.

Yinger, M. (1986), 'Intersecting Strands in the Theorisation of Race and Ethnic Relations', in J. Rex and D. Mason (eds), *Theories of Race and Ethnic Relation*, Cambridge: Cambridge University Press, pp. 1–19.

Zolberg, A.R., Suhrke, A. and Aguayo, S. (1989), *Escape from Violence: Conflict and the Refugee Crisis in the Developing World*, Oxford: Oxford University Press.

Chapter 8

Interrogating Identity, Ethnicity and Diaspora: Three Case Studies of the Ethnic Chinese*

Chan Kwok Bun

I would like to begin this chapter with an autobiographical note. Sociologists rarely take on a comparative project. Over the past decade, I happened to have the privilege and the fortune of doing fieldwork on the ethnic Chinese of three different places: Thailand, Singapore, and Hong Kong. Thailand has been my research site since I went from Canada to Southeast Asia in 1987 where the ethnic Chinese are a significant minority group in economic terms. The only place in Southeast Asia where the ethnic Chinese are a majority group, Singapore was where I taught for 14 years. Born in China, I grew up in Hong Kong and left for Canada for university studies in 1969; I returned to Hong Kong in 2001. Between 1980 and 1987, I published several works on the Chinese of Canada (Chan, 1983, 1987; Chan and Helly, 1987). The changing, multiple ethnic identities of the Hongkongers since the return of the former British colony to China in 1997 have been a matter of deep personal and scholarly concern to me. In the past three years, I have published three book manuscripts on, respectively, the ethnic Chinese of Thailand (Tong and Chan, 2001), Chinese business networks (Chan, 2000), and the social history of Singapore (Chan and Tong, 2003). In a way, the two strands of research, on the identities of the ethnic Chinese and on the Chinese business networks, have come to a head – precisely at a moment when I am using the occasion of writing this essay to reflect on the ethnic Chinese experiences of the three places – all in an attempt to interrogate words such as Chinese diaspora, identity, ethnicity, and Chineseness. I hope to critique existing, as well as offer alternative, ways of conceptualising what it means to be Chinese in the post-modern world. Not entirely satisfied with the Chinese diaspora term but not able to find a substitute, I wonder what it means to be hyphenated, to carry one's house and home on one's back, to exist in a transit, third zone 'where words do not stick' (Alexander, 1999) because one is sometimes much better off to remain nameless when language fails.

Thailand

In our earlier attempt to study and rethink the case of the ethnic Chinese in Thailand (Chan and Tong, 1993), we made several assertions. Firstly, we underscored the continuous need for alternative conceptualisations to the Skinnerian idea of assimilation (Skinner, 1957a, 1957b, 1962, 1973) and for creative theory-building in race and ethnic relations studies. Secondly, methodologically speaking, this need is best met by focusing one's sociological gaze at how the ethnic Chinese go about conducting themselves as a group and as persons in their daily social transactions with those of their own kind and with 'others'. The sociologist is to sample a wide range of 'ethnic relations situations' unfolding in their natural settings (Lal, 1990, p. 164), circumstances of contacts, mixings, crossings, traversings and interminglings – all toward a phenomenology and anthropology of everyday interethnic life. Human actors continue to meet their own needs by trying out a myriad of strategies in daily social transactions. Thirdly, with the above theoretical and methodological considerations, we argued that assimilation cannot be seen as a one-way, lineal process of the Chinese becoming Thai. Rather, it is a two-way process which, in the long run, will leave the Chinese with something Thai, and the Thais with something Chinese. Such a process highlights the mutual, reciprocal, multidimensional, multidirectional and syncretic character of culture contact – itself a problematic, highly complex, human drama. Fourthly, we noted the tenacious persistence of Chinese ethnicity in modern-day Thailand.

There is also the reality of cultural and social modernisation in contemporary Thailand. In recent decades, both the Thais and the Chinese have been exposed to outside Western or, if you like, global elements during the modernisation and industrialisation of Thailand. It is not only that the Chinese and the Thais have become more like each other because the Chinese are assimilated into the Thai culture (and vice versa), but also because both are, to a certain extent, assimilated into a common, new cultural and social environment. As observed by Bao (2001), Western influences cross ethnic and class boundaries. As a process started at the time of the original formation of the Thai capitalist class in the middle of the nineteenth century, Western style consumerism as well as the reciprocal relationships between Western consumer culture and class status are by now deeply entrenched in the Thai social structure and social order. Amara (2001) thus viewed this process in terms of the Chinese *and* the Thais *both* making adjustments to the national capitalistic development ideology of the Thai government – and thus becoming increasingly similar to each other. It is a process of two dissimilar cultures evolving a shared culture, perhaps a third cultural zone, between themselves as a result of common exposure to the powerful homogenising effects of a third global force, that of capitalism and consumerism.

Of course, there is also the anthropology of intra-ethnic diversity or heterogeneity. Despite mutual ethnic stereotyping that accentuates in-group sameness and between -group differentness, the Thais and the Chinese themselves are not homogeneous ethnic groups. For most ordinary Thai people, the concept of ethnicity seems abstract enough; the majority do not feel able to talk about it. In the Thai language, the word ethnicity is rather problematic. There seems to be no equivalent Thai word for ethnicity. The closest term used by Thai anthropologists is *Chaad Phalli* (birth race) which only makes sense to the academics. To the lay people, the concept of ethnicity can only be described in separate terms, *chya chaad* (race), *Phaa Saa* (language), *caariid themnian* (tradition and/or custom), etc. In present-day Thailand, apart from the southern region, there are three major subethnic Thai groups: the Siamese in the central region, the Laos in the northeastern region, and the *Khon Muung* in the northern region (which are further subdivided into many more, smaller cultural groupings). Each of these subethnic groups has a distinct identity of its own. Geographical movements of these subethnic groups, as a result of wars or economic conditions, have reshaped the boundaries of these cultural regions and transformed many parts of the country into a multicultural society of different subethnic groups and diverse sets of cultural standards. In general, the Thais do not seem to have an integrated, whole concept of ethnicity.

For the ethnic Chinese, their ethnicity is not based on a common set of cultural or sentimental attachments either. Chinese ethnicity in Thailand derives from various historical backgrounds, different dialect groups and many plural forms of cultural practices – though most still identify themselves as 'Chinese'. Among Chinese of the same dialect group, one witnesses changes in cultural practices due to discrepant cultural interpretations among different generations, hence the diversity and heterogeneity observed. As it happens, there is no single set of Thai cultural practices into which one can say the Chinese are assimilated. Neither can one say all Chinese share the same cultural pattern in their encounters with the Thais.

While articulating our critique of the classical idea of assimilation as such, we of course have not lost sight of the reality of a Sino-Thai morality being constructed, as Bao (2001) put it, out of an emerging synthesis, 'a *combination of Chinese Confucianism and Thai Buddhism which influences their ethnic identity*'. What results is a Sino-Thai morality shaped by their Chinese past (wherever they *are from*), albeit adapted, and by the Thai society where they have lived and put down roots (wherever they were *at* and headed towards as a personal as well as collective ethnic project). To Bao, as she has discovered in her studies of marriage rituals practised among the Sino-Thai, these two aspects are 'deeply intertwined and virtually inseparable'.

Ethnicity is invoked and, sometimes, 'manufactured' in the host society, not simply imported or transplanted wholesale from the past (Chan, 1997; Chan and Ong, 1995). While it is true that immigrants bring along with them an 'original' culture that shapes their initial behaviours, it is the structural (thus, sociological, not cultural) conditions in the local *context* that will significantly shape their long-term adaptation patterns – an idea anticipated by Yancey (1976) in his formulation of the 'emergent ethnicity' concept. In the long haul, immigrant culture and ethnicity is rarely transplanted as is, but rather reproduced and produced, deconstructed and reconstructed, in exploitation of structural advantages as well as in adaptation to structural constraints.

What emerges here is the synthesis of two or more cultures – such a process unites and integrates, but does not completely homogenise the groups in question (Chan and Tong, 1993, p. 147). Following Glazer and Moynihan (1970) who first stressed the processual, emergent and transformative character of integration in interethnic contacts, Femminella (1961) coined the concept of *impact* to articulate 'a booming collision (of two or more cultures) resulting in a forced entanglement ...'. Postiglione (1983, pp. 22–3) suggested that 'out of the process of impacting and integration evolves a new synthesis which gives a new meaning and importance to the developing nation' – the myriad forces of this culture contact yield a creative, adapted, transformed ethnicity, a kind of syncretism, or hybridity.

The above discussion has provided us with the necessary theoretical building blocks for the construction of a conceptual model within which a comprehensive analysis of Chinese (and, for that matter, Thai) ethnicity in Thailand (and in much of Southeast Asia) can be undertaken. The model would consist of five intertwined elements: Firstly, *differential Chinese ethnicity* or '*differential Chineseness*' due to intra-ethnic differences in place, generation, class, religion, language, and gender; secondly, 'differential Thainess' due to the same factors bearing on the first element; thirdly, influences of global culture, trade flows and transnationalism subsumable under at least three subentities: global and local capitalistic consumerism and material culture; the Chinese transnational economy with its numerous interlocking modes and networks that transcend political and geographical boundaries; and accelerated economic growth of the People's Republic of China (and, perhaps, correspondingly, re-sinification as a possibility); fourthly, national political socialisation, Thai citizenship and nation-building; and fifthly, influence of the local place, local history and local customs throughout Thailand in creating a common civic identity shared by all ethnic groups in residence (Pornchai et al., 2001). This model maps out the orbit within which culture contact takes place; it takes special notice of the plausibility of dynamic interactions as well as mutual and reciprocal influence between the Chinese culture and the Thai culture; between the global, the national and the local; and also the macro, the mezzo and the micro. More importantly, the model explicitly recognises and allows for the coexistence of seemingly contradictory forces – thus the tension between them and the strategies adopted to resolve such tension – for example, sameness and differentness, globalisation and indigenisation, the global/transnational and the native/local, homogenisation and differentiation, national integration and ethnic maintenance, and so on. It views ethnic identification as much a tension-ridden process as it is complex, interactional and dynamic, thus underscoring its emergent, evolving, dialectical character, all in the context of self-others encounters, at a multiplicity of levels. As a new configuration, a new Rubric's cube of Chinese-Thai ethnicity, larger but little-known factors like the Chinese transnationalism need to be taken into account seriously, so is the homogenising and integrative role of socio cultural and economic realities of Chinese-Thai encounters at the national as well as the local, village levels – the anthropology of shared place, shared history, shared nationality, shared civic identity (Pornchai et al., 2001).

Given its aspirations to comprehend the ethnic realities operating on multiple levels and being shaped by multiple, and sometimes contradictory, forces, the model has its fair share of paradoxes. Contact between cultures and groups has potential integrative *and* divisive consequences; it creates conditions for cooperation and fusion, as well as for conflict and differentiation, partly because sameness and differentness are simultaneously accentuated by the groups' co-presence. Also, global culture homogenises group differences but is rarely not met with the respective groups' own idiosyncratic attempts at indigenisation and incorporation through invoking the socio- psychological mechanisms of perception, selection and infiltration. Local cultures strive to decide when and in what form they are being homogenised by the global culture – thus the paradox of homogenisation, indigenisation, sameness *and* differentiation (Roberts, 1992). Homogenisation in intent is not necessarily followed by homogenisation in process, certainly not in consequence. While the Chinese and the Thais begin to strive towards a common civic identity at the local, village level by virtue of having a shared place and shared history, or towards a national identity as Thai citizens by virtue of their participation in the political socialisation process and in nation building, the equally potent countervailing forces of resinification because of the emerging economic significance of China cannot be ignored – given the continuing identification of the Thai-Chinese with business interests. The calculus of ethnic identification has many permutations. The sociologist is often faced with a *new ethnicity, each time, every time.*

Ethnic identification is often a process of working out the contradictions and tensions of maintaining one's own *and* becoming like others, or, possibly in the course of time, of creating a *third* cultural space, a marginal area, a shared community in which all parties can partake, communicate, cooperate and *do things together*. In the case of Thailand, this third culture, this third space, is an outgrowth of mutual cultural borrowing, of multiple two-way cultural flows, of hybridisation. What will emerge, as Ang (1993, p. 13) put it, are 'new forms of culture at the collision of two: hybrid cultural forms out of a productive, creative syncretism'.

At the very least, in Thailand, Chinese of middle class (or higher) background, the professional and business elite of the third, fourth generations, owe their ethnic and cultural sustenance to all of these sources: Chinese and Thai (and their varieties), the local, the national, the global, and the transnational. However, the tenacity and persistence of Chinese ethnicity and sentiments in contemporary Thailand is still repeatedly observed today; the Chinese in Thailand still continue to identify themselves as Chinese and maintain their ethnic distinctiveness and consciousness. Much of the time, they probably engage in what Hurh and Kim (1994, p. 190) called 'additive or adhesive sociocultural adaptation' resorted to by Korean immigrants in America: though absorbed into the host society both culturally and socially, 'such assimilation would not replace or weaken any significant aspect of Korean traditional culture and social networks'. Spivak (1990) would call this 'strategic essentialism'. The ethnic person has a primary, core ethnic identity, an inner self (Lebra, 1994), a constant, best nurtured and expressed in private. This is his master ethnic identity, his 'central life interests' (Dubin, 1992). He also has a secondary ethnic identity, a Goffmanian 'presentational self' (Lebra, 1994), a variable, the acquisition of which is anthropologically problematic. Just like the core ethnic identity, this *presentational ethnic identity* needs to be acquired, internalised, nurtured, displayed and validated (Chan and Tong, 1993, p. 146). As Nagata (1991, p. 277) pointed out, everywhere, the modern-day man and woman, 'whether Chinese or others, must simultaneously manage their identities, statuses and relationships in the states where they set anchor'. They invoke their identity *in context. By* strategically balancing these multiple identities, they open up many more options for themselves – they have increased their 'degree of freedom'. They have widened their choice in their deliberations about their ethnicity; like Lifton's (1970) Protean man, they wear different masks on different theatrical stages; their competence is in 'staging' (Tong and Chan, 2001). In an importance sense, this 'pick-and-choose' ethnicity (or call it symbolic ethnicity, if you like) is itself a potent cause of 'differential Chineseness' – of the heterogeneity and multiplicity observed amongst the Chinese within and outside Thailand, in Southeast Asia, everywhere.

In an essay tracing the history and sociology of knowledge as far as the study of Chinese overseas in Southeast Asia is concerned, Qiu (1990) identified three waves of theoretical ideas. The first wave was that of 'ethnic persistence theory' right after the war – which saw the ethnicity of Chinese in Southeast Asia as unchanging, ever persistent. Victor Purcell (1965) was the theory's chief proponent. The dominant image of the overseas Chinese was that of a sojourner who always looked homeward – China. Overseas Chinese were studied as a window to a larger agenda of understanding China. To loosely paraphrase two Chinese sayings: 'Change is coped with by no change'; and 'All changes in the periphery are finally traceable to the origin, the centre' – China. The intellectual spirit here was rather akin to what critics in the field of cultural studies now call essentialism. At the crest of the second wave was of course the extremely influential idea of assimilation advocated by Skinner in the late fifties in his famous works on the Chinese in Java and Thailand. His prediction that the Chinese in Thailand would have completed their assimilation by the fourth generation was a well-known one within the academic as well as the policy making communities. As an idea, assimilation can perhaps be seen as a counter-reaction, an antithesis, to the earlier thesis of ethnic persistence. The two ideas represented two contrasting orientations on the part of the theorists as well as the Chinese themselves. According to the former, one looks towards, or some say, backward to, China. According to the latter, one orients oneself towards Thailand – to solve 'the Chinese problem', assimilation is the only way out. Or so they say.

If the ideas of ethnic persistence and assimilation represented two polarities, the Chinese as individuals and groups/communities on the one hand, and the theorist on the other, were faced with the dilemma of choice. As it happened, the dilemma turned out to be more apparent than real upon a *discovery* of the complexity of 'the Chinese problem' – and perhaps of most instances of ethnic group relations. What has emerged is a third idea, a third image of the Chinese, a third ethnicity which is a product of structural and cultural integration. Borne out of an intellectual heritage that speaks vehemently of pluralism and a variety of multi-culturalisms, this third wave stresses the *multiple faces of ethnicity* while interacting with the social structures of class, politics, gender, generation, and so on. In contemporary Thailand, there are many ways of being Chinese and, for that matter, of being Thai.

Several core concepts inform this third wave, this third ethnicity. The first is the discovery of one's *multiple rootedness;* it conjures up an image of plurality, not singularity, of a succession of sinking roots as process, and of multi-stranded roots as outcome (Chan 1997, p. 207). Each and every Chinese is at the tension point of a multiplicity of forces intersecting with each other, be they nationalism, neo-colonialism, transnationalism, localism, capitalistic consumerism, traditionalism, modernism, and so on. A related concept is that of hybridity borne out of multiple rootedness and consciousness. The ethnic actor is forever mixing and mixed, forever crossing, traversing, translating linguistically, culturally and psychically. He is not either/or, but both. Thainess interacts with Chineseness. The third concept is 'enabled' or 'made possible' by the first two: that of *positionality.* Because of his plural consciousness and hybridity, to the ethnic actor, identity is mere positioning. The ethnic actor invokes his identity in context; his ethnic competence is in what Berger (1986, p. 68) calls alternation, which is 'the possibility to choose between varying and sometimes contradictory systems of meaning'. In alternating his identities, an ethnic Chinese person of Thailand develops 'the perception of oneself in front of an infinite series of mirrors, each one transforming one's image in a different conversion' (Berger, 1986, p. 77). A Chinese thus has as many selves or faces as the number of mirrors he cares to hold up for himself or herself. This metaphor stresses the agency of the ethnic actor though the real sociological drama in reality is not all romance because the validity of a face presented is in part determined by the extent to which it is *socially* recognised. Identity alternation has its own limits and is often a matter of social and political permission by others (Chan and Tong, 2001).

Singapore

In Singapore, what used to be a Chinese 'community' has by now largely disappeared. Traditionally and partly due to British policies, the Chinese were segregated from the other ethnic communities. They tended to live in close-knit and clearly marked out territorial areas. However, rapid urban renewal and development and ethnically integrated housing policies have by and large broken down these physical boundaries and mixed the various communities.

In modern-day Singapore, territoriality, language, and religion no longer serve as markers of ethnicity for *all* Chinese. Rather, these factors have become part of a contested discourse in defining ethnicity. The core features of ethnicity have over time become closely tied to ascriptive features of phenotype, bloodline and lineage, resulting in a strong sense of sociological boundary, of who can and cannot be a Chinese. A person is 'born Chinese', cannot become 'un-Chinese'; people from other races who adopt 'Chinese cultural values' cannot and will never become or be accepted as Chinese. It is probably this sense of exclusiveness that provides the bonds holding together a Chinese 'community' in Singapore – in spite of the loss of place (Rushdie, 1988, p. 63).

The fragmentation of Chinese ethnicity manifests itself on many fronts. There are severe differences in whether language is a defining characteristic of Chineseness. One thus observes great diversity, multiplicity and heterogeneity in conceptions of being Chinese. Among the Chinese-educated, Chinese language is central; among the English-educated, it is filial piety. Among the older Chinese, it is a sense of China as homeland (which itself is quickly disappearing), while among younger Chinese, one observes a 'disembedding' of place in that China and homeland have become unimportant in their sense of Chineseness. For them, being born in Singapore, a sense of ancestral place is missing. Many have never been to China and have little sense of what it is like. For the few who visited China, they came back with very negative feelings. This disembedding process is important to note as it allows one, at one level, to define the uniqueness of Chinese in Singapore, that is, they are Singaporean Chinese, as opposed to the 'China Chinese', 'Taiwanese', 'Hong Kong Chinese', and so on. At the same time, the ascription to blood and lineage allows the Chinese in Singapore to identify and affiliate with the Chinese worldwide, when the appropriate contexts present themselves.

There are in fact disembeddings at several levels and at different points of time and place. On one level, there was a disembedding of the self from mainland China, Chinese history, culture, tradition and heritage, resulting in a sense of loss of place; and on another level, disembedding from the local community in Singapore. This is important in articulating a discourse on the unity and diversity, sameness and differentness, of Chineseness in Singapore. It allows, in a sense, an individual to say that 'I'm a Chinese, they are also Chinese, but they are *so different from me*'. The self, over time, has experienced a closer identification with family and family history rather than community or community organisations. Identity has become more individualised, personalised, or if you like, subjectivised. A movement of ethnic identity being tied to the individual self is becoming more prevalent. Finally, there is a separation of self-identity from nationality. It is no longer necessary to be a citizen of China to be Chinese, and there is no problem for them to be 'Singapore Chinese', to be *both* Singaporean *and* Chinese, to be Singaporean precisely by being ethnically Chinese. One may surmise that once outside Singapore, the Singapore Chinese, like those from Hong Kong, Taiwan, America, and Europe, will decide whether or not to attach, and how much, importance to their Chinese label, to their nationality, thus enjoying some liberty in articulating their sameness versus differentness in the arena of the Chinese transnational space. This may well be their strength.

Ethnicity is no longer entirely ascriptive. This new ethnicity, whether symbolic (Gans, 1979) or emergent (Yancey et al., 1976), will wear as many masks as individual members care to present themselves and to others. Ethnicity is a variable (Cohen, 1974, p. XV) in terms of differences in manifestation. The ethnic actor, at any point of time and place, has in front of him or her a plurality of 'identity options on offer' (Rex and Josephides, 1987). One face (racial), many masks (cultural), or none.

One often-discussed issue in the journalistic literature on Chinese business is the motive behind the rush by ethnic Chinese from Southeast Asia, including Chinese Singaporeans, to invest in mainland China since 1979 (Chan and Beoy, 1999, 2000). One widely held view (especially among Indonesian newspapers) is that 'overseas Chinese', including Chinese Singaporeans, invest in China for emotive reasons, particularly to participate in the development of their ancestral homeland. Such a perception may have been true before the 1950s. Wang (1995) suggested two models of this perception. The first is the Tan Kah Kee model. Tan Kah Kee, a Chinese businessman who was loyal to his motherland, China, mobilised financial resources in Malaya and Singapore and channelled funds to China to fight the Japanese during the World War II. After the war, Tan donated a large sum of money to help build China, before eventually returning to his homeland for good. Under this model, Wang (1995, p. 21) argued, 'philanthropy was extended to cover investments in local industry, but mainly to support the philanthropic projects that had been started' in a person's hometown. This type of philanthropy is almost extinct among present-day Singaporean Chinese businessmen, especially the younger entrepreneurs.

In an earlier study (Chan and Tong, 2000) of Chinese Singaporeans doing business in China, we found sufficient differences in cultural ethos and business conduct that set the two peoples apart. A mainland Chinese sees socialising with his business associates as part of 'the deal' whilst keeping himself busy in inferring the latter's moral character and judging whether he is sincere, honest, trustworthy, worthy of a relationship, and so on. Unlike the Singaporean, the China Chinese does not separate the social, moral, and economic realms of his business conduct, seeing all of them equally integral to the larger whole. A mainland Chinese businessman works with a minimum of written agreements while relying on trust, sincerity and goodwill to realise verbal agreements and to orally interpret the written. The spoken substantiates and fills in the written. He also prefers a slow, gradual build-up in his business conduct – his conception of time differs markedly from that of a Singaporean. As far as the mainland businessman is concerned, this emphasis on the social, moral, oral, and temporal realms of his business conduct lends himself readily to the creation, development and maintenance of *quanxi* networks. As socia/interpersonal relations, *quanxi* is precarious and thus requires vigilant accommodation and adjustment on the part of both parties. In China, *quanxi* is fundamental to business success, a fact the Singaporean businessman feels uncomfortable about but has learned not to ignore.

Hong Kong

One way to read Wong's recent essay (1999) on Hong Kong Chinese identities is to pay attention to the language he uses while describing Hong Kong's contemporary situation. He used words and phrases such as 'troubled by doubts and uncertainties, difficulties and dilemmas'; 'an articulate sense of unease in the community'; and 'a transition that has been complex, subtle and profound'. In describing identities of the Chinese in Hong Kong, he used such descriptors as 'mixed and ambivalent'; 'mobile, not fixed to a locality'; 'split'; 'multiple and pluralistic'; 'flexible and situational'; 'diverse'; and so on. Purists looking for things fixed, unchanging, homogeneous will be disappointed.

Hong Kong is a transitional society, a society in flux, which has engendered a multiplicity of historical experiences for the individual – among the most salient were experiences of emigration, immigration, and return migration or 'experimental migration'. These multiple experiences with psychosocial transitions inscribe onto the identity many *layers of meaning*. As such, these experiences, together, force the sociologist to think and rethink, many times over. Theorising about identity in a postmodern world is a tricky, complicated business.

Identity is a slippery thing. It is elusive, hard for the theorist to pin down; it is complex and multifaceted because it is sometimes displayed or positioned depending on the nature of the audience, or, to use a social psychological phrase, the presence of the other. As such, the form or symbolic value of identity as intended by the ethnic actor should be as interesting as its contents or substance, whatever they may be.

Wong constructed four types of Hong Kong identities on which I offer the following observations. First, as prototypes and as persons, the loyalists (to China), the locals, the waverers (between the orientations of the first two types), and the cosmopolitans do not exist in isolation of each others. Each is positioned in the presence of others, thus sharpening each other's identities – sort of one mirroring the other in a complicated context of rational dialectics. What separates them, though not necessarily perpetually, is their unequal access to class resources or capital, which necessitates a materialist conceptualisation of identity. This relational dialectics suggests numerous sites of tension between and amongst the four identities (for example, between the locals and the cosmopolitans) – indeed a goldmine for the sociologists. Secondly, as Wong rightly pointed out, one's identity is rooted in family experiences partly because identity, like love, is too important a matter to be left to the individual. Family sociologists have noted this fact long, long ago. Migration is a family affair. But it will be naïve on the part of the sociologist to assume homogeneity of identity patterns within a particular family. A façade of family harmony uniting husband and wife, parents and children, is either a methodological artefact or a front a family desires to project onto itself or to the world. A family identity can hardly subsum individual identities without some degree of coercion or violence by the powerful against the powerless.

My third observation has perhaps been anticipated by Wong's typology itself. Theoretically speaking, an individual can come in and out of these four types of identities, perhaps many times in one's life time. This observation thus bears out an important principle of identity: that of indeterminacy.

Wong's fourth type, the cosmopolitans, interests me a great deal. For them, home is where he hangs his hat. The compression of time and place in a post-modern world lands him inadvertently in a multiplicity of circumstances. Adaptability and pragmatism is his ticket to survival. Before the theorist gets too carried away by his romance with his cosmopolitans, Wong reminds us that while 'such a form of modernity has its dynamism and its charm', others may find this way of life not so endearing. Moralists or nationalists demand 'authenticity', 'sincerity' and commitment. They may find the cosmopolitans' or even the waverers' indeterminacy morally wanting, if not offensive. Hybridity is enabling because it puts one in the best of all possible worlds. Much has been written about this by the postmodernists. But hybridity can also be disabling because the hybrid man or woman has to live with others, sometimes bringing forth discrimination by the other. Hybridity as identity thus has its own psychic costs. In a sense, Park (1928) and Stonequist (1937) had long anticipated this dark side of the double or multiple consciousness in their classical writings on the marginal man. Though expanded in their intellectual horizons and unstrained in their movements, the hybrid man has his moments of nervousness. Others must ask questions about his identity, or more precisely, his allegiance. A study of identity is as much a study of the self of the person, as of the other and the latter's capacity for tolerating difference. The question of identity is thus first and foremost a political one.

Discussion and Conclusion

In a recent essay, Wang Ling-chi (1991, pp. 181–206) constructed five different types of Chinese identity in terms of *variant* orientations of Chinese overseas to China, the various host countries in the West and Southeast Asia, and different meanings attached to one single Chinese word, *gen* (roots). They are *yeluo guigen* (fallen leaves return to the roots, the origin, the soil), or the classic, 'old-fashioned' sojourner mentality; *zancao chugen* (to eliminate grass, one must pull out its roots), or total, complete assimilation; *luodi shenggen* (settle down or 'sink roots' in a foreign land and accommodate to the host society), or accommodation, not assimilation; *xungen wenzu* (search for one's roots and ancestors, return to China, to the ancestral village), or ethnic pride and consciousness; and *shigen lizu* (lose contacts with one's roots and ancestors), or the uprooted, the alienated, the 'wandering intellectuals away from their roots in historic China', in exile.

In addition to these five types of identity, the identity of the Chinese transilient, the new middle class, the transnational Chinese bourgeoisie may well represent – a sixth, new, emergent type (Chan, 1997). He has long since overcome or exorcised his desire to search for and sink his roots back in ancestral China. He may or may not go back; he has a choice; he has always made efforts to strive for integration, *without assimilation*, in whatever country of abode he happens to find himself; strictly speaking, he is not really experimenting with accommodation in the host society, either because he cannot see himself settling down and sinking his roots in any one single place or because his consciousness is not tied to one origin, one ethnicity, but to many. A new ethnicity each time, every time. Neither is he the classic, much caricatured 'uprooted' migrant, sad, unhappy, spiritually dispossessed, disgruntled, alienated, disheartened with the present *and* the past because he finds both dissatisfying and unacceptable, thus suspended in the air, rootless or uprooted, unable to go home again, psychically and physically speaking.

One may call this sixth emergent type of Chinese identity *zhonggen,* or multiple rootedness or consciousness. The Chinese word *zhong* has three meanings: first, multiple, not singular; second, regenerative, as in 'born again'; third, to treasure, to value (one's many diverse roots). It conjures up an image of a succession of sinking roots as process and multi-stranded roots as outcome. It is akin to what Lee (1991, p. 215) called 'Chinese cosmopolitanism.' Himself calling the term a loose epithet, Lee further explained it as 'one that embraces both a *fundamental intellectual commitment* to Chinese culture and a multicultural reciprocity, which effectively cuts across all conventional national boundaries' (emphasis added). It is, in other words, 'a purposefully marginal discourse'. To a Chinese cosmopolitan, again in Lee's words, 'the boundaries are again not so much geographical as intellectual and psychological'. Of course, I am aware that, in a certain discourse, roots or *gen* always means ground, earth – the antithesis of trans-locality. There is thus the potential paradox of a translocal, indeed transoceanic, rootedness – a decidedly mixed image.

With this sixth new, emergent type of Chinese identity, he is perhaps the first, 'old fashioned' sojourner type, reconstructed, and brought 'back in vogue, in a rather more respectable form' (Nagata. 1991, p. 277). The new cosmopolitan is not the nineteenth-century sojourner, forever yearning to return to China, to go home, in mind or body. The new overseas Chinese *may or may not* go home, just like his Jewish contemporaries, muttering quietly and privately to themselves, 'Next year in Jerusalem, *every* year.' (Clifford. 1993). Yet at any one given time and place, he is also sojourning, not intent on eventually going home to China, but rather, willing to go anywhere, everywhere, provisionally. It is his provisionality that seems particularly salient and needs to be foregrounded. He makes a chronicle of brief appearances in a succession of geographic places, but always on the world stage. He has a suitcase at the door, always ready to go.

Lest this be mistaken for or confused with the idealist's notion of a romantic, cosmopolitan man with absolutely no physical, materialist anchorage – the *wugen* (the rootless), the one who does it all *without* (*wu* in Chinese) roots, transcending it all, who may or may not empirically exist – the 'sixth' type being sketched here is one in whom 'a certain *elemental* awareness of Chinese identity at its most basic seems to *persist* uninterrupted beneath the surface (emphasis added)' (Nagata, 1985, p. 22). He may or may not 'spontaneously invoke a Chinese identity in context'. Or, as Ang (1993, p. 14) put it, 'sometimes it is and sometimes it is not useful to stress our Chineseness, however defined.

In other words, the answer (to the question, why still identify ourselves as 'overseas Chinese' at all?) is *political.*

My three case studies of the ethnic Chinese of Thailand, Singapore, and Hong Kong have unearthed several ideas about the ethnic persons as individuals and in a group, which can now be used to 'interrogate' the 'Chinese diaspora' label. The first idea of differential Chineseness or Chinese variety, that Chinese everywhere taken as a whole are *varied* and *heterogeneous* in composition, is an empirical reality that is often glossed over or outrightly ignored, whatever the underlying motives. They are indeed less similar than they seem (to the outsiders, the non-Chinese). The internal homogeneity or sameness of the ethnic Chinese as a group is a social construction of those external to the group – the social psychology of intergroup perception. For instance, not all Chinese in Asia are successful businessmen. Not all successful businessmen in Asia are Chinese (Chan and Ng, 2000). Not all Chinese in Asia aspire to become entrepreneurs, at least, not now anymore – the claim that ethnic Chinese naturally possess business acumen, we now know, is an artefact, a myth. But this stereotypical artefact persists in contemporary Thailand and, I argue, throughout Southeast Asia. I argued elsewhere (2000) that many of them may well be 'reluctant merchants', having been 'pushed' by society and family into a career in business because of blocked opportunities in the profession and the bureaucracy in many Southeast Asian countries. The observed internal heterogeneity of the Chinese as a group can be tested empirically as well as logically if the sociologist decides to focus his gaze at the gender and generation politics that divide the Chinese family, the harmony of which is another populist allegation (Chan and Dorais, 1998). As members of a quickly developing field of studies, observers of the ethnic Chinese worldwide seem more interested in (and thus know more about) forces that integrate the family and the community than opposite forces that divide, disturb and disembed.

One may want to couple the Chinese variety idea with the idea of emergent culture of the Chicago School of symbolic interactionism. Here the sociological gaze is at the personal and group conduct of the ethnic Chinese while acculturating themselves into the many, varied cultures of the host society. The outcome of this process is as varied as it is unpredictable partly because the process is sometimes conflict-laden, and other times less so, largely depending on the orientations and policies of the respective nation-states. I have documented this process of deliberating on the identity options on offer (Rex and Josephides, 1987) on the part of Hong Kong immigrants making adaptation in Singapore (Chan, 1994). Their ethnicity paradox (Lal, 1990,

p. 3) is a real one, not simply for academic consumption. My idea of multiple rootedness as the sixth type of identity of the ethnic Chinese is one possible outcome of this process which is unfolding everyday in different parts of Asia. The Southeast Asian societies are indeed as heterogeneous as the sociologist can imagine (Chan and Tong 1993). What happens to such a multiply-rooted identity in an ethnically heterogeneous society? There is not a singular ethnicity for one to assimilate into – thus my 'discovery' of the complexity of the problem. In my studies of the ethnic Chinese of Thailand, I introduced Berger's idea of alternation – that an ethnic person alternates, changes, mutates in form and structure, oscillates between positions as identities and ethnicities – or, positionality as identity, positionality to replace identity as concept. Thus this rather graphic, dramatic image of one face, many masks – Chinese now, not Chinese later; one type of Chinese now, another type later, depending on the nature of the audience. The Chinese cosmopolitan is forever 'on stage', always engaged in some form of performance – the Goffmanian actor, the Parkian marginal man par excellence. I now have an idea of identity firmly grounded in heterogeneity and hybridity, which fascinates as much as it abhors the nationalists who insist on borders, boundaries, purity, loyalty, oneness, singularity.

Conceptualised and properly understood as such, and in the theoretical and empirical terms I have discussed in this essay, the ethnic Chinese the world over do not constitute a diaspora like the Jews or the Greeks do. In Cohen's (1997, p. 25) 'consolidated list of the 'common features' of a diaspora', an adaptation of Safran's (1991) list, five out of the nine features of his diaspora make reference to homeland, home which is remembered, idealised and, sometimes, returned to by a dispersed people who seem compelled to find various ways in a foreign land to make themselves more similar than before to each other – thus their alleged 'strong ethnic group consciousness' and 'coethnic empathy and solidarity' (Cohen's other diasporic features). As I attempt to show in this essay, all these descriptors and narratives are untenable as far as the ethnic Chinese case is concerned. As Wang (1999) might have intimated, there are Chinese diasporas, in their plural or, may I add, pluralistic form and structure, not a singular, unified Chinese diaspora the world over. A historically informed study of these 'Chinese diasporas' that take family histories and generations seriously will remind us that this alleged orientation of ethnic Chinese towards China as homeland, imaginary or not, is at best empirically untenable, and at worst politically harmful or even dangerous (the recent race riots against the ethnic Chinese of Indonesia may be a case in point). Wirth, in his preface to Mannheim's *Ideology and Utopia* (1991), reminded us that 'since the world is held together to a large extent by words, when these words have ceased to mean the same thing to those who use them, it follows that men will of necessity misunderstand and *talk past one another*'. While looking for a better vocabulary, itself a task of much import, the term diaspora-as-heterogeneity (Mckeown, 1999) is problematic. For one, I would much prefer to think in terms of the ethnic Chinese *of* Thailand, not *in* Thailand, certainly not of the Chinese diaspora in Thailand. The dispersal idea suggests a traumatic, involuntary separation followed by a yearning for unity, unification, of going home, of favouring the origin, the pure – the lack of (or, the variation from) which suggests, torture, suffering and agony. I find this empirically untenable. As I argued elsewhere (Chan, 1997), Chinese families separate as a coping strategy now in order to unite later – a deep paradox traceable to the family portfolio idea in economics.

Now, does this mean nothing holds the ethnic Chinese together anymore? I think there is. And I think the cementing factor is a symbolic, or if you like, a sentimental one. It takes the form of an idea, an ideology (thus a utopia), a sentiment, an *awareness* of the individual Chinese as an ethnic person belonging to a borderless, groundless, non-ground, non-physical, extra-territorial, imagined space (Ma Mung, 1998) which I am struggling to find a word to name. So, the ethnic Chinese person can be here, there, and everywhere, simultaneously. Whether this feeling will take the form of an affinity, a 'coethnic empathy and solidarity', an 'ethnic advantage' to be exploited for business or other causes is a sociological problematic never to be taken for granted. The Chinese businessmen of Singapore have only recently come to this sober realisation when they invest in China. It is hard to disagree with Wirth's (1991, p. xxv) assertion that 'a society is possible in the last analysis because the individuals in it carry around in their heads some sort of picture of that society'. But then, what can one do or what is one supposed to do with this picture in the head? My feeling is that the 'usefulness' of this picture has been exaggerated in the literature on the ethnic Chinese and their business (Chan, 2000).

Note

*   A shorter version of this chapter, bearing a different title, appears in Wong-Siu-lun (ed.) (2003), *Comparative Perspectives on the Chinese and Indian Diasporas*, Hong Kong: Centre of Asian Studies, University of Hong Kong.

References

Alexander, M. (l999), 'Ethnic Selves, Auto-biographical Identities', paper presented at Department of English Language and Literature, National University of Singapore, 14 August.

Amara, P. (2001 'Chinese Settlers and their Role in Contemporary Thailand', in Tong Chee Kiong and Chan Kwok Bun (eds), *Alternate Identities: The Chinese of Contemporary Thailand*, Singapore: Times Academic Press, and Leiden: Brill Academic Publishers, pp. 85–106.

Ang Ien (1993), 'To be or Not to be Chinese: Diaspora, Culture and Postmodernist Ethnicity', *Southeast Asian Journal of Social Sciences*, 21 (1), pp. 1–17.

Bao Jiemin (2001), 'Sino-Thai Identity: Married Daughters of China and Daughters-in-law of Thailand', in Tong Chee Kiong and Chan Kwok Bun (eds), *Alternate Identities: The Chinese of Contemporary Thailand*, Singapore: Times Academic Press, and Leiden: Brill Academic Publishers, pp. 271–98.

Berger, L.P. (1986), *Invitation to Sociology. A Humanistic Perspective*, Harmondsworth: Penguin.

Chan Kwok Bun (1983), 'Coping with Ageing and Managing Self-identity: The Social World of the Elderly Chinese Women', *Canadian Ethnic Studies*, 15 (3), pp. 36–50.

Chan Kwok Bun (1991), *Smoke and Fire: The Chinese in Montreal*, Hong Kong: Chinese University Press.

Chan Kwok Bun (1994), 'The Ethnicity Paradox: Hong Kong Immigrants in Singapore', in R. Skeldon (ed.), *Reluctant Exiles? Migration from Hong Kong and the New Overseas Chinese*, Armonk, NY: M.E. Sharpe, pp. 308–24.

Chan Kwok Bun (1997), 'A Family Affair: Migration, Dispersal, and the Emergent Identity of the Chinese Cosmopolitan', *Diaspora*, 6 (2), pp. 195–214.

Chan Kwok Bun (2000), *Chinese Business Networks: Economy, Culture and Society*, Singapore: Prentice Hall and Copenhagen: Nordic Institute of Asian Studies.

Chan Kwok Bun (2000), 'State, Economy and Culture: Reflections on the Chinese Business Networks', in Chan Kwok Bun (ed.), *Chinese Business Networks: State, Economy and Culture*, Singapore: Prentice Hall and Copenhagen: Nordic Institute of Asian Studies, pp. 1–13.

Chan Kwok Bun and Dorais, L.J. (1998), 'Family, Identity, and the Vietnamese Diaspora', *Sojourn*, 13 (2), pp. 285–308.

Chan Kwok Bun and Helly, D. (eds) (1987), 'Coping with Racism: the Chinese Experience in Canada', Special Issue. *Canadian Ethnic Studies*, XIX (3).

Chan Kwok Bun and Ng Beoy Kui (2000), 'Myths and Misperceptions of Ethnic Chinese Capitalism', in Chan Kwok Bun (ed.), *Chinese Business Networks: State, Economy and Culture*, Singapore: Prentice Hall and Copenhagen: Nordic Institute of Asian Studies, pp. 285–302.

Chan Kwok Bun and Ng Beoy Kui (2001), 'Singapore', in E.T. Gomez and M.H.H. Hsiao (eds), *Chinese Business in Southeast Asia*, Surrey: Curzon, pp. 38–61.

Chan Kwok Bun and Ong Jin Hui (1995), 'The Many Faces of Immigrant Entrepreneurship', in Robin Cohen (ed.), *Cambridge Survey on World Migration*, Cambridge: Cambridge University Press, pp. 523–31.

Chan Kwok Bun and Tong Chee Kiong (1992), 'Rethinking Assimilation and Ethnicity: the Chinese in Thailand', *International Migration Review*, XXVII (1), pp. 140–68.

Chan Kwok Bun and Tong Chee Kiong (2000), 'Singaporean Chinese Doing Business in China', in Chan Kwok Bun (ed.), *Chinese Business Networks: State, Economy and Culture*, Singapore: Prentice Hall and Copenhagen: Nordic Institute of Asian Studies, pp. 71–85.

Chan Kwok Bun and Tong Chee Kiong (2001), 'Positionality and Alternation: Identity of the Chinese of Contemporary Thailand', in Tong Chee Kiong and Chan Kwok Bun (eds), *Alternate Identities:The Chinese of Contemporary Thailand*, Singapore: Times Academic Press, and Leiden: Brill Academic Publishers, pp. 1–8.

Chan Kwok Bun and Tong Chee Kiong (eds) (2003), *Past Times: A Social History of Singapore*, Singapore: Times Editions.

Clifford, J. (1993), 'Sites of Crossing: Borders and Diasporas in Late 20th century Expressive Culture', *Cultural Currents 1*, Program for Cultural Studies, East-West Centre, 1 (3–4).

Cohen, A. (1974), 'Introduction', in A. Cohen (ed.), *Urban Ethnicity*, London: Tavistock, pp. ix–xxv.

Cohen, R. (1997), *Global Diasporas: An Introduction*, London: UCL Press.

Dubin, R. (1992), *Central Life Interests: Creative Individualism in a Complex World*, New Brunswick, NJ: Transaction.

Femminella, F.X. (1961), 'The Impact of Italian Migration and American Catholicism', *American Catholic Sociological Review* (Fall), pp. 223–41.

Gans, H. (1979), 'Symbolic Ethnicity: the Future of Ethnic Groups and Cultures in America', *Ethnic and Racial Studies*, 2 January, pp. 1–20.

Glazer, N. and Moynihan, D.P. (1970), *Beyond the Melting Pot*, Cambridge, MA: MIT Press.

Hurh Won Moo and Kim Kwang Chung (1993), 'Adhesive Sociocultural Adaptation of Korean Immigrants in the United States: an Alternative Strategy of Minority Adaptation', *International Migration Review*, XVIII (2), pp. 188–215.

Lal, B.B (1990), *The Romance of Culture in Urban Civilisation: Robert E. Park on Race and Ethnic Relations in Cities*, London: Routledge.

Lebra, T.S. (1994 'Self in Japanese Culture', in N.R. Rosenberger (ed.), *Japanese Sense of Self*, Cambridge: Cambridge University Press, pp. 105–20.

Lee, L.O. (1991), 'On the Margins of the Chinese Discourse: Some Personal Thoughts on the Cultural Meaning of the Periphery', *Daedalus*, 5, pp. 239–73.

Lifton, R.Jay (1970), *History and Human Survival*, New York: Random House.

Ma Mung, E. (1996), 'Groundlessness and Utopia: The Chinese Diaspora and Territory', in E. Sinn (ed.), *The Last Half Century of Chinese Overseas*, Hong Kong: Hong Kong University Press, pp. 35–48.

Mannheim, K. (1991), *Ideology and Utopia*, London: Routledge.

Mckeown, A. (1999), 'Conceptualising Chinese Diasporas', *The Journal of Asian Studies*, 58 (2), pp. 306–37.

Nagata, J. (1984), 'Religion, Ethnicity and Language: Indonesian Chinese Immigrants in Toronto', paper presented at the Symposium on Changing Identities of the Southeast Asian Chinese Since World War II, Australian National University, Canberra, Australia, June.

Nagata, J. (1991), 'Local and International Networks Among Overseas Chinese in Southeast Asia and Canada', in B. Mathews (ed.), *Quality of Life in Southeast Asia*, Canadian Council for Southeast Asian Studies XX, No. 1, Canadian Asian Studies Association, pp. 255–81.

Park, R.E. (1928), 'Human Migration and the Marginal Man', *American Journal of Sociology*, May, pp. 881–93.

Pornchai, T., Chan Kwok Bun and Tong Chee Kiong (2001), 'Wang Tong: Civic Identity and Ethnicity in a Thai Market Town', in Tong Chee Kiong and Chan Kwok Bun (eds), *Alternate Identities: The Chinese of Contemporary Thailand*, Singapore: Times Academic Press and Leiden: Brill Academic Publishers, pp. 227–70.

Postiglione, G.A. (1983), *Ethnicity and American Social Theory: Towards Critical Pluralism*, Lonham: University Press of America.

Purcell, V. (1965), *The Chinese in Southeast Asia*, London: Oxford University Press.

Qiu, Li (1990), 'Changes in Ideas in Studies of Southeast Asian Chinese', paper presented in Conference on Overseas Chinese Communities toward the 21st Century, Singapore.

Rex, J. (1987), 'Introduction: The Scope of a Comparative Study', in J. Rex, D. Joly and C. Wilpert (eds) (1987), *Immigrant Associations in Europe*, Aldershot: Gower, pp. 1–10.

Rex, J. (1973), *Race, Colonialism and the City*, London: Routledge and Kegan Paul.

Rex, John and Josephides, S. (1987), 'Asian and Greek Cypriot Associations and Identity', in J. Rex, D. Joly and C. Wilpert (eds) (1987), *Immigrant Associations in Europe*, Aldershot: Gower, pp. 11–41.

Roberts, M.(1991), '"World Music" and the Global Cultural Economy', *Diaspora*, 2 (2) (Fall), pp. 229–42.

Rushdie, S. (with G. Grass) (1988), 'Writing for a Future', in B. Bourne et al. (eds), *Writers and Politics*, Nottingham: Spokesman Hobo Press, pp. 52–64.

Safran, Wi. (1991), 'Diasporas in Modern Societies: Myths of Homeland and Return', *Diaspora*, 1 (1), pp. 83–99.

Skinner, G.W. (1957a), *Chinese Society in Thailand: an Analytical History*, Ithaca: Cornell University Press.

Skinner, G.W. (1957b), 'Chinese Assimilation and Thai Politics', *Journal of Asian Studies*, 16, p. 238.

Skinner, G.W. (1962), 'The Thailand Chinese: Assimilation in a Changing Society', lecture presented at the Thai Council of Asian Society.

Skinner, G.W. (1973),'Changes and Persistence in Chinese Cultures Overseas: a Comparison of Thailand and Java', in J.T. McAlister (ed.), *Southeast Asia: the Politics of National Integration*, New York: Random House, pp. 383–415.

Spivak, G.C. (1990), *The Post-Colonial Critic*, ed. S. Harasym, New York: Routledge.

Stonequist, E.V. (1937), *The Marginal Man: a Study in Personality and Culture Conflict*, New York: Russell & Russell.

Tong Chee Kiong and Chan Kwok Bun (2001), *Alternate Identities: the Chinese of Contemporary Thailand*, Singapore: Times Academic Press and Leiden: Brill Academic Publishers.

Tong Chee Kiong and Chan Kwok Bun (2001), 'One Face, Many Masks: the Singularity and Plurality of Chinese Identity', *Diaspora*, 10 (3), pp. 316–89.

Wang Gungwu (1995), 'The Southeast Asian Chinese and the Development of China', in Leo Suryadinata (ed.), *Southeast Asian Chinese and China: the Politico-Economic Dmension*, Singapore: Times Academic Press.

Wang Gungwu (1999), 'A Single Chinese Diaspora?', paper presented at Chinese Southern Diaspora Centre, Australia National University.

Wang Ling-chi (1991), 'Roots and Changing Identity of the Chinese in the United States', *Daedalus*, 120, pp. 181–206.

Whitten, N.E. and P.S. Whitten (1972), 'Social Strategies and Social Relationship', *Annual Review of Anthropology*, Vol. 1, ed. B.I. Siegel, Palo Alto, CA: Annual Review Inc., pp. 247–70.

Wirth, L. (1991), 'Preface', in Karl Mannheim, *Ideology and Utopia*, London: Routledge.

Wong Siu-lun (1999), 'Changing Hong Kong Identities', in Wang Gungwu and J. Wang (eds), *Hong Kong in China: The Challenges of Transition*, Singapore: Times Academic Press, pp. 182–202.

Yancey, W.L., Ericsen, E.P. and Juliani, R.N. (1976), 'Emergent Ethnicity: a Review and Reformulation', *American Sociological Review*, 41, June, pp. 391–403.

Chapter 9

Ethnicity, Racism and Discrimination

Michel Wieviorka

Any analysis of the links between racism and ethnicity today, must begin with a precise definition of these two concepts. I am therefore going to differentiate them analytically and then endeavour to see how they are related in the context of the European societies to which I shall confine myself in this exposé.

Ethnicity in Modernity

I will begin with ethnicity and start by pointing out that the term itself is problematic and that its use and its meaning vary considerably from one language to another. For example, the spell-check programme in French on my computer systematically rejects the word each time I use it.

In my opinion, from the outset the question of ethnicity must be formulated on the basis of a conception which incorporates the much larger concept of culture. In contemporary European societies, ethnicity is a special form of cultural identity. It belongs to a much larger set of identity phenomena. Some are relatively close to it, or contribute to defining it, like religion or language; national identity is different mostly on political grounds in so far as the national project aspires to a state. Other identities are even more remote; I have in mind in particular those associated with gender, or again with a chronic illness or disability, like deafness, for example.

Ethnicity is often reduced – particularly in everyday language – to the idea of an essence of a primordial nature, inherited from a past which is said to go back almost as far as the beginning of time, and whose present manifestations are said to be the proof of its capacity to resist the rise of modernity, political domination, colonisation or yet again, in more economic terms, the destruction by capitalism, money and markets. It is obvious that we have to break with this type of representation and, instead, ask a sociological and historical question: in the ethnicities which we observe, how much is related to reproduction, and therefore resistance to modernity, and how much is related to production. Usually, ethnicity has dimensions which make of it an inheritance from the past, the transmission of characteristics specific to a group with a history, or at least, steeped in a temporal dimension. From this point of view, it is a projection of the past into the present, and possibly a form of resistance. But it is also, and much more so than is usually assumed, an invention, a production, the construction of an identity. This production is itself a complex process; it owes a great deal to the actors themselves, but also, on the one hand, to the society in which they live, the systems of action in which they are embedded, and on the other, to the existence of traditional elements which they may borrow, reconstruct, and *'cobble together'* to use Claude Lévi-Strauss' well-known words. The ethnicity of social anthropologists, in Africa or in Asia, owes a great deal to a logic of reproduction and, in particular, to the role of the colonisers, who have contributed considerably to its invention, and which they themselves may have contributed to forging. Today, in Europe, it is often to a large extent, a production in which actors construct a past which may or may not be mythical, a culture which in reality has scarcely known any previous existence; or else they find a language which they revive but which is nevertheless very different from this language as it was spoken one or two centuries previously.

One paradox is that the level of production of ethnicity is all the more active as our societies are; more modern and individualistic; what some would call hypermodern, others postmodern; the greater the degree of ethnicity. Contrary to an oversimplified idea, it is a mistake to contrast two sociological images, – one stressing the rise of individualism and the other very differently stressing phenomena of identity, communitarianism, the return to religious themes, tribalism the rise of ethnic identities, and others. It is quite the reverse: the emergence of identities owes a great deal to the rise in individualism which sustains them. To belong to an identity is increasingly an individual choice, an assertion of the self as subject, as the personal actor of one's own life. To use an old terminology, cultural identities, including ethnic ones, tend to be in the sphere of *achievement* and not of *ascription*. In France, young people of immigrant origin are choosing to be either Arab or Muslim; it is a personal decision which is often the outcome of intense work on the self, and moreover, one which can always be reviewed. Naturally, the importance of personal subjectivity should not lead us to underestimate the weight of either the group or the community of origin, or the way in which other people perceive them. These are individuals who are often racialised and are pressurised to define themselves as different. This is a well-known mechanism which Sartre strongly illustrated while speaking of Jews, as he explained that the Jew is nothing other than the creation of the anti-Semite. 'It is the anti-Semite who creates the Jew', he says.

These remarks could be formulated in a totally different way. If ethnicity is indeed a production, and not only a reproduction of a form or a resistance to modernity, if it is linked with modern individualism and not opposed to it, then any sort of evolutionism should be totally eliminated from our analyses. I think that contemporary ethnicity is one way in which our societies invent tradition, and that the level of production of tradition depends on the degree of modernity. Hypermodernity involves the invention of an increasingly abundant and varied set of traditions, amongst which is ethnicity, by which I mean ethnic groups.

Ethnicity, Social Inequality and the Naturalisation of Culture

The production of ethnicity is to a large extent the outcome of the interaction between on one hand the system and other actors and on the other hand the ethnic actors. In a period of growth, relative economic prosperity, and confidence in the future, ethnicity develops in a way which is relatively random in social terms; it is not particularly associated with processes of poverty, downward social mobility, or with an unbearable degree of inequality. This for example was true of the end of the 1960s and the beginning of the 1970s in Europe when ethnic identities began to be asserted – or reasserted – as such; in France, for example, we saw the emergence of regional identities, but also of Jewish identity which became ethnicised, breaking with the Republican model of assimilation inherited from the Enlightenment and Napoleon 1. But more recently, it is obvious that the question of ethnicity has become closely linked to exclusion, the *underclass*, poverty and also downward social mobility, especially when it is a question of 'poor whites' who become ethnicised in a nationalist mode. It would be interesting to envisage more specifically the relationship between the rise of forms of identity, in this instance, ethnic identity, and social change specifically speaking. Let us simply say that it is not enough to stress poverty or exclusion. Another dimension of the production of ethnicity is that it may, on the contrary, also be associated with wealth or with the material well-being of groups for whom the control of capital and considerable resources goes along with cultural assertions which may assume an ethnic dimension.

Amongst the poorest or the most threatened populations, ethnicity, is produced, in part at least, or reinforced by the processes in which the most wealthy and most influential groups, or quite simply those who are best placed to do so, deprive the weakest and the most highly dominated, of access to resources, money, employment, health, education and accept or promote discriminatory forms of behaviour or social segregation. This can easily be linked with cultural differentiation and, by extension, with racial differentiation. In situations where a social definition of self becomes difficult, or impossible, people may be led to adopt another definition in cultural terms; this is the path of ethnicity. Therefore the production of ethnicity is closely linked to racism, which conveys to victims that they are different, and with the social processes of exclusion and precariousness. It can also be observed that in industrial society there was a powerful and central working class movement embedded in the conflictual relationship which structured all collective life. This social definition of people meant that there was less need for them to assert an ethnic identity than in post-industrial society in which the structural and structuring relationships which characterised the class conflict are no longer present.

Nonetheless, some will say that at the time of industrial society there were many immigrant workers who were frequently quite specifically ethnicised, by which I mean characterised by their difference. In France, for example, immigrant workers in the 1950s and 1960s were socially integrated at work and culturally excluded. They remained confined to their home cultures, took little part in civic life, lived in immigrant hostels with other immigrants, spoke their own language and had only one idea – to go back home and to live in their own culture. This brings me to a very important point: ethnicity today in Europe is very different from what we meant a few years ago. It is no longer a characteristic of groups or distant peoples living in other parts of the world – what I would tend to refer as the ethnicity of social anthropologists. It is not even the characteristic of groups which are isolated from the rest of society, who may be integrated socially but are culturally very marginal and do not envisage any sort of integration. If we are interested in ethnicity today it is because it is present at the very heart of our societies, of which it is a constituent element – a participant in community life. To put it differently: ethnicity may indeed come from without and therefore be an aspect of the questions posed by immigration. But in fact it is, and will increasingly be, a problem internal to our own societies, a social problem, similar to racism – often a factor which contributes to its production. I might add that this does not mean that the boundaries of ethnic groups coincide with those of the society and the state under consideration: ethnicity is also a transnational phenomena – an element of the diaspora.

Tensions within Ethnicity

At least, some of these remarks can be summarised by using the image of a triangle of ethnicity, which I suggested in my book *La démocratie à l'epreuve* (1993). This triangle defines the space within which ethnic actors move, circulate or, on the contrary, settle. One apex refers to the collective identity of the actor and, more specifically, to communitarianism. This identity is itself a mixture which includes references to culture and others to nature. Another apex refers to the fact that the actor participates in the social and political life of the society in which he lives. He is not external to it. He is a person who, like others, expresses himself, consumes, works, wants to have access to health and educational facilities for his children, and so on. Finally, a third apex refers to the actors' subjectivity; he wishes to construct his life, make choices, work out his own trajectory, his own existence and, as far as possible, be in control of his personal biography.

Within this space, some people clearly choose the apex of collective identity at the risk of encountering sectarianism or the ghetto. Others, on the contrary, avoid collective identity; some prefer to participate as individuals in modernity and others to assert their personal subjectivities by, for example, taking part in cultural expressions which have little to do with ethnicity, in certain forms of music, dance or literature for example. However, many also move around as best they can, endeavouring, despite difficulties, to articulate the individualism of participating in modern life, personal subjectivity and belonging to a collective identity. Danièle Joly and I were thus able to see that this image of a triangle within which the actors move did offer young Afro-Caribbeans a pertinent representation of their identity and of their difficulties (Joly, 2001).

Racism plays here a fundamental role. On the one hand, it contributes to pushing people towards ethnicity, by saying to those who do not necessarily see themselves as different at the outset: you are different, with the colour of your skin, your name, the area where you live, you cannot be considered the equal of the Whites and those of English stock. Racism discredits, and sociologists are well aware of the mechanism by which the stigmata are reversed, in which an individual asserts himself by internalising the discourse of the dominator and reversing it: as a result of telling someone he is different, it is possible that the outcome be his appropriation of the difference which is attributed to him. And on the other hand, racism makes moving around within the triangle of ethnicity particularly difficult and particularly necessary at the same time. The person who does want to participate as an individual in modern life is rejected in the process of discrimination and segregation which encourage the assertion of collective identity. But racism, by exposing collective characteristics, specific to the ethnicities which it naturalises, pushes people into retreating into group or communities, which cannot possibly correspond to most people's desires, given the power of the attraction of consumption and money or, equally important, the desire for personal recognition. Moreover, racism exacerbates the unhappy character of subjectivity. The latter may at that point tend towards self-destruction – since I am not considered a member of the human race, I might as well disappear – either by committing suicide or by becoming a drug addict. Another possibility is the expression of the self in artistic practices in which the stigmata is not reversed but is instead sublimated. In short, racism skews ethnicity by exerting a pressure which distorts the whole area of the triangle of ethnicity.

Racism and Ethnicity

Contrary to what might have been hoped in the 1950s and 1960s, racism is not in a historical long phase of regression which would have begun with the realisation of the implications of Nazi barbarism and decolonisation. The tendency is much closer to a phase of recomposition. The most summary ideologies, the doctrines which informed what can be referred to as classical, scientific racism, have certainly been weakened, even if, in a country like the United States their immense vitality can still be observed as testifies, for example, the success of the book *The Bell Curve* by Herrnstein and Murray. But over the past 20 years, the best analysts have understood that racism is undergoing a considerable transformation. Now, on both sides of the Atlantic, this transformation has precisely been concomitant with the rise of ethnic identities, or, as some might prefer to say, the ethnicisation of our community life.

I will simply recall here what is well known to the specialists – that is, the way in which the social sciences have become aware of this transformation in the process of forging closely related concepts on both sides of the Atlantic but also on both sides of the Channel. In the United States, the term *symbolic racism* has been used to refer to the way in which prejudice with respect to Black Americans is increasingly expressed: the latter are considered to be inferior not so much for biological, physical or racial reasons but for reasons related to their culture and their presumed incapacity to adapt to the values of American society, including work which they are said to refuse, the sense of personal responsibility, effort and the family. In Great Britain, Martin Barker has coined the term 'New Racism' and has demonstrated how there is no direct reference to immigrant's natural characteristics; racism stresses this cultural difference of the immigrants; this is said to be a threat to the cultural identity of the dominant group. In France and in Belgium, several researchers have also stressed the theme of 'differentialist' or 'cultural' racism, a 'neo-racism' which is developing by stressing not so much the inferiority and physical inequality of 'races' but the incompatibility of cultures which are in fact naturalised.

This transformation in the research categories obviously corresponds to a social transformation in which cultural difference, naturalised to some extent, becomes a central issue in discussions and conflicts. Not only does it coincide with the emergence of new ethnicities which are to varying degrees the product of the immigration process; but it also coincides with transformations in which the groups become ethnicised when previously they were endowed with, or had been endowed by society with, definitions of their identity which were in no way ethnic. I will give two examples. On the one hand, the Jews have become increasingly ethnicised throughout Europe since the end of the 1960s by which I mean that they no longer adhere to models confining them either to isolation in the ghetto, or to assimilation, or quasi-assimilation, and that they are increasingly visible in the public sphere, while continuing to participate in the general life of the society to which they belong. On the other hand, Black Americans who, until the 1980s were primarily defined in physical terms, are now increasingly gaining a degree of recognition which ethnicises them by making of them a cultural group endowed with a memory and a culture; in these cases they are referred to as African-Americans. It must be recognised that the racism of post-industrial societies, is neither solely a heritage from the past, the survival of its classical, scientific forms, nor purely the product of the decomposition of the social relationships specific to the age of industry. It is of course the former and above all the latter, and is indeed closely related to the decline of the working class movement and the crisis in the institutions of solidarity and welfare specific to industrial society. But it is also intimately linked with ethnicity – a phenomenon which is expected to develop in the future. As we have seen, racism contributes to the production of ethnicity; it is also one of the forms which can be taken by the clash of ethnic groups, when they are unable to enter into an intercultural dialogue. It is the culmination of processes in which ethnic groups decline in strength, and gradually become natural rather than cultural.

But we have to be more specific here. The relationship between racism and ethnicity may correspond, in a highly paradoxical manner, to two diametrically opposed logics. The first and most obvious is the approach whereby racism conveys the opposition between one cultural, ethnic or national group, and another. In this case, racism is the opposition between two identities one of which reduces the other, and in the last resort, itself, to a race. In the second logic, an ethnic group is the victim of discrimination or, at least, of a refusal of recognition, which may go as far as taking on the appearance of racism, in the name of the universalist refusal of difference. If, for example, it is impossible to assert oneself in the public sphere in the name of a particular ethnic identity because the public sphere only recognises individuals who are free and equal in rights, we have an instance in which the refusal of the public recognition of a specific ethnic identity can become a negation of this identity; this is close to racism. In other words: racism may focus on members of ethnic groups, either in the name of other groups of the same type which are also dominated, or dominant – like the nation – or in the pursuit of universalism by refusing to allow the assertion of cultural differences in the public sphere.

This duality is not only a paradox; within Europe itself, it stands for two types of society. The first type, which is open to the recognition of cultural difference in the public sphere, is illustrated by Anglo-Saxon countries, where racism is primarily associated with the clash of ethnicities, either with one another, or with the dominant cultural group. The second type corresponds to the countries which develop or maintain an abstract form of universalism which only admits individuals to the public sphere; theoretically this is the case of France, where racism is henceforth in part at least, the outcome of the refusal of difference by the political culture of the Republic. This observation also reminds us that to build Europe we will have to find ways of articulating or harmonising political cultures which are so different that what is defined as racism for some is not necessarily so for others.

Three Positions

Let us take this argument to its logical conclusion. If ethnicity constitutes the present and the future of European societies, including in particular the most modern ones, and if racism is not only a heritage from the past but also the price to be paid given the very fact of the existence of ever more numerous and varied ethnic groups, then any consideration of the political treatment of minorities or cultural differences, and of racism, must be combined. In contemporary political philosophy there are three main democratic positions as regards cultural differences. The first can be referred to as assimilation: this position demands not only that the expression of cultural differences be forbidden in the public sphere but also that they be actively encouraged to disappear in the private sphere. This is a very 'French' hypothesis which was expressed by the Count of Clermont-Tonnerre during the French Revolution when he declared that the Jews had the right to everything as individuals but nothing as a nation. Today, this approach seems to me untenable. On the one hand, it rapidly becomes repressive; on the other, it embodies a particularly negative attitude towards the groups in question, stigmatising them to the point that it is experienced as a sort of racism. How can a child construct his or her identity, at school for example, if his family is discredited because it belongs to a minority identity which is ordered to disappear?

The second position is one of tolerance. It enables each group to do as it likes in the private sphere, and even to appear in the public sphere as long as it is not disruptive or a source of conflict. This position does tend to be less racist, at least in its universalist dimensions, but obviously, it does retain a demeaning dimension for those who are only tolerated.

Finally, a third approach, which can be described as one of recognition, pleads in favour of the recognition in the public sphere of differences which are recognised and which benefit from cultural rights. This position should not be confused with communitarianism, in so far as it demands simultaneously the respect of universal values by and for all, whereas communitarianism may permit each community to live under its own law and further its own values. It challenges universalist racism by not demeaning ethnic groups and their demands when they emerge in the public sphere; it also challenges differentialist racism, by specifically recalling the need to respect universal values, law and reason.

The conditions which promote racism in a hypermodern society in which cultural identities are many and of varying degrees are therefore those related to the way in which the latter are dealt with politically. When universalism results in their visible existence being forbidden, or when communitarianism challenges universal values, there is more likelihood of racism flourishing than when an attempt is made to find ways of articulating the two demands: respect for difference and the maintenance of universal values. This remark is valid for institutional and political actors, of course, but also for those who, in a specific minority, endeavour to navigate a course within the triangle of ethnicity.

References

Barker, M. (1981), *The New Racism*, London: Junction Books.
Herrnstein, R.J. and Murray, C. (1994), *The Bell Curve*, New York: The Free Press.
Joly, D. (2001), *Blacks and Britannity*, Aldershot: Ashgate.
Sartre, J.-P. (1954), *Réflexions sur la question juive*, Paris: Gallimard.
Wieviorka, M. (1993), *La démocratie à l'épreuve*, Paris: La Découverte.

Chapter 10

Dual Citizenship as Overlapping Membership

Thomas Faist

Introduction[1]

Dual citizenship has rapidly increased all over the world in the past decades. More and more sovereign states tolerate or even accept multiple nationalities for various reasons (Goldstein and Piazza, 1996). Even in countries such as Germany, which do not tolerate dual citizenship as a rule, about one-fourth to one-third of all naturalisations from the 1970s through the 1990s resulted in multiple citizenship (Beauftragte der Bundesregierung, 1999, p. 27).[2] This is a puzzling state of affairs. Until very recently, public opinion and political theory regarded citizenship and loyalty to a nation as indivisible. Yet the new developments now raise doubts that border-crossing ties and loyalities of citizens violate the principle of popular sovereignty and contradict full sovereignty claimed by national and multinational states.

Dual citizenship raises the fundamental question of whether citizenship across borders in democratically legitimated states can be designed in such a way that it upholds the feedback loops between the governed and the governing. Ideally, citizens are the basic law-givers in a democratic society. And, at least theoretically, all political power taming unrestrained social power flows from citizens to their elected representatives. This principle of popular sovereignty requires socially functioning communities. Empirically, we observe that citizenship – understood as the set of ties between the governed and the governing, which are based upon social and symbolic ties among citizens – has developed over time in territorially deliminated, socially relatively coherent and intergenerational political communities. Therefore, the implications of citizenship overlapping at least two political communities are in need of closer analysis, keeping in mind the two fundamental dimensions of full political membership: the legal status of equal political liberty *and* the ties of citizens amongst each other. These relations reflect citizens' affinity to a political community claiming sovereign statehood, often called a nation (cf. Weber,

1968, p. 395). Concerning the legal status of citizens, dual citizenship raises the issue whether border-crossing ties violate basic principles of democracy, such as 'one person, one vote'. As to the ties between citizens, we may ask whether loyalty is divisible, and what kinds of border-crossing ties actually affect the core of citizenship. It is only from answers to such questions that we can evaluate whether dual citizenship is an evil to be avoided, or a status to be tolerated or even accepted or welcomed.

Three perspectives throw light on the potential consequences of dual citizenship. From a stylised national viewpoint, dual citizenship can be viewed as either contributing or hindering the integration of newcomers to a political community. The specific verdict depends on whether one takes a more exclusive ethnic or a more assimilatory republican perspective. An equally stylised postnational perspective would emphasise the need for democratically legitimate procedures for making decisions 'beyond' the sovereign state in order to politically embed those border-crossing realities that impact upon citizens' lives. In such a view, dual citizenship is primarily of transitory importance only, a step from national citizenship to regional or even global citizenship. By contrast, a transstate perspective sees dual citizenship as a political and legal expression of relatively dense, continuous and life-world ties of would-be citizens and citizens themselves– with transstate ties overlapping several states.

The term used here is transstate because the analysis concerns ties spanning states but not necessarily nations. There are several multinational states such as Canada, Indonesia, India and Belgium. Within the borders of these sovereign political entities, we find ties crossing nations. It is not primarily relations within states that matter for the analysis of border-crossing phenomena, although these may become relevant in the case of civil wars and secessionist movements – just think of the conflicts between 'Turks' and 'Kurds' in Turkey, or the continuing quarrels over minority rights between 'Québecois' and the rest of Canada. In addition, border-crossing ties not only refer to nations but also to other collectives such as kinship systems, village communities, churches, religious congregations and professional groups – to name only the most obvious ones. Decades ago, the Canadian politician William Henry Moore put the difference between state and nation succinctly:

> At first sight, allegiance to a common state, appears to be the test of nationality; and in that sense the word is probably most frequently used. But the word nationality should not be confused with the word nation in the sense of a state. The state is the casing; the nationalities are the encased (Moore, 1918, p. 5).

The proposition advanced here is that dual citizenship in neither an evil nor an intrinsic value in political communities. Dual citizenship mirrors border-crossing social and symbolic ties of citizens and thus emanates from transstate life worlds. Analytically, this insight flows out of a transstate perspective. Such a vantage point analyses the potentials for exchange, reciprocity and solidarity within border-crossing spaces which are neglected or shortcut in the national perspective. And unlike the postnational-cosmopolitan perspective, the transstate view does not need to make heroic assumptions about a quantum leap of collective identity from the sovereign level state to 'Europe' or even humankind.

The following analysis firstly differentiates between nationality and citizenship. Secondly, it explicates the notion of dual citizenship and the main reasons for its growth. Thirdly, a discussion of three perspectives sheds light on the characteristics of dual citizenship – national, postnational and transstate. Fourthly, the use of these stylised perspectives allows to gauge the significance of border-crossing ties for citizens' life worlds. Ultimately, political socialisation and social cooperation within and across state borders form a societal basis for citizenship. This leads to the final question of whether dual citizenship – when viewed against national and postnational perspectives – primarily fulfils a complementary or a substitutive function.

Nationality and Citizenship

Nationality means full membership in a state and the corresponding tie to state law and subjection to state power. The interstate function of nationality is to clearly define a nation within a relatively clearly delineated territory and to protect the citizens of a state against the outside, at times hostile, world. The intrastate, or domestic, function of nationality is to define the rights and duties of members. According to the principle of *domaine réservé*, each state decides within the limits of sovereign self-determination which criteria it requires for access to its nationality. One general condition set is that nationals have some kind of close social and symbolic set of ties to the respective state, a *genuine link* (Rittstieg, 1990, p. 1402). By contrast, *citizenship* essentially concerns two broader dimensions which condition each other. Firstly, the legal status of equal individual liberty, which implies the paradoxical unity between governing and governed in a democracy (cf. Aristotle, 1962, III.1274b32–1275b21). Without democratic procedures guiding citizens' political self-determination, citizenship would be meaningless. Secondly, citizenship requires some affinity to a political community with a distinct collective identity.

The constitutions of modern states enshrine human and fundamental rights of liberty belonging to citizenship as a legal status. In general, citizens' rights fall into various realms, for example, civil rights, political rights to participation such as the right to vote and to associate, and social rights such as education, entitlements to services in case of sickness, unemployment or old age (Marshall, 1992). It is highly contested whether, to which degree and for which category of citizens there are cultural or even group-differentiated rights (for example, Kymlicka, 1995). The duties corresponding to citizens' entitlements are the duty to serve in the armed forces in order to protect state sovereignty toward the exterior, while the duty to pay taxes, to acknowledge the rights and liberties of other citizens and to accept democratically legitimated decisions of majorities structure pertain to the internal sphere (cf. Habermas, 1992, p. 371).

Also, citizenship rests on an affinity of citizens to certain political communities (cf. Rex, 1991), the partial identification with, and thus loyalty to, a self-governing collective. Normatively speaking, citizenship rests on popular sovereignty which is empirically grounded in continuous, intergenerational social and symbolic ties between citizens in a political community (Faist, 2000a, ch. 4).[3] Affiliation to a collective, expressed as a set of relatively continuous, symbolic ties of citizens otherwise anonymous to each other, is linked to the status dimension because citizenship means the formalisation of reciprocal obligations of members in a political community, akin to a social treaty (Dahrendorf. 1992, p. 116). By means of laws and official norms, government institutions hold in trust networks of reciprocity and collectives of solidarity, which cannot be produced by the state itself.

The Diffusion of Dual Citizenship

A few decades ago most states agreed that multiple citizenship should be avoided as far as possible. State laws, bilateral treaties – such as the famous Bancroft Treaties the USA concluded with European countries around the middle of the nineteenth century – and interstate conventions such as the Hague Convention of 1930 and the *European Convention on the Reduction of Multiple Nationality* (Council of Europe, 1963) bear testimony to this dominant belief. While these conventions did not carry the binding character of interstate regimes, such as the human rights regime, they guided sovereign states' declared policies. The preamble to the Hague Convention reads: 'All

persons are entitled to possess one nationality, but one nationality only'
(League of Nations, 1930). Political commentators connected dual citizenship
to treason, espionage and a whole range of subversive activities. Two rules
dominated law and state practice from late nineteenth century until the Cold
War. Firstly, acquiring a new nationality meant losing the previous one. Most
states automatically excluded a citizen from membership when this person
acquired the nationality of another state, or when other signs suggested that
a citizen expressed loyalty to foreign potentate – for example, serving in its
army or voting in elections (cf. Spiro, 1997). In many cases, countries of
immigration required release from the original nationality upon naturalisation.
Secondly, since dual citizenship could never be avoided completely, some
states dealt with the actual increase in multiple nationalities in providing for
an optional rule. Upon reaching majority age the respective person had to
choose one of the two nationalities; otherwise, they risked expatriation (cf.
Bar-Yaacov 1961, chs 5 and 10).

Despite all these provisions, dual citizenship multiplied. People continued
to migrate across state borders, settled upon their territories beyond the right
to hospitality, or even came as immigrants who were set on the road to
citizenship. Thus, dual nationality usually arose when a person was born on
the territory of a state where *jus soli* reigned supreme, while the parents of the
child held a nationality transmitted by *jus sanguinis*. Actually, all countries
have *jus sanguinis* rules. The question is whether they are supplemented by
jus soli and other regulations. In addition, increasing gender equality in law
also contributed to the rise of dual nationality. The New York Protocol of
1957 revised the status of women who automatically lost their nationality
when marrying a foreign man. Women used to be totally dependent on the
citizenship status of their husbands. Increasingly, most countries have remedied
this discrimination, and now allow for eased naturalisation to ensure family
cohesion (de Groot, 1989, p. 308). Even more far-reaching is the new *European
Convention on Nationality* (Council of Europe, 1997). This agreement demands
that both parents may transfer their nationality to their children. This rule opens
new venues for the multiplication of full state memberships.

Over the past years, a great many sovereign immigration states have made
naturalisation less and less dependent upon giving up former citizenship.
This trend clearly pervades nationality laws and regulations. For instance,
the rules of loss have changed. Some states who required release from former
citizenship now tolerate multiple nationalities to a much higher degree
– examples include France in 1973, Portugal in 1981 and Italy in 1992. It is
certainly no coincidence that emigration states outside Europe have changed

their laws to permit continued citizenship even upon naturalisation in an immigration country. Other measures include the renaturalisation of former citizens and eased access to property and heritage for former citizens. Such countries include Mexico, Turkey, Tunisia, El Salvador, Colombia and the Dominican Republic (cf. Freeman and Ögelman, 1998). Even those states who, in principle, strive to avoid multiple citizenship, usually have some exempting rules (cf. Hailbronner, 1992). In general, such rules apply when the former state refuses to release the citizen from nationality, or makes the release dependent upon unreasonable conditions; for example, the rule that young men need to serve in the army before being discharged from citizenship.

Three Perspectives on Dual Citizenship: National, Postnational and Transstate

Three models help us understand dual citizenship: national, postnational and transstate perspectives. All three vantage points emphasise the central dimensions of dual citizenship in different ways: legal status based upon equal political liberty of citizens amongst each other and the ties among citizens – which may cross state borders.

The National Perspective: Dual Citizenship as a Mechanism of Domestic Integration for Minorities

As a sort of anomaly, citizens living abroad belong to territorially and intergenerationally bounded political communities. In countries with a strong ethno-national tradition, the transmission of citizenship may proceed for several generations. It is no coincidence that many countries are usually more tolerant towards multiple memberships of their own citizens living abroad if compared to immigrant newcomers in their territory. In a national perspective there may be a strong reason for tolerating or even accepting dual citizenship. The most persuasive is that dual citizenship increases the propensity among immigrants to naturalise in the country of settlement. All available empirical surveys suggest that immigrants prefer maintaining their old citizenship when naturalising in another country (cf. Chavez, 1997, p. 131). Even more telling are actual tendencies: for example, from 1992 until 1997, The Netherlands did not make naturalisation dependent upon release from the old citizenship. During this period the naturalisation quota increased from 5 per cent to 12 per cent. By early 1997, 55 per cent of Turkish and 40 per cent of Moroccan immigrants held Dutch citizenship. Although Turkish immigration to Germany occurred around the same time as in The Netherlands and the legal non-citizen status of Turks was similar in both countries, the rate of naturalised citizens was much lower in Germany, only around 10 per cent (Groenendijk, 1999, pp. 76–9). However, there are also critics of dual citizenship from a national perspective – arguing that it creates problems of loyalty should the two respective states of membership go to war with each other (cf. Kammann, 1984).

Run-of-the mill distinctions such as the one between ethno-national and civic conceptions of nationhood and citizenship offer no guideline to evaluate *de jure* tolerance or rejection of dual citizenship. Often, analysts have contrasted countries with an ethno-national tradition and an emphasis upon the *jus sanguinis* principle are contrasted with those upholding a more civic tradition, thus complementing *jus sanguinis* with the *jus soli* principle. A common hypothesis is that citizenship laws in those countries with a civic, or republican, tradition are more amenable to naturalisation of immigrants than those with an ethno-national tradition (Brubaker, 1992). However, *jus sanguinis* on the one hand, and *jus sanguinis* complemented by *jus soli*, on the other hand, are overstylised types. Virtually all countries have additional and diverging rules – which also apply to the children of immigrants, the so-called 'second generation'. Among these are optional rules, grounding access to citizenship upon socialisation in the country of settlement such as in Sweden, or quasi-automatic access at majority age based upon birth in the country such as in France. Even when awarding optional rules to *jus sanguinis* and quasi-automatism to *jus soli*, no consistent correlation emerges between the overgeneralised dichotomy and the attitudes or rules towards dual citizenship. Quite to the contrary, *jus sanguinis* countries such as Sweden and Norway have passed (2001) the most liberal laws concerning dual citizenship, while a *jus soli* country such as the USA has consistently opposed an official acceptance of dual citizenship. Germany, where a recent reform of citizenship law (2000) has resulted in one of the most liberal rules on the European continent for the second generation – matched only by Portugal and the UK – does not officially recognise dual citizenship as a rule when naturalising new citizens. Of course, it should not be forgotten that even in such restrictive cases the reality of law has been more tolerant than the letter.

By contrast, emigration countries have been generally interested in maintaining ties to their citizens living abroad, in order to ensure the continued retransfer of economic and human capital. Moreover, quite a few emigration states have an interest in using emigrants to influence the foreign policy of immigration country governments (cf. Schmitter Heisler, 1984). While the principle of *jus sanguinis* was meant to guarantee these ties in the age of nationalism, contemporary emigration countries favour dual citizenship as the most appropriate legal mechanism.

One of the weaknesses of the national perspective on dual citizenship is, however, that it does not take into account the importance of transstate ties of citizens and the resources inherent in relations, such as reciprocity and solidarity. These resources may be helpful for the integration in political communities. Also, the realm of eventual integration is an open question: Whether immigrants and minorities only integrate within immigration countries, or whether other realms of integration should also be considered, can only be determined by exacting empirical analysis.

The Postnational Perspective: Dual Citizenship as a Transitory Phenomenon

The postnational concept comes in three variants: postnational membership, suprastate citizenship, and global democracy. Postnational membership focuses on the impact of interstate norms upon national citizenship. Suprastate citizenship asks about the rights of citizens in multi-level governance systems such as the European Union (EU), and global democracy addresses the implications of transstate societies for democratic participation of citizens beyond sovereign states.

Postnational membership The main idea is that the two main components of citizenship – in this concept simply rights and duties and collective identity – have increasingly decoupled over the past decades. Thus, for example, human rights, formerly tightly connected to nationality, nowadays also apply to non-citizen residents. In other words, settled non-citizens also have access to significant human, civil and social rights. Therefore, citizenship as a 'right to have rights' (Arendt, 1981) is not any more the fundamental basis for membership in political communities. Instead, discourses tied to interstate norms such as the various charters of the United Nations are supposed to contribute to postnational membership (Soysal, 1994). This perspective, however, cannot comprehend the democratically legitimated part of citizenship status. As a consequence, it is no coincidence that analysts speak of postnational membership instead of citizenship. For example, political rights – the very expression of equal political liberty – are still almost exclusively tied to formal citizenship. The popular legitimation of membership in political communities, of utmost importance for any democratic regime, gets lost. Instead, the focus is on courts who uphold interstate norms – 'rights across borders' (Jacobson, 1995).

Suprastate citizenship The concept primarily concerns citizenship in political multi-level systems such as the EU. At first sight, this form of citizenship appears as the logical next step in the centuries-old evolution of citizenship in what nowadays are liberal democracies. It is a process similar to the way in which sovereign states have gradually centralised and assimilated local and regional citizenships over the past centuries. In our times, this may proceed under propitious political-economic conditions and under the umbrella of proto-federative systems such as the EU. The formidable obstacles on the road to substantive EU citizenship include the acceptance of democratic majority decisions and suprastate social policies, and resources necessary for the integration of political communities, such as trust and solidarity (Offe, 1998; cf. Delanty, 1996, p. 6). European Union citizenship, as it has developed since the Treaty of Maastricht (1991), is not coterminous with dual citizenship, overlapping several sovereign states. Rather, it is a sort of multiple citizenship nested on several governance levels – regional, state and suprastate (Faist, 2001a). Only citizens of a member state are citizens of the Union. Although only a few entitlements such as participation in elections to European Parliament are tied to Union citizenship, there are the rudimentary signs of European consciousness which are necessary for the evolution of a collective political identity on the EU level (Bauböck, 1997). In such a suprastate perspective dual citizenship is ultimately of a secondary importance only. Nevertheless, it could be argued that European integration has fostered the mutual recognition of multiple citizenship in the member states. For example, Germany does not require citizens of other member states to ask for release from their former citizenship when acquiring German nationality.

Global democracy The supposedly minor importance of dual vis-à-vis postnational citizenship becomes even more apparent in the third concept, cosmopolitan, or global, democracy (Held, 1995). Such a consideration aims to bolster interstate and suprastate organisations and regimes 'from below', or to go even further in creating a confederal framework for politics on a global scale. In essence, global democracy strives to replace or at least complement territorial with functional criteria of governance (cf. McGrew, 1998). Global democracy means to ensure that the citizens affected by border-crossing phenomena in obvious areas such as the environment and economic transactions do have a vote in decision making. The view of democracy most congenial to this effort, deliberative democracy (cf. Elster, 1998), tries to embed the expressions of world society, such as transstate organisations and social movements, into the world of states by attributing individual rights to citizens across states. However, emerging visions of global democracy cannot yet point to a feasible political community to which the citizens of the world should feel attached. In sum, it is hard to imagine a quantum leap from the sovereign state level to the world level.

The Transstate Perspective: Dual Citizenship Reflects Overlapping Ties

Detailed analyses of border-crossing exchange show that different states and distinct economic, political and social sectors have been impacted by border-crossing exchanges in very different ways and to varying degrees (for example, Held et al., 1999). It is necessary to move beyond this insight. Geographically mobile persons, in contrast to goods, capital and information, frequently form dense and continuous border-crossing networks, communities and organisations which connect the relatively sedentary and the more mobile parts of citizenries. In short, they form transstate spaces. Descriptions of transstate spaces paint a picture of life worlds and the efforts of states and other organisations to regulate border-crossing exchange. In essence, four stylised types of transstate spaces can be discerned. Firstly, there are contact fields of goods, persons, ideas and services. These include processes of diffusion, for example, of social movement strategies (cf. Tarrow, 1996), such as the Kurdish New Year's celebration *Newroz*, or *Nevroz*, which remigrated among Kurdish groups via Germany to Turkey and has even been declared an official holiday by the Turkish government. Secondly, there are small groups such as kinship systems. Examples include nurses from Jamaica working in New York City hospitals, while their mothers care for their offspring in the Caribbean. Of central importance for dual citizenship are also binational partnerships. The partners usually settle in one country but frequently entertain symbolic and social ties abroad (cf. Brown, 1997). Thirdly, a multitude of non-governmental organisations has mushroomed in world society, forming 'transnational advocacy networks' (Keck and Sikkink, 1998); not to forget networks of economic entrepreneurs who venture beyond state borders. Fourthly, there are numerous communities and organisations whose reach crosses state borders. The most obvious examples include village communities with emigrants abroad, and classical diasporas with a strong sense of an imagined homeland. Border-crossing organisations not only comprise multinational companies and political parties such as the Socialist International, but also religious institutions, the most prominent being the Catholic Church (cf. Faist, 2000b, ch.

1). Small kinship groups with geographically mobile members, and transstate communities and organisations in particular, foster a life-style which implies frequent and dense social and symbolic transactions across state borders. And quite a few of those involved possess genuine links reaching into different states (cf. the case studies in Smith and Guarnizo, 1998).

All of this suggests that relatively dense and continuous interstitial ties of citizens are not located beyond states but criss-cross state borders. A transstate perspective also implies that dual citizenship is not a separate form of membership in political communities such as national citizenship in sovereign states or suprastate, or nested, citizenship in multilevel governance systems. Rather, dual citizenship essentially is a form of political membership complementing national citizenship when life-world ties of citizens overlap state borders. And dual citizenship may even support postnational forms of citizenship if suprastate integration fosters the mutual recognition of other nationalities in case of naturalisation – such as in the EU. Unlike the national perspective on dual citizenship, the transstate angle offers a way to recognise the potentials for reciprocity and solidarity in border-crossing social and symbolic ties. And unlike the postnational vantage point, a transstate perspective can take border-crossing identities into account without making excessively optimistic assumptions about cosmopolitan 'we-feelings'.

Socialisation and Social Cooperation as a Basis for Citizenship

To answer the question about the potentials for reciprocity and solidarity inherent in dual citizenship, it is inevitable to specify the mechanisms that turn citizens' border-crossing ties into relevant elements of political membership. Citizenship not only concerns legal ties between the state and citizens. Eventually, states hold in trust direct and personal ties in small groups and indirect ties in bigger communities and organisations. This double coding of citizenship through both a legal and a socio-cultural dimension implies a more 'liberal' and not a strong 'republican' view of citizenship. Both concepts differ fundamentally: The republican perspective emphasises the active and 'good' citizen in the Aristotelian tradition, the *zoon politikon*. The liberal concept starts in a more Lockean vein from the freedom of citizens in the private sphere of the *eoconomia*, with the competition of citizens in markets (cf. Locke, 1980). In the republican view the ties of persons are especially relevant when concerning virtuous citizens who engage in public affairs (Rousseau, 1966). In a liberal perspective, it is the totality of social and symbolic ties between citizens – including both the private and the public sphere that matters for membership in political communities.

The socialisation and cooperation argument says that loyalities of citizens to political communities emerge out of their ties to other persons – for example, parents, siblings, partners and children (cf. Easton, 1965, ch. 20). In other words, the affiliation to the country of birth or settlement closely correlates with affective ties towards significant others. This is true for diverse settings such as childhood and binational partnerships. From the process of political socialisation via transmission it can also be concluded that ties towards state are intrinsically linked to feelings towards members of such political communities. This implies that there is a close correlation between specific reciprocity and focused solidarity, on the one hand, and generalised reciprocity and diffuse solidarity, on the other hand. Without socialisation in small communities on the basis of specific reciprocity and focused solidarity there would be no grounds for a more far-reaching reciprocity and solidarity among citizens. Reciprocity in its specific forms refers to situations in which known partners exchange items of equivalent value in a strictly delimited sequence. If any obligations exist, they are clearly specified in terms of rights and duties of a particular actor. Specific reciprocity pertains to varied situations, for example, when children care for their elderly parents. Generalised reciprocity means that equivalence is less precise, one's partners may be viewed as a group in a community or a country, rather than as particular actors, and the sequence of events is less narrowly bounded. It involves conforming to generally accepted standards of behaviour. Generalised reciprocity is of utmost importance in upholding the welfare function in sovereign states. For example, public old age insurance in continental Europe usually rests on a 'contract of generations' – persons of working age finance the pensions of the retired. As a prerequisite, those still in the active labour force trust tat the succeeding generation will do the same for them. Similarly, solidarity can be either focused, directed towards a narrow kin group and thus frequently bounded by household and blood lineage, or it can extend to more diffuse forms. Diffuse solidarity pertains to larger aggregates, such as territorial and symbolic community groupings (nations) and organisations (insurance schemes or even states), in which participants and members largely lack face-to-face contact (cf. Faist, 2000a, ch. 4). Diffuse solidarity exists, for example, if citizens recognise moral claims of needy fellow citizens and pay taxes to finance some kind of social assistance. For specific reciprocity to turn into generalised reciprocity and for focused solidarity to come into diffuse solidarity, ties between citizens need to go beyond dyads and refer to 'third' persons: Citizens (X_i) should help others (Y$_i$) who need the kind of help they (X$_i$) may require from others (Z$_i$) in the future; also, citizens (X$_i$) should help others (Y$_i$) who now need the kind of help which they (X$_i$) received from third citizens (Z$_i$) in the past (cf. Ekeh, 1974, p. 206–7).

Thus, reciprocity and solidarity can go beyond small groups and reach to generalised reciprocity and diffuse solidarity in larger groups and even nations. The main mechanism here is participation in voluntary associations which might lead to social structures of cooperation. Such structures underpin civic engagement (cf. Putnam, 1993, ch. 6; of course, the *locus classicus* is de Tocqueville, 1966, Vol. 1, Part II, ch. 4). Citizens socialised in small groups have a necessary, albeit not sufficient, grounding to apply forms of reciprocity and solidarity to larger aggregates in the political community, and to the polity itself.

In principle, these considerations also apply to citizens' border-crossing ties. Dual citizenship is not only a recognition of border-crossing ties to another political community but also of concrete ties on the substate level. As to specific reciprocity, for example, immigrants take care of their elderly parents living abroad. They sometimes fulfil an implicit contract of generations in sending remittances or sponsoring the immigration of their parents to the new country of settlement. Conversely, grandparents may commute in transstate spaces to care for their grandchildren. In short, citizens claim and fulfil specific obligations towards significant others – to inherit, to purchase property, to aid to relatives, or to travel (cf. Jones-Correa, 1998). Such life world relations signify crucial aspects of socialisation and continued attachments to the communities of origin.

Also, generalised reciprocity can be found in organisations which exchange informations across state borders and diffuse solidarity floats in networks of non-governmental organisations – for example, when financial resources are transmitted among human rights associations. To contribute to democratic governance and to mutual recognition of rights among citizens, such voluntary associations – akin to those without border-crossing ties – need not necessarily be organised internally along democratic principles. Most associations in civil society are rather agnostic (Eckstein, 1966, Appendix A); examples include soccer clubs and choirs. Nevertheless, it is only upon the existence of voluntary structures of cooperation, based upon generalised reciprocity and diffuse solidarity that the informal claims and codified entitlements of other citizens are recognised. Dual citizenship implies the recognition or at least toleration of citizens' border-crossing ties in small groups, networks and organisations.

A transstate perspective, taking the life world of border-crossers seriously, leads to a balanced evaluation of the potentials and dangers of dual citizenship.

It sounds utterly unrealistic when critics of dual citizenship claim that dual citizens are in danger of developing a very instrumental – action oriented to realise explicit goals efficiently – and not enough of affective ties to the new countries of citizenship, the countries of immigration (Schuck, 1998, p. 219). Firstly, to claim that new, dual citizens acquire another citizenship primarily for instrumental reasons is a pure invention. This is so because settled immigrants with a permanent residence permit generally have access to most civil and social rights available to citizens. Therefore, naturalisation in the country of settlement will give permanent residents primarily additional political rights. Thus, naturalisation in those cases is very unlikely to be of an instrumental nature. Secondly, if the goal of the applicant to citizenship is to more effectively participate in the polity of settlement, it is a kind of instrumental orientation to be welcomed from a normative basis. It is in tune with democratic virtues. Thirdly, it is very likely that the wish to naturalise is usually also connected to two other 'modes of orientation': expressive – action directed at realising emotional satisfactions – and moral – action concerned at realising standards of right and wrong (cf. Parsons, 1951, p. 58). Again, if naturalisation does not yield substantial additional material rights when compared to the status of permanent residency, chances are that extra-instrumental orientations also play a role. What could be criticised from a normative point of view, however, is rather the practice of some states in the Caribbean and the Pacific to purposely offer their citizenship for sale.

Dual Citizenship: not an Evil, but also of no Intrinsic Value

The question now is whether dual citizenship violates fundamental principles of democratically legitimated membership and governance – such as 'one person, one vote', additional exit and/ or entry rights not available to 'single' citizens, lacking loyalty – or even contributes to the spread of democratic forms of governance.

In principle, dual citizens have the right to vote in two countries. At first sight, this situation seems to violate the principle 'one person, one vote'. First, however, overlapping membership does not violate equal political liberty. This is so because dual citizens have voting rights in states formally sovereign and independent. These states are unified by a common political authority. This would be different in nested and multiple-level governance systems with a central government. This could be the case in the EU in some future time – for example, a common government in Brussels, based upon popular sovereignty. Multiple votes on the same level – for example national level – could indeed lead to inequalities between citizens. Just think of a situation in which there is a common government in Brussels, based upon popular sovereignty. Imagine dual citizens who vote in both France and the UK. True, in such a scenario, they would have more than one vote within the common political system. Secondly, however, fears of multiple voting and participation are vastly overdrawn for really existing political systems. Empirical research shows that even highly mobile persons such as the proverbial 'astronauts' – business people from Hong Kong whose families prefer to live in North America – have a definite geographical centre of their life (Wong, 1997); in spite, or perhaps, indeed, because of their cosmopolitan lifestyle. And in cases in which duties of citizens may conflict – such as tax payments or service in the armed forces – bilateral arrangements or even the instrument of dormant citizenship are available. Dormant citizenship means that citizens can activate full citizenship only in the country of actual settlement, while full rights and duties in the partner country are temporarily suspended until the person relocates the place of habitual residence. In practice, dormant citizenship can easily be implemented through bi- and multilateral treaties. The agreements between Spain and 12 Latin American countries are just one case in point (Chavez, 1997, p. 141).

One may also object to dual citizenship that emigrants living abroad may exit the political community at any time, although they have participated in bringing about the laws and regulations they prefer to escape from. This seems to constitute a particularly favourable combination of exit and voice. However, the exit-option is a fundamental freedom available to all citizens in all countries on earth, codified in the Charter of Fundamental Rights of the United Nations (UN). This means that dual citizens do not have an additional exit-option but a supplementary entry-option if they possess the passport of the respective state(s). The high volume of refugee migration and the human suffering involved, as evidenced by interstate wars and proliferating civil wars in disintegrating and authoritarian states, shows how important such added entry options actually are. Many refugees use the additional entry option as a temporary device. Indeed, the majority of refugees usually intends to return to the home country when the armed conflicts and the most dire threats to life cease (cf. UNHCR, 1997). Also, it is useful to place this entry-option in perspective: 'single' citizens in Western liberal democracies usually have more entry options than 'dual' citizens of the 'South' and the 'East'.

A popular and widespread argument against multiple citizenship is that dual citizens' loyalties are torn in case of war between the respective countries of membership (Aron, 1974). Firstly, however, the loyalty nexus between universal conscription and nationality is becoming less and less relevant, as many liberal democracies reorganise their armed forces into voluntary and professional armies. For the past, the argument could muster somewhat more support because 'nation-building' proceeded with an a trade between the right to vote and compulsory military service (Bendix, 1996, p. 114). But this correlation only applies to liberal democracies. In more authoritarian regimes such as nineteenth century Prussia, universal conscription did not entail voting rights on an equal and free basis. Secondly, all empirical evidence indicates that new citizens are the ones who are most eager to show loyalty to their new home country in case of war. As to populist reactions against lacking loyalty, these have been usually directed against certain categories of new citizens, not against dual citizens in particular; take the discrimination directed at German-Americans during World War I and Japanese-Americans during World War II in the USA as examples. Also, there are no indications that dual citizens have been more prone to engage in espionage than 'single' citizens (Hammar, 1989, p. 90). And the charge from a national perspective that dual citizenship encourages the import of political conflicts from emigration to immigration countries misses the point (Brieden, 1996). Exports and imports of conflicts are quite independent of formal nationality because fundamental rights such as the freedom of association are also available to permanent residents – as evidenced by the activity of authoritarian social movements such as the Kurdish PKK in Germany. More generally, it can be said that that stable democracies allow for diverse and plural ties of citizens. In fact, plural loyalties to organisations may even foster democratic practice as long as citizens do not single-mindedly pursue the interests of a specific class or set of organisations (cf. Truman, 1951, p. 168). Again, there are no plausible reasons to limit citizens' plural ties to the container box formed by the people of a state, the state government and the state territory.

A more plausible scenario of objections emerges when looking at national minorities instead of immigrants. After all, dual citizenship not only occurs in immigration settings but also in situations of secession and state succession. In the case of transstate migration and settlement, the parameters for the political triangle are: emigration country, immigration country and immigrants. In the second case – for example, the emergence of new states out of faltering empires – dual citizenship is framed by the relations between the old imperial power, the newly independent state and the respective national minorities; Russians in the Ukraine are a recent example (Shevchuk, 1996). Other cases concern the relationship between an ancestral country of settlement, an external patronage state and national minorities; think of the Hungarian minority in Romania. Compared to labour immigrants and refugees, autochthonous national minorities tend to be more adamant, persistent and often more successful in claiming a distinctive 'national' collective identity. National minorities often pursue (limited) rights of limited self-government within the traditional country of settlement. In cases of ethnic and nationals strife this often means that it tends to be easier for patronage states to instrumentalise national minorities abroad for political purposes in supporting irredentism (Brubaker, 1996, pp. 6–7). But it would be far-fetched to explain potential irredentism in the Ukraine or Romania as a direct result of the recognition or tolerance towards dual citizenship. At the most, dual citizenship could be one instrument in political, public debates to bolster the belonging of certain national minorities to the external patronage state, especially if rights granted to a national minority set in motion a spiral of rising expectations and demands. However, it is equally likely that dual citizenship serves as a moderating influence in ethnic and national conflicts because dual citizens entertain ties intersecting multiple states. In essence, the function of dual citizenship in conflictual settings depends on factors external to the intrinsic values of multiple membership.

While the dangers of dual citizenship in the national perspective seem to be widely exaggerated, the hopes invested in this form of supplementary membership in political communities from a postnational viewpoint are equally overrated. One hypothesis says that dual citizenship may help to make the transition to democracy in certain emigration countries (Spiro, 1997, p. 1477). There is some truth to this claim when arguing that the export of democracy as a creative mix of exit from the authoritarian regime and voice from abroad carries more weight today than in the early decades of the twentieth century. In the past, examples such as the Spanish Civil War and anti-fascist movements during World War II indicate that emigrés did contribute to the fall of authoritarian or totalitarian regimes but were not the main cause – which can be found in lost wars and economic recessions (cf. Shain, 1989). Nowadays, the conditions for an effective mix of exit and voice have increased. Most emigration countries do not resemble the 'strong' authoritarian states of the early and mid-twentieth century. Activists in transstate spaces thus encounter somewhat more propitious conditions to reinforce political transitions towards democratic life in their home countries. However, the same caveat as in the case of negative implications of dual citizenship has to be added here as well: dual citizenship is neither the main prerequisite nor the principal mechanism of democratic transition. Rather, it can fulfil the role of an intervening factor.

An interesting future development would be a radical individualisation of the first dimension of citizenship – democratically legitimated rights and duties – towards borderless transactions. Such a thought experiment could be derived from 'constitutional democracy'. Citizens could purchase public goods such as protection from military threats, collective and club goods such as social welfare and individual goods such as life insurance in places most convenient for them. Even more further reaching would be a trade with nationalities (Tullock, 1997). However, such a policy would totally disregard the danger that it would be impossible to institutionalise generalised reciprocity and diffuse solidarity beyond particular single group interests on a sovereign state or global level. Especially those citizens rights and duties, which are not only instrumentally but also morally and expressively demanding – such as welfare and social entitlements and obligations – cannot be easily universalised beyond individual welfare regimes to a regional or even global level. This hunch is borne out by the fact that the collectivisation of social rights on the European Union level lags far behind civil, economic and even political rights.

In contrast to the 'national' fears of instrumentalised loyalties and the violation of principles such as 'one person, one vote' and 'postnational' hopes towards a central role of dual citizenship for the 'third wave' of democratisation in developing countries, a transsate perspective renders a more realistic description of multiple membership's functions. Fundamentally, dual citizenship is a recognition of border-crossing ties of citizens in certain life worlds – binational partnerships, socialisation in another country, or national minorities. It is primarily a form of symbolic policy with real advantages for dual citizens concerning freedom of movement, inheritance, property purchase and even political participation. Nevertheless, dual citizenship also carries obvious disadvantages, not for states but for citizens themselves: a potential lack of diplomatic protection. For example, there are refugees living abroad and whose country of origin denied to expatriate them. When travelling back to this country, these dual citizens are exclusively subject to the respective laws and the immigration country cannot protect them. Nevertheless, the advantages of dual citizenship usually far outweigh this drawback.

Concluding Remarks: the World of Societies and its Representation in the World of States

All three conceptual perspectives help to understand the spread and the functions of dual citizenship – national, postnational and transstate views.

But only the transstate perspective deflects overdrawn hopes and overblown dangers and leads to the centre of dual citizenship's function: the representation of citizens' border-crossing ties and the significance of citizens' genuine links in life worlds for the integration of political communities. It is an open question which function dual citizenship may fulfil in governance systems beyond sovereign states. We would need to probe the proposition that dual citizenship could be a link between national and postnational concepts of membership, without necessarily being a transitory phenomenon. This link could foster the acceptance of forms of membership beyond sovereign states. The definite advantage of dual citizenship over other, existing forms of membership beyond sovereign states – for example, European Union citizenship – is that it does not impact upon the link between the governing and the governed. It leaves the principle of popular sovereignty intact and does not create additional problems of democratic accountability and legitimacy. Dual citizenship as membership overlapping distinctive political communities rather aims at the recognition of ties in transstate spaces populated by mobile and sedentary citizens. A long time ago, Immanuel Kant has drawn attention to the alternative of a 'federation of free republics' on the level of states to avoid the twin dangers of postnational tyranny, on the one hand, and the anarchy of sovereign states, on the other (Kant 1970). In this perspective, dual citizenship interfaces the world of states by institutionalising the overlapping ties in the world of societies.

Notes

1   For helpful criticism on an earlier version of this article I would like to thank Jürgen Gerdes and Rainer Bauböck.
2   Dual citizens in Germany encompass four categories of persons: 1) children of German fathers or mothers and foreign mothers or fathers; 2) ethnic Germans (*Aussiedler*, since 1993: *Spätaussiedler*) who are allowed to keep the citizenship of the country of origin upon arrival in Germany, and members of the German minority in Poland; 3) exceptions in regular naturalisations; 4) since the reform of the Citizenship Act in 2000 the so-called optional rule has been added. Children of foreign parents who hold a permanent resident permit may keep two nationalities until the age of 23.
3   Social ties constitute continuous series of interpersonal transactions – bounded communications between at least three actors. The participants attribute common interests, obligations, expectations and norms to these ties. By contrast, symbolic ties are steady transactions to which the participants connect common meanings, memories, future expectations and symbols. Social and symbolic ties may reach beyond immediate viz. direct ties between persons, referring to indirect transactions regarding religion, language, ethnicity, and nationality.

References

Arendt, H. (1981 [1949]), 'Es gibt nur ein einziges Menschenrecht', in O. Höffe, G. Kadelbach and G. Plumpe (eds), *Praktische Philosophie/Ethik*, Vol. 2, Frankfurt: Fischer, pp. 152–67.

Aristotle (1962), *The Politics*, trans. T.A. Sinclair, revised and represented by T.J. Saunders, London: Penguin Books.

Aron, R. (1974), 'Is Multinational Citizenship Possible', *Social Research*, 41, pp. 638–56.

BMAS (Bundesministerium für Arbeit und Sozialordnung) (1995), *Repräsentativuntersuchung '95*, Bonn: Friedrich-Ebert-Stiftung.

Bar-Yaacov, N. (1961), *Dual Nationality*, London: Stevens and Sons.

Bauböck, R. (1994), *Transnational Citizenship. Membership and Rights in International Migration*, Aldershot: Edward Elgar.

Bauböck, R. (1997), 'Citizenship and National Identities in the European Union', in E. Antalovsky, J. Melchior and S.P. Riekmann (eds), *Integration durch Demokratie. Neue Impulse für die Europäische Union*, Marburg: Metropolis, pp. 297–331.

Beauftragte der Bundesregierung (1999), *Daten und Fakten zur Ausländersituation*, Bonn: Mitteilungen der Beauftragten der Bundesregierung für Ausländerfragen.

Bendix, R. (1996 [1964]), *Nation-Building and Citizenship. Studies of Our Changing Social Order*, New Brunswick, NJ: Transaction Books.

Brieden, T. (1996), *Konfliktimport durch Immigration. Auswirkungen ethnischer Konflikte im Herkunftsland auf die Integrations- und Identitätsentwicklung von Immigranten in der Bundesrepublik Deutschland*, Hamburg: Dr. Kovac.

Brown, D. (1997), 'Workforce Lessons and Return Migration to the Caribbean: a Case Study of Jamaican Nurses', in P.R. Pessar (ed.), *Caribbean Circuits. New Directions in the Study of Caribbean Migration*, New York: Routledge, pp. 197–223.

Brubaker, W.R. (1992), *Citizenship and Nationhood in France and Germany*, Cambridge, MA: Harvard University Press.

Brubaker, W.R. (1996), *Nationalism Reframed. Nationhood and the National Question in the New Europe*, Cambridge, MA: Cambridge University Press.

Chavez, P.L. (1997), 'Creating a United States-Mexico Political Double Helix: the Mexican Government's Proposed Dual Nationality Amendment', *Stanford Journal of International Law*, 33, pp. 119–51.

Council of Europe (1963), 'European Convention on Reduction of Cases of Multiple Nationality and Military Obligations in Cases of Multiple Nationality', 6 May, ETS No. 43, http://www.coe.fr/eng/legaltxt/43e.htm.

Council of Europe (1997), 'European Convention on Nationality', 6 November, ETS no. 166, http://www.coe.fr/eng/legaltxt/166e.htm.

Dahrendorf, R. (1992), 'Citizenship and the Modern Social Conflict', in R. Holme and M. Elliot (eds), *1688-1988. Time for a New Constitution*, Basingstoke: Macmillan, pp. 112–25.

de Groot, G.-R. (1989), *Staatsangehörigkeitsrecht im Wandel*, Köln: Bund.

de Tocqueville, A. (1966), *Democracy in America*, trans. G. Lawrence, ed. J.P. Mayer, New York: Harper and Row.

Delanty, G. (1996), *Inventing Europe: Idea, Identity, Reality*, Houndmills: Macmillan.

Easton, D. (1965), *A Systems Theory of Political Life*, Chicago: University of Chicago Press.

Eckstein, H. (1966), *Division and Cohesion in Democracy: A Study of Norway*, Princeton, NJ: Princeton University Press.

Ekeh, P.P. (1974), *Social Exchange Theory. The Two Traditions*, Cambridge, MA: Harvard University Press.

Elster, J. (1998), *Deliberative Democracy*, Cambridge, MA: Cambridge University Press.

Faist, T. (2000a), *The Volume and Dynamics of International Migration and Transnational Social Spaces*, Oxford: Oxford University Press.

Faist, T. (ed.) (2000b), 'Transstaatliche Räume. Politik, Wirtschaft und Kultur in und zwischen Deutschland und der Türkei', Bielefeld: transcript.

Faist, T. (2001a), 'Social Citizenship in the European Union: Nested Membership', *Journal of Common Market Studies*, 39 (1), pp. 39–60.

Faist, T. (2001b), 'Integrationen von Polen – Assimilation, "Polonia" und Diaspora', in Z. Krasnodębski and C. Krampen (eds), *Polen in Deutschland – eine unsichtbare Minderheit?*, Bremen.

Freeman, G.P. and Ögelmann, N. (1998), 'Homeland Citizenship Policies and the Status of Third Country Nationals in the European Union', *Journal of Ethnic and Migration Studies*, 24, pp. 769–88.

Goldstein, E. and Piazza, V. (1996), 'Naturalization. Dual Citizenship and the Retention of Foreign Citizenship – a Survey', *Interpreter Releases*, 517, pp. 61–73.

Groenendijk, K. (1999), 'Stellungnahme zu den Gesetzentwürfen zur Reform des Staatsangehör igkeitsrechts', *Deutscher Bundestag, Stellungnahmen der Sachverständigen zur öffentlichen Anhörung des Innenausschusses. Ausschußdrucksache*, 14 (14), pp. 71–83.

Habermas, J. (1992 [1990]), *Faktizität und Geltung*, Frankfurt a.M.: Suhrkamp.

Hailbronner, K. (1992), *Einbürgerung von Wanderarbeitnehmern und doppelte Staatsangehörigkeit*, Baden-Baden: Nomos.

Hammar, T. (1989), 'State, Nation, and Dual Citizenship', in W. Rogers Brubaker (ed.), *Immigration and the Politics of Citizenship in Europe and North America*, Lanham, MD: University Press of America, pp. 81–95.

Held, D. (ed.) (1995), *Cosmopolitan Democracy*, Cambridge: Polity Press.

Held, D., McGrew, A., Goldblatt, D. and Perraton, J. (1999), *Global Transformations. Politics, Economics and Culture*, Stanford, CA: Stanford University Press.

Jacobson, D. (1995), *Rights Across Borders: Immigration and the Decline of Citizenship*, Baltimore: Johns Hopkins University Press.

Jones-Correa, M. (1998), *Between Two Nations. The Political Predicament of Latinos in New York City*, Ithaca, NY: Cornell University Press.

Kammann, K. (1984), *Probleme mehrfacher Staatsangehörigkeit; unter besonderer Berücksichtigung des Völkerrecht*s, Frankfurt a.M.: Lang.

Kant, I. (1970 [1781]), 'Perpetual Peace. A Philosophical Sketch', in *Kant's Political Writings*, ed. H. Reiss, trans. H.B. Nisbet, Cambridge, MA: Cambridge University Press, pp. 93–130.

Keck, M. and Sikkink, K. (eds) (1998), *Activists Beyond Borders. Transnational Advocacy Networks in International Politics*, Ithaca, NY: Cornell University Press.

Kymlicka, W. (1995), *Multicultural Citizenship. A Liberal Theory of Minority Rights*, Oxford: Oxford University Press.

League of Nations (1930), 'Treaty Series, Convention on Certain Questions Relating to the Conflict of Nationality Laws, April 12, 1930. Treaties and International Engagements Registered with the Secretariat of the League of Nations', Vol. 179, No. 4137 (1937–38).

Locke, J. (1980 [1689]), *Second Treatise of Government: an Essay concerning the True Original, Extent, and End of Civil Government*, ed. C.B. Macpherson, Indianapolis, IN: Hackett.

Marshall, T.H. (1992 [1949]), *Citizenship and Social Class*, London: Pluto Press.

McGrew, A. (1998), 'Demokratie ohne Grenzen? Globalisierung, demokratische Theorie und Politik', in U. Beck (ed.), *Politik der Globalisierung*, Frankfurt a.M.: Suhrkamp, pp. 374–422.

Moore, W.H. (1918), *The Clash! A Study in Nationalities*, Toronto.

Offe, C. (1998), 'Demokratie und Wohlfahrtsstaat: Eine europäische Regimeform unter dem Streß der europäischen Integration', in W. Streeck (ed.), *Internationale Wirtschaft, Nationale Demokratie. Herausforderungen für die Demokratietheorie*, Frankfurt a.M. and New York: Campus, pp. 99–136.

Parsons, T. (1951), *The Social System*, New York: The Free Press.

Putnam, R.D. (1993), *Making Democracy Work. Civic Traditions in Modern Italy*, Princeton: Princeton University Press.

Rex, J. (1991), 'The Political Sociology of a Multi-cultural Society', *European Journal of Intercultural Studies*, 2, pp. 7–19.

Rittstieg, H. (1990), 'Doppelte Staatsangehörigkeit im Völkerrecht', *Neue Juristische Wochenschrift*, 43, pp. 1401–5.

Rousseau, J.-J. (1966 [1762]), *Du contrat social: ou Principes du droit politique,* Paris: Garnier.

Schmitter Heisler, B. (1984), 'Sending Countries and the Politics of Emigration and Destination', *International Migration Review*, 19, pp. 469–84.

Schuck, P.H. (1998), *Citizens, Strangers, and In-betweens. Essays on Immigration and Citizenship*, Boulder: Westview.

Shain, Y. (1989), *The Frontier of Loyalty. Political Exiles in the Age of the Nation-state*, Middletown, CT: Wesleyan University Press.

Shevchuk, Y. (1996), 'Dual Citizenship in Old and New States', *Archives Européennes de Sociologie*, 37, pp. 47–73.

Soysal, Y.N. (1994), *The Limits of Citizenship*, Chicago: University of Chicago Press.

Spiro, P.J. (1997), 'Dual Nationality and the Meaning of Citizenship', *Emory Law Journal*, 46, pp. 1411–86.

Smith, M.P. and Guarnizo, L.E. (eds) (1998), *Transnationalism from Below*, New Brunswick: Transaction Books.

Tarrow, S. (1996), 'Fishnets, Internets and Catnets: Globalization and Transnational Collective Action', Madrid: Instituto Juan March de Estudios e Investigaciones. Working Paper 1996/78.

Truman, D.B. (1951), *The Governmental Process. Political Interests and Public Opinion*, New York: The Free Press.

Tullock, G. (1997), 'Trading Citizenship', *Kyklos*, 50 (2), pp. 251–3.

UNHCR (United Nations High Commissioner for Refugees) (1997), *The State of the World's Refugees: a Humanitarian Agenda*, Oxford: Oxford University Press.

Weber, M. (1968), *Economy and Society*, ed. G. Roth and C. Wittich, Berkeley, CA: University of California Press.

Wong, L.L. (1997), 'Globalization and Transnational Migration: a Study of Recent Chinese Capitalist Migration from the Asian Pacific to Canada', International Sociology, 12, pp. 329–52.

Index

Notes: page numbers in italics refer to figures and tables; numbers in brackets preceded by *n* are note numbers.